Practical Suggestions for Teaching

REAL ESSAYS

with Readings

Fourth Edition

Eddye S. Gallagher
Tarrant County College

BEDFORD/ST. MARTIN'S   *Boston • New York*

Manufactured in the United States of America.
7 6 5 4 3 2
f e d c b a
For information, write: Bedford/St. Martin's, 75 Arlington Street, Boston, MA 02116
(617-399-4000)

ISBN: 978–0–312–56664–7

Instructors who have adopted *Real Essays,* Fourth Edition, as a textbook for a course
are authorized to duplicate portions of this manual for their students.

Acknowledgment:
Linda B. Nilson, *Getting Students to Do the Readings: Why Students Skip the Readings.*
National Education Association. Vol. 25, No. 2. December 2007.

Contents

1

How to Use Real Essays *in Your Course*

(with icebreaker exercises from Billy P. Jones, *Miami Dade College*)

Welcome to *Real Essays*, and (if you are a new instructor) welcome to developmental writing instruction. This instructor's manual will, I hope, give you some practical ideas for using *Real Essays* and its support materials as aids to understanding and helping your students, teaching the course, and facing the challenges of our profession.

This chapter starts with first things first: what to do the very first day you walk into the class with *Real Essays* in your hands and a collection of new students in front of you. After that come overviews of *Real Essays* and its ancillary package, and some sample syllabi and class schedules that demonstrate how to integrate *Real Essays* into the course.

Susan Anker, the editors at Bedford/St. Martin's, and I have tried to make this instructor's manual and the other parts of *Real Essays* as helpful to you as possible. We're interested in hearing your feedback, particularly if you have ideas about how to improve the coverage or make it more useful. Please write to us at *Real Essays*, Bedford/St. Martin's, 75 Arlington Street, Boston, MA 02116.

What to Do on Day One

The first day of class can set the tone for the entire semester, so prepare yourself and your plans carefully. If you approach the day with a great attitude and a smile on your face, your students will probably be quite receptive to you and your course. How much you can accomplish during the first day will depend on the length of your class, the promptness of your students, and your own preparedness.

PREPARATION. Before class, read through this chapter of *Practical Suggestions;* if you are a new instructor, also read Chapter 2, Tips for New Instructors, and Chapter 3, Working with Developmental Writers. If you have time, read the preface in *Real Essays* to acquaint yourself with the book and its features; skim through Chapter 1 of *Real Essays* if you intend to assign that chapter or go over it in class. Plan out the activities you want to cover on the first day, figuring out approximately how much time you will spend on each activity. (It's better to plan too much than too little.) Bring your copy of *Real Essays* and samples of any supplies that you'll want students to have (journals, portfolio folders, and so on). Also prepare any of the following handouts to distribute to your students:

- Student Information Form (sample on p. 3)

- Syllabus (sample on p. 9)

- List of required texts and supplies

- Grading policy

- Attendance policy

- Class schedules or assignment schedules (samples on pp. 15–28)

- Acknowledgment of Student Responsibilities (sample on p. 37)

- Writing Questionnaire (see p. 4 of this manual; in *Additional Resources,* and available for downloading at **bedfordstmartins.com/realessays /catalog**)

- Critical thinking activities to use as icebreakers (samples on pp. 75–89)

Arrive at the classroom early so that you can write important information on the board; this aid enables ESL or slower students to get a head start and saves time for other activities. Greet your students as they come into the room.

INTRODUCTIONS. Begin the class by welcoming your students to the course and introducing yourself. Yes, your name may be on their class schedules, but saying your name lets students know how to pronounce it and reinforces your identity. Because my first name is an unusual one for a female, many students expect a male teacher, so I usually make some kind of joke about their being surprised to discover I'm a woman; I also stress the importance names have for all of us. As I begin to call roll, I say, "Please let me know if I'm mispronouncing your name or calling you something that you prefer not to be called." If a student's name is particularly hard for me to pronounce, I ask the student to bear with me as I learn the pronunciation and to remind me if I forget.

OVERVIEW. After roll call, you may want to give a brief course overview. You can distribute the course syllabus and class schedule (see pp. 9–28 for samples) and discuss student responsibilities, course focus, the grading system, and text and supply requirements. I wouldn't go into a tremendous amount of detail. Basically, just walk your students through the syllabus, pointing out various sections of particular importance. You could even make reading the syllabus a homework assignment for the next class. Keep the presentation very short. You will discover that students will forget much of what you say on the first day; therefore, you will need to repeat some information during another class period. Although many students will not retain the introductory information, most will appreciate knowing from the beginning what to expect. Every few minutes throughout class, ask for questions. Although you may get few, if any, you are at least establishing that you encourage questions.

LOGISTICS. When introducing necessary supplies, follow the same guidelines—keep the discussion short and ask if students have questions. Have your textbooks handy and hold them up as you refer to them. If you use more than one, you might want to mention how each will be used. This is a great time to present any computer access codes and urls that your students will need. Also, present guidelines for submitting papers. To help keep your students organized, consider asking them to purchase a three-ring binder to hold all their class assignments and writings. Explicitly tell your class the purpose of the binder and how it should be organized and maintained.

ENCOURAGEMENT AND RAPPORT. You will probably want to give a pep talk about how much the students can learn during the semester and how you are going to be their guide to success. In my school, students receive no credit for developmental courses, so I usually emphasize the benefits the course will provide as they move into the credit (and graded) classes. I tell them that the composition teachers love to get students from the developmental writing classes because those students are well prepared, ready to work, and not afraid to write. I want them to see the connection between my class and their success in other classes (not just English), their careers, and their everyday lives.

Try to establish a feeling of comfort and openness from day one. My students (and perhaps yours also) enter the course through various avenues: a low score on the state exam or the college's placement test, their own recognition of their weaknesses in grammar and/or writing, or the recommendation of a counselor or another teacher. Those who have not passed the placement tests sometimes resent having to be in my class, so I discuss why they "may" have entered the class. I even mention negative attitudes they have because of low test scores or previous failures in English classes. Then I say, "But, let's put all that aside now. We're all here together, so let's establish goals for the semester. Do you want to improve your grammar skills, develop strong thesis statements, learn how to gather research, and write coherent essays? Let's focus on what you want to accomplish this semester and how we are going to work together to reach your goals. I'm not going to tell you how you must write, but I will offer suggestions to make the writing process easier for you. I don't expect you all to leave my class saying, 'I love to write; I love English,' but if I can get you to say, 'Oh, the semester was okay; writing's not too bad,' then I will have succeeded and you will have made a giant step toward reaching your goals." I also stress that the class is designed to help students learn and improve, and that no one in the class should be afraid of making mistakes—which, of course, is often a means of learning.

Student Information Form

Name:_____   Class Time:_____

Address: _____   Phone:_____

_____   E-mail:_____

Other Courses Currently Taking:

_____

_____

_____

Current Employment: _____

Work Schedule: _____

Have you taken this class before? _____

If yes, when? _____

Is there anything about you that I need to know in order to help you do your best this semester?

_____

_____

_____

_____

_____

_____

_____

_____

Writing Questionnaire

Name: _____ Date: _____

Course:_____

Real-World Goals

Use the spaces below to list at least five specific goals you have set for yourself.

_____

_____

_____

_____

_____

Course Goals

Think about your writing and comments you have received about it in the past. What do you think your major problems with writing are? What should you work on improving? List a few answers to these questions in the spaces that follow.

_____

_____

_____

_____

_____

_____

When you have jotted down a few ideas, list three writing skills you want to learn or practice. Be as specific as possible. For example, "Learn to write better" is too general to mean anything much or to help you focus on the areas you want to improve. Expanding on your answers to the questions above, write three specific skills you want to address and improve during this course.

1._____

2._____

3._____

BASIC INFORMATION. You may want to ask students to complete a Student Information Form that will include their home or campus address, phone number, e-mail address, class load, and workload. You can also ask for pertinent information that will help you help them: learning or physical disabilities, travel requirements for work, and so on. I usually say, "Tell me anything about yourself that might prevent your 100 percent effort in this class, such as being the single parent of ten kids." Giving such an exaggerated example can help students feel comfortable revealing personal information. (See p. 3 for a sample form.)

REAL ESSAYS. Ask students to familiarize themselves with their textbooks and let them know how important *Real Essays* is to their success in the class, to the improvement of their writing, and to their careers (both in college and at work) outside your classroom. Consider assigning *Real Essays'* Chapter 1, Succeeding in College, to be read before the next class meeting. (You can discuss the introduction in class to ensure that students have completed this assignment.) Many developmental students are unfamiliar with basic success strategies, so they will benefit from this overview.

ICEBREAKER. Depending on the length of the class, you might have time for an icebreaker. Billy P. Jones of Miami Dade College suggests two exercises to get students acquainted with one another and prepare them for some of the grammar work they'll be doing later in the course. Although these exercises are great for the first week of class, they can also be used as an in-class assignment later in the course.

OPTION 1

1. Using a chalkboard, whiteboard, or overhead projector, write down the following parts of speech and the numbers in parentheses:
   a. Noun (1)   c. Adjective (2)
   b. Verb (1)   d. Pronoun (2)

2. With input from students, briefly define each of the parts of speech. Write the definitions by the parts of speech.

3. Break students into groups of two or three.

4. For ten to fifteen minutes, have the students interview one another to learn more about each other (for instance, birthplace, favorite foods, favorite things to do). The interviewers should make notes on what they learn.

5. After the interviews, ask students to write a paragraph describing their interviewees. They should try to use each part of speech at least the number of times indicated in parentheses.

6. Ask students to read their paragraphs aloud.

7. Optional: If you want students to hand in their work, ask them to highlight or label the parts of speech in their paragraphs.

OPTION 2

1. Before class, write the following parts of speech on separate scraps of paper: noun, verb, pronoun, adverb, adjective. Make sure that the number of slips you create equals the number of students in the class. Fold the slips in half and put them in a can or other container. (Remember to bring the container to class.)

2. In class, write the same parts of speech on a chalkboard, whiteboard, or overhead transparency.

3. With input from students, briefly define each of the parts of speech. Write the definitions by the parts of speech.

4. Walk around the room with the slips of paper, and ask each student to pick one.

5. Once all students have selected a slip, ask them to write one sentence that introduces them to the class and uses the part of speech they've selected.

6. Ask students to read their sentences and identify the word or words that fit the part of speech they selected. You might want to write some of the sentences on the board.

A critical thinking activity from Chapter 6 of this manual could also serve as a great icebreaker. Or, you can try one of these:

- Ask students to line themselves up by a specific characteristic: alphabetically by last name, by place of birth, by academic major, or by birthday. They will inevitably introduce themselves and learn about one another as they figure out the correct order in which to line up.

- Conduct a scavenger hunt for people in the class. Divide the students into groups and give each group a list of people to find: the person who has read the most books in the last three months; someone who grew up in the town the college is in; anyone born in a foreign country.

See also: The Cooperative Learning Environment, in How to Begin, in Chapter 7 of this manual.

GOALS WORKSHEET AND WRITING SAMPLE. Students need to begin thinking of themselves as writers, and you need to get samples of their writing so that you can assess their needs; it is therefore important to have them do some actual writing on the first day of class. Ask them to fill out the Writing Questionnaire. Make copies of this form in advance and distribute. On the form, students list their real-world goals, course goals, and specific writing skills they want to learn. I usually have my students write a paragraph (100 to 150 words), in which they expand on one of the goals they listed on the questionnaire. You could also introduce a new topic as a paragraph prompt. I like to ask students to describe the best or worst English class they have ever taken: Most students have experienced either a good or a bad class, so they have content to impart, and their descriptions tell me a great deal about their attitudes and expectations. You may want to end the class period with the request for the writing sample so that those who write slowly won't feel pressured and those who write quickly can leave when they finish.

CLOSURE. Some teachers like to end the first class meeting early because most students are not yet prepared for a long lecture. I, however, tell students that I'm a firm believer in giving them their money's worth, so they will seldom get out early. End the class by reemphasizing your positive attitude toward the semester and by making an assignment for the second class. You can make the assignment as simple as reading the syllabus/class schedule and purchasing texts and supplies, or you can jump right into a reading assignment from *Real Essays*. You can see the sample class schedules starting on page 15 for suggested assignments during the first week. Also encourage students to call you, or e-mail you, or come by your office if they have questions or to jot down the questions to ask at the next class. As you dismiss the class, tell them to have a nice day (or evening) and cheerfully call out, "I'll see you next class!"

THE REST OF THE FIRST WEEK. During the rest of the first week of class, make sure you accomplish any of the goals that you weren't able to fit in on the first day. In addition, give students a diagnostic grammar test so that you can assess their needs both as individuals and as a class. (See *Additional Resources* for several ready-made tests keyed to the chapters in *Real Essays*. Diagnostic tests are also available on the *Testing Tool Kit* CD that you can get with this book.) If you are going to be teaching in a computer lab or otherwise requiring the use of computers, build in time for acquainting students with the computer-related logistics. Also talk about other resources on campus, such as the writing center or library; you may even want to plan a visit. Finally, you may want to discuss plagiarism and give your students a written statement (such as the one found in Chapter 2 of this book) to clarify both the concept and its consequences.

Overview of *Real Essays*

Real Essays is organized to be both straightforward and flexible. The book is divided into eight parts: Part 1, College Thinking, Reading, and Writing (which discusses how to read in college and surveys the general writing process); Part 2, Writing Different Kinds of Essays (which covers each type, or mode, of essay that students are typically asked to write: narration, illustration, description, process analysis, classification, definition, comparison/contrast, cause/effect, and argument); Part 3, Special College Writing Projects (which discusses essay exams and research papers); Part 4, The Four Most Serious Errors; Part 5, Other Grammar Concerns; Part 6, Word Use; and Part 7, Punctuation and Capitalization. The final section, Readings for Writers, contains nine chapters: eight chapters with readings that illustrate each of the rhetorical methods addressed in the text, and a mini-casebook (Chapter 49) that presents argument readings and assignments on one theme.

How to Use **Real Essays**

Most instructors find it useful to begin the course with Part 1, which explains the expectations in a college writing course; introduces active, critical reading; surveys the writing process; and establishes the context for the rest of the book. Chapter 1 contains helpful suggestions for adapting to the college learning environment. Chapter 2 discusses critical thinking and what it means in the context of college work. Chapter 3 stresses the importance of reading closely and critically in college and beyond and introduces students to writing about readings, an important academic skill that is treated in more depth (with assignments) later in *Real Essays*. Chapter 4 covers writing basics, describing the importance of purpose and audience, outlining paragraph and essay structures, and providing an overview of the writing process. If you prefer to spend more time teaching each step of the writing process before asking students to produce an entire essay, you can use the assignments in Chapters 5 through 9, the chapters that delve into each writing step in greater depth.

After completing one of these assignments from Part 1, students will be well prepared for the writing chapters in Part 2. Each of these chapters includes a step-by-step Writing Guide that makes the process manageable. If students need more information on a particular step, cross-references in the Writing Guide direct them back to the chapters in Part 1.

Part 3 includes instruction for completing specialized writing tasks such as a research essay and a timed writing assignment. Use these chapters if they suit your course structure and your students' needs.

Different instructors have different ways of integrating grammar instruction into class time. Consider assigning Chapter 22, The Basic Sentence: An Overview, early in the semester; it contains an excellent review of the basics and should help allay some students' fears about grammar. *Real Essays* emphasizes the four most serious grammar errors (fragments, run-ons, problems with subject-verb agreement, and verb problems), so you may want to assign the chapters that address these errors to the class as a whole and discuss them during class time; you can assign other grammar chapters as needed, either to individual students or to the entire class.

Part 8, Readings for Writers, is organized according to rhetorical strategy, which should make it easy for you to integrate the selections into your class schedule and to connect reading with writing. When students are working on their process analysis paragraphs, for example, you can easily direct them to the professional examples in Chapter 44. Consider assigning the mini-casebook (Chapter 49) if you would like students to write about multiple readings grouped by theme.

Real Essays is filled with features designed to make the course useful to your students and to help them become better writers. I recommend reading through the first few pages of the *Instructor's Annotated Edition for Real Essays* and the preface to give yourself an overview of these features.

Sample Syllabus and Class Schedules

As I am using the terms, a *syllabus* is a written description of a course's content, requirements, and policies whereas a *class schedule* outlines what work is to be completed each day or week during the semester. Regardless of what terminology you use, I hope the following examples will be useful to you.

Sample Syllabus

Your school's or state's requirements may determine how much information you need to include in the syllabus that you distribute to your students. As a minimum, you will probably want to include a course description, a statement of attendance and grading policies, a list of required texts and supplies, and an explanation of available resources. The syllabus on pages 9–12 is used in Texas, a state where students are required to either pass a mandated test showing readiness for Freshman Composition or be placed in developmental writing until they pass the test; it may be more detailed than one you would need if you are teaching outside of Texas, but it can be used as a model nonetheless.

Developmental English Course Syllabus

INSTRUCTOR: OFFICE:

OFFICE HOURS: PHONE:

                                         E-MAIL:

Course Description

Developmental English is a basic writing course designed to prepare you for Freshman Composition.

Course Focus

The course focuses on principles of grammar, usage, sentence structure, paragraph development, and essay writing.

Texts and References

Anker, Susan. *Real Essays,* Fourth Edition. Boston: Bedford/St. Martin's, 2012.
A college dictionary.

Course Goals

Classes will have some lecture, discussion, and media presentations. In addition, during some classes, you will write and revise your assignments. The course covers the following content goals, although sequence may vary.

- A. Usage and Mechanics
    1. Use nouns and pronouns correctly as subjects or objects.
    2. Use correct verb forms.
    3. Use modifiers effectively in a sentence.
    4. Identify unnecessary shifts in verb tense.
    5. Identify shifts in person.
    6. Display standard punctuation and capitalization skills.
    7. Display standard spelling skills.
    8. Complete classroom and/or laboratory assignments.
- B. Sentence Structure
    1. Write clear and correct sentences.
    2. Write parallel sentence structures.
    3. Correct comma splices or run-on/fused sentences.
    4. Correct sentence fragments.
    5. Demonstrate understanding of subject-verb agreement.
    6. Write sentences that combine ideas correctly.
- C. Unity and Focus
    1. Select writing topics.
    2. Practice prewriting strategies.
    3. Focus writing topics.
    4. Distinguish between effective and ineffective topic sentences.
    5. Formulate topic sentences.
    6. Formulate thesis statements.
    7. Demonstrate use of appropriate transitional words and phrases.

D. Organization and Development
    1. Identify an essay's thesis.
    2. Identify an essay's support points.
    3. Identify an essay's concluding sentence.
    4. Identify methods of ordering ideas in an essay.
    5. Outline essay content.
    6. Convert outlines into essays.
    7. Write different kinds of essays (e.g., narration, illustration, cause/effect, argument, etc.).
    8. Develop ideas and arguments.
E. Appropriateness
    1. Identify writing purpose.
    2. Identify audience.
    3. Demonstrate appropriate and varied word choice.
    4. Demonstrate appropriate personal style and voice.
    5. Proofread essays.
F. Exit Skills
    1. Complete timed in-class writings.
    2. Review THEA [Texas Higher Education Assessment] skills.
    3. Complete final essay sample.

Student Contributions

1. You need to spend at least six hours per week preparing for class. Timely completion of class work and home assignments is crucial.

2. If you need additional computer time to work on your papers, you may visit the Writing Center or the Computer Learning Center.

3. You can also improve your reading and writing skills through independent study in the Learning Mall or Computer Learning Center and conferences with your instructor.

4. You should attend class regularly because major concepts are explained in class and much of the writing and daily work will be done in class. In addition, state law requires that students who enroll in remedial classes because of THEA scores attend and participate fully in those remedial classes. Therefore, those THEA-liable students with nine absences on MWF or six on TTH or MW will be automatically withdrawn from all courses in which they are enrolled.

5. If you miss roll call because you are tardy, contact the instructor as soon as class is over, or you will be counted absent.

6. If absent, you are responsible for discovering what you missed and for preparing assignments for the next class. Makeup work is allowed only at the instructor's discretion.

7. Complete and submit course work by specified deadlines. Papers turned in after the due date will not receive full credit. Your absence from class on the day an assignment is due does not excuse the assignment from being late. If the instructor approves, some late work may be made up by a specified deadline.

8. If you must withdraw from this course, you are responsible for contacting the registrar.

Course Evaluation

The final grade will be *credit* or *no credit*. To receive credit, you must either (a) make an average of at least 70 in the course and complete a timed persuasive essay at the end of the semester, or (b) pass the THEA test.

Your semester grade will be based on the following:

Homework, in-class activities	10%
Spelling tests + comprehensive final	10%
Unit tests on mechanics, usage, sentence structure + comprehensive final	30%
Essay assignments	40%
Final writing exam (timed essay)	10%

Credit for the course does not guarantee passage to Composition I. Your next English course will be determined on the basis of the following criteria:

1. If you have been placed in English 0324 on the basis of PTT (Pre-THEA test) scores, you must pass the essay portion of the PTT in order to advance to English 1301.

2. However, if you have been placed in English 0324 on the basis of PTT scores and did not pass the THEA writing test during the semester, you must pass the THEA writing test to advance to English 1301.

3. If you have been placed in English 0324 on the basis of THEA scores, you must pass the THEA writing test in order to advance to English 1301.

Important Note: THEA scores will always override timed essay scores. Furthermore, passing the end-of-semester essay does not exempt you from the THEA, nor does it guarantee success on the THEA test.

Performance Objectives

Your mastery of the performance objectives will be evaluated in several ways, with a score of 70 considered mastery. Your recall of text assignments, laboratory practice, lecture notes, and class assignments will be tested according to each instructor's directions. Your responses must be consistent with the text and lectures. Individual instructors may emphasize, in a personal manner, course content, order, and related topics. Writing assignments are also a critical part of demonstrating mastery of the performance objectives. Performance will be satisfactory if these skills are practiced and applied in your paragraphs and essays. To show mastery of course goals, you will be required to

1. Write sentences that demonstrate correct usage of the parts of speech, punctuation, and capitalization.

2. Demonstrate precision and variety in choice of words.

3. Write sentences, paragraphs, and essays free of sentence errors.

4. Write sentences, paragraphs, and essays free of shifts in person and errors in verb tense.

5. Determine the audience and purpose of a paragraph or essay.

6. Demonstrate the ability to write a clear focus statement for both a paragraph and an essay.

7. Demonstrate the ability to develop ideas and arguments in appropriate order to produce an effective, unified, coherent paragraph and/or essay.

8. Demonstrate the ability to write a well-developed multiple-paragraph essay (300–600 words). Performance will be satisfactory if the writing sample effectively communicates a whole message to the specified audience for the stated purpose.

9. Demonstrate the ability to proofread and revise paragraphs and essays.

10. Complete the timed persuasive essay. Performance will be satisfactory if the writing sample effectively communicates a whole message to the specified audience for the stated purpose and if the student scores 70 percent correct on the objective test.

Special Instructions

A. *Materials*

You will need the following supplies for this course:
- paper for class notes
- journal notebook
- portfolio folder
- pens, pencils
- computer access

B. *Special Help or Instruction*

Several areas are available for assistance with special problems and your assignments. Some areas will require you to show a current student ID.

The Skills Center, located in ACB 109, is open 7:30 A.M. to 10:00 P.M. (M–Th) and 7:30 A.M. to 5:00 P.M. (F) during the long terms, and 7:30 A.M. to 9:00 P.M. (M–Th) during the summer. Sometimes you will have a required assignment that uses the center's materials; therefore, it is important that you arrange your schedule so that you can use this learning facility.

Also located in ACB 109, *The Writing Center* operates from 7:30 A.M. to 9:30 P.M. (M–Th) and 7:30 A.M. to 4:30 P.M. (F) during long terms only. An English consultant is available to help you understand your assignments and improve your writing skills. The area also has Macintosh computers available for your use.

The Computer Learning Center, located in LRC 101, is open from 7:45 A.M. to 9:45 P.M. (M–Th), 7:45 A.M. to 4:45 P.M. (F), and 7:45 A.M. to 3 P.M. (Sat) during long terms. Summer hours are 7:30 A.M. to 10 P.M. (M–Th). You can work on your own as you see a need, or your instructor may assign you a specific software program to complete. The CLC personnel are trained to assist you with the computers.

Sample Class Schedules

Whether or not you distribute a class schedule to your students, you will probably want to create one for your own use. Always plan more than you think you can cover. Doing so can prevent the embarrassment of not knowing what to do with extra time; besides, eliminating assignments rather than adding assignments can enhance your reputation with your students.

The four sample schedules included here model different configurations based on different numbers of weeks and different emphases (e.g., focus on invention, organization, and drafting, or focus on practicing the essay). These schedules can easily be adapted for use in a computer classroom or lab by setting aside one day during the first week to introduce students to the computers and one day during the second week for an introduction to the word processing software. Allow students to plan and/or draft some of their writing at home and then use class time for typing the assignment into the computer, editing, and revising. In addition, you can substitute appropriate chapters when you have determined the type of grammar, sentence structure, word usage, and punctuation assistance your students need. Furthermore, if your school or state requires an exit essay, you may want to include two to three in-class essays and concentrate on the particular rhetorical mode or modes in which your students will be required to write.

Class Schedule: Emphasis on Invention, Organization, and Drafting of the Essay (16 weeks)

Note: This class schedule focuses on three modes of writing: narration, illustration, and argument.

Week One
Reading Assignment: Ch. 1, "Succeeding in College: What You Need to Know." Ch. 2, "Thinking Critically: Developing Your Power of Mind." Ch. 3, "Reading Critically: Developing Your Understanding." Ch. 4, "Writing Basics: Audience, Purpose, and Process."
Classroom Activities: Introduction to course. In-class diagnostic writing. In-class diagnostic test. Overview of the writing process and journal writing.
Writing Assignment: Prewriting practice. Journal entries.

Week Two
Reading Assignment: Ch. 5, "Finding and Exploring Your Topic: Choosing Something to Write About." Ch. 10, "Narration: Writing That Tells Stories." Ch. 22, "The Basic Sentence: An Overview."
Classroom Activities: Practice choosing topics. Review homework exercises.
Writing Assignment: Find and explore a topic.

Week Three
Reading Assignment: Ch. 6, "Making a Point: Writing Your Thesis Statement." Ch. 23, "Fragments: Incomplete Sentences."
Classroom Activities: Group work on effective thesis statements. Review homework exercises.
Writing Assignment: Write thesis statement. Find details, examples, and facts.

Week Four
Reading Assignment: Ch. 7, "Supporting Your Point: Finding Details, Examples, and Facts." Ch. 24, "Run-Ons: Two Sentences Joined Incorrectly."
Classroom Activities: Working with and ordering major events and supporting a thesis with relevant details. Review homework exercises.
Writing Assignment: Arrange details in an outline.

Week Five
Reading Assignment: Ch. 8, "Writing a Draft: Putting Your Ideas Together." Ch. 25, "Problems with Subject-Verb Agreement: When Subjects and Verbs Do Not Match."
Classroom Activities: In-class work on essay outline. Review homework exercises.
Writing Assignment: Write narration draft.

Week Six
Reading Assignment: Ch. 9, "Revising Your Draft: Improving Your Essay." Ch. 26, "Verb Problems: Avoiding Mistakes in Verb Tense."
Classroom Activities: Introduction to peer evaluation. Review homework exercises.
Writing Assignment: Revise narration draft.

Week Seven
Reading Assignment: Ch. 11, "Illustration: Writing That Shows Examples." Ch. 36, "Commas."
Classroom Activities: Freewrite, brainstorm, and cluster for illustration essay. Review homework exercises.
Writing Assignment: Find and explore a topic for illustration essay.

Week Eight
Reading Assignment: Ch. 38, "Quotation Marks." Ch. 39, "Other Punctuation."
Classroom Activities: Group work on effective thesis statements and finding important examples. Review homework exercises.
Writing Assignment: Write thesis statement. Find important examples.

Week Nine
Reading Assignment: Ch. 34, "Word Choice: Avoiding Language Pitfalls."
Classroom Activities: Evaluating the order of importance for examples. Review homework exercises.
Writing Assignment: Arrange examples in an outline.

Week Ten
Reading Assignment: Ch. 30, "Coordination and Subordination: Joining Ideas."
Classroom Activities: In-class work on essay outline. Review homework exercises.
Writing Assignment: Write illustration draft.

Week Eleven
Reading Assignment: Ch. 32, "Sentence Variety: Putting Rhythm in Your Writing."
Classroom Activities: Peer evaluation. Review homework exercises.
Writing Assignment: Revise illustration draft.

Week Twelve
Reading Assignment: Ch. 18, "Argument: Writing That Persuades." Ch. 27, "Pronouns: Using Substitutes for Nouns."
Classroom Activities: Discuss ideas for argument. Review homework exercises.
Writing Assignment: Find and explore a topic for argument essay.

Week Thirteen
Reading Assignment: Ch. 35, "Commonly Confused Words: Avoiding Mistakes with Sound-Alikes."
Classroom Activities: Prewrite to explore positions on issues. Consider thesis statement. Review homework exercises.
Writing Assignment: Write thesis statement and support for argument.

Week Fourteen
Reading Assignment: Ch. 37: "Apostrophes."
Classroom Activities: Discuss order of ideas in argument. Review homework exercises.
Writing Assignment: Argumentative paragraph. Arrange ideas for argument in an outline.

Week Fifteen
Reading Assignment: Ch. 19, "Writing under Pressure: Tests and Essay Exams."
Classroom Activities: In-class work on essay outline. Review homework exercises.
Writing Assignment: Practice writing summaries. Write argument draft.

Week Sixteen
Classroom Activities: Review for/complete final.
Writing Assignment: In-class essay final. Revise argument draft.

Class Schedule: Emphasis on Practicing the Essay (16 weeks)

Note: Assignments from grammar chapters will be made as need is determined. Chapter 21, "Writing the Research Essay: Using Outside Sources," may be assigned if needed.

Week One

Reading Assignment: Ch. 1, "Succeeding in College: What You Need to Know." Ch. 2, "Thinking Critically: Developing Your Power of Mind." Ch. 3, "Reading Critically: Developing Your Understanding." Ch. 4, "Writing Basics: Audience, Purpose, and Process." Ch. 5, "Finding and Exploring Your Topic: Choosing Something to Write About."

Classroom Activities: Introduction to course. Introduction to journal writing. In-class diagnostic test. Overview of the writing process. Practice choosing topics. Group work on effective topic sentences.

Writing Assignment: In-class diagnostic writing. Prewriting practice. Journal entries. Find and explore a topic for first paragraph.

Week Two

Reading Assignment: Ch. 6, "Making a Point: Writing Your Thesis Statement." Ch. 7, "Supporting Your Point: Finding Details, Examples, and Facts." Ch. 30, "Coordination and Subordination: Joining Ideas."

Classroom Activities: Working with, evaluating, and organizing supporting details. Review homework exercises.

Writing Assignment: Write paragraph. Journal entries.

Week Three

Reading Assignment: Ch. 8, "Writing a Draft: Putting Your Ideas Together." Ch. 9, "Revising Your Draft: Improving Your Essay."

Classroom Activities: In-class work on paragraph draft. Introduction to peer evaluation. Review homework exercises.

Writing Assignment: Continuing assignment, steps five and six. Revise paragraph draft.

Week Four

Reading Assignment: Ch. 11, "Illustration: Writing That Shows Examples." Ch. 31, "Parallelism: Balancing Ideas."

Classroom Activities: Discuss connection between single paragraphs and body paragraphs of an essay. Select topic and write thesis statement for illustration essay. Review homework exercises.

Writing Assignment: Thesis statement for illustration essay.

Week Five

Reading Assignment: Reread Ch. 8, "Writing a Draft: Putting Your Ideas Together."

Classroom Activities: Plan essay and start draft. Review homework exercises.

Writing Assignment: Topic sentences, support details, and rough draft of illustration essay.

Week Six
Reading Assignment: Reread Ch. 9, "Revising Your Draft: Improving Your Essay." Ch. 32, "Sentence Variety: Putting Rhythm in Your Writing."
Classroom Activities: Continue work on essay. Peer editing. Review homework exercises.
Writing Assignment: Revise illustration essay.

Week Seven
Reading Assignment: Ch. 10, "Narration: Writing That Tells Stories." Ch. 34, "Word Choice: Avoiding Language Pitfalls."
Classroom Activities: Discuss, plan, draft, revise, and edit narration essay. Review homework exercises.
Writing Assignment: Narrative essay.

Week Eight
Reading Assignment: Ch. 13, "Process Analysis: Writing That Explains How Things Happen."
Classroom Activities: Discuss, plan, draft, revise, and edit process analysis essay. Review homework exercises.
Writing Assignment: Process essay.

Week Nine
Reading Assignment: Ch. 14, "Classification: Writing That Puts Things into Groups."
Classroom Activities: Discuss, plan, draft, revise, and edit classification essay. Review homework exercises.
Writing Assignment: Classification essay.

Week Ten
Reading Assignment: Ch. 16, "Comparison and Contrast: Writing That Shows Similarities and Differences."
Classroom Activities: Discuss, plan, draft, revise, and edit comparison/contrast essay. Review homework exercises.
Writing Assignment: Comparison/contrast essay.

Week Eleven
Reading Assignment: Ch. 17, "Cause and Effect: Writing That Explains Reasons or Results."
Classroom Activities: Discuss, plan, draft, revise, and edit cause/effect essay. Review homework exercises.
Writing Assignment: Cause/effect essay.

Week Twelve
Reading Assignment: Ch. 18, "Argument: Writing That Persuades."
Classroom Activities: Discuss, plan, and draft argument essay. Review homework exercises.
Writing Assignment: Argument essay draft.

Week Thirteen
Classroom Activities: Edit, revise, and peer-evaluate argument essay.
Writing Assignment: Argument essay.

Week Fourteen
Reading Assignment: Ch. 19, "Writing under Pressure: Tests and Essay Exams."
Classroom Activities: Practice planning answers to essay exams. Review homework exercises.
Writing Assignment: Sample essay exam.

Week Fifteen
Reading Assignment: Ch. 20, "Finding and Evaluating Outside Sources: Preparing to Write a Research Essay."
Classroom Activities: Group and individual work on summary writing. Comprehensive grammar final.
Writing Assignment: Sample summaries.

Week Sixteen
Classroom Activities: In-class review of writing.
Writing Assignment: In-class essay final.

Class Schedule: Emphasis on Practicing the Essay (10 weeks)

Note: Assignments from grammar chapters will be made as need is determined. Chapter 21, "Writing the Research Essay: Using Outside Sources," may be assigned if needed.

Week One

Reading Assignment: Ch. 1, "Succeeding in College: What You Need to Know." Ch. 2, "Thinking Critically: Developing Your Power of Mind." Ch. 3, "Reading Critically: Developing Your Understanding." Ch. 4, "Writing Basics: Audience, Purpose, and Process." Ch. 5, "Finding and Exploring Your Topic: Choosing Something to Write About."

Classroom Activities: Introduction to course. Introduction to journal writing. In-class diagnostic test. Overview of the writing process. Group work on choosing topics and writing effective topic sentences. Review homework exercises.

Writing Assignment: In-class diagnostic writing. Prewriting practice. Journal entries. Develop topic sentence for first paragraph.

Week Two

Reading Assignment: Ch. 7, "Supporting Your Point: Finding Details, Examples, and Facts." Ch. 8, "Writing a Draft: Putting Your Ideas Together." Ch. 9, "Revising Your Draft: Improving Your Essay." Ch. 30, "Coordination and Subordination: Joining Ideas."

Classroom Activities: Working with and evaluating supporting details. In-class work on paragraph draft. Introduction to peer editing. Review homework exercises.

Writing Assignment: Complete full paragraph.

Week Three

Reading Assignment: Ch. 11, "Illustration: Writing That Shows Examples." Ch. 31, "Parallelism: Balancing Ideas." Ch. 32, "Sentence Variety: Putting Rhythm in Your Writing."

Classroom Activities: Discuss connection between single paragraphs and body paragraphs of an essay. Select topic for illustration essay. Plan essay and start draft. Review homework exercises.

Writing Assignment: Illustration essay.

Week Four

Reading Assignment: Ch. 34, "Word Choice: Avoiding Language Pitfalls."

Classroom Activities: Continue drafting essay. Edit essay. Review homework exercises.

Writing Assignment: Illustration essay.

Week Five

Reading Assignment: Ch. 16, "Comparison and Contrast: Writing That Shows Similarities and Differences."

Classroom Activities: Discuss, plan, draft, revise, and edit comparison/contrast essay. Review homework exercises.

Writing Assignment: Comparison/contrast essay.

Week Six

Reading Assignment: Ch. 17, "Cause and Effect: Writing That Explains Reasons or Results."

Classroom Activities: Discuss, plan, draft, revise, and edit cause/effect essay. Review homework exercises.

Writing Assignment: Cause/effect essay.

Week Seven

Reading Assignment: Ch. 18, "Argument: Writing That Persuades."

Classroom Activities: Discuss, plan, and draft argument essay. Review homework exercises.

Writing Assignment: Argument essay draft.

Week Eight

Classroom Activities: Edit, revise, and peer-evaluate argument essay.

Writing Assignment: Argument essay.

Week Nine

Reading Assignment: Ch. 19, "Writing under Pressure: Tests and Essay Exams."

Classroom Activities: Discuss and practice writing essays. Review writing process. Comprehensive grammar final.

Writing Assignment: Sample essay.

Week Ten

Reading Assignment: Ch. 20, "Finding and Evaluating Outside Sources: Preparing to Write a Research Essay."

Classroom Activities: Group and individual work on summary writing. Review homework exercises.

Writing Assignment: Sample summaries. In-class essay final.

Class Schedule: Using Computers to Teach the Essay (16 weeks)

Week One

Reading Assignment: Ch. 1, "Succeeding in College: What You Need to Know." Ch. 2, "Thinking Critically: Developing Your Power of Mind." Ch. 3, "Reading Critically: Developing Your Understanding." Ch. 4, "Writing Basics: Audience, Purpose, and Process."

Classroom Activities: Introduction to course. Introduction to journal writing. In-class diagnostic test. Overview of the writing process. Introduction to the computer.

Note: Plan about 50 minutes for introducing students to the computers. If your computer has a self-guided tour, you may want to make up short-response questions that your students can answer while they complete the tour. Using the self-guided tour enables students to work at their own pace while picking up the useful information and terms that will prove beneficial throughout the semester. If your computer doesn't have a tour, then show students how to turn on the computers, get in and out of applications, save to their own thumbdrives, open and close documents, scroll or move through documents, cut and paste, print, and so on. Also introduce any terminology that you will be using. Printed instructions will help those students who are not familiar with computers.

Writing Assignment: In-class diagnostic writing. Prewriting practice. Journal entries.

Week Two

Reading Assignment: Ch. 5, "Finding and Exploring Your Topic: Choosing Something to Write About." Ch. 6, "Making a Point: Writing Your Thesis Statement." Ch. 7, "Supporting Your Point: Finding Details, Examples, and Facts." Ch. 22, "The Basic Sentence: An Overview."

Classroom Activities: Practice choosing topics. Group work on effective topic sentences. Review homework exercises. Introduce the word processing software.

Note: After completing the self-guided tour or your own introduction, students should be ready to type, edit, save, and print a short document. You could have them do a journal entry or their paragraph preparation on the computer.

Writing Assignment: Develop topic sentence for first paragraph.

Week Three

Reading Assignment: Ch. 8, "Writing a Draft: Putting Your Ideas Together." Ch. 23, "Fragments: Incomplete Sentences."

Classroom Activities: Working with and evaluating supporting details. In-class work on paragraph draft. Review homework exercises. Introduce students to the format you want for paragraphs (margins, line spacing, headings, titles, etc.). Then have them type their drafts and save them to their own disks. Ask students to print copies to take home for review and editing.

Writing Assignment: Complete full paragraph.

Week Four

Reading Assignment: Ch. 9, "Revising Your Draft: Improving Your Essay." Ch. 11, "Illustration: Writing That Shows Examples." Ch. 24, "Run-Ons: Two Sentences Joined Incorrectly."

Classroom Activities: Introduction to peer evaluation. Introduce the Writing Guide Software for *Real Essays*. Discuss, plan, and draft illustration paragraph. Review homework exercises. Remind students how to cut and paste as they revise their paragraphs. Introduce editing software, and explain how it works and how to use it. Have students type their illustration paragraphs into the computer. Ask students to print copies to take home for review and editing.
Writing Assignment: Illustration draft.

Week Five
Reading Assignment: Ch. 30, "Coordination and Subordination: Joining Ideas."
Classroom Activities: Revise and edit illustration essay. Review homework exercises. Have students print copies of their illustration essays to exchange for peer editing, or have students trade computers and evaluate one another's paragraphs on the computer screen. Run editing software on all paragraphs.
Writing Assignment: Complete illustration essay.

Week Six
Reading Assignment: Ch. 16, "Comparison and Contrast: Writing That Shows Similarities and Differences." Ch. 25, "Problems with Subject-Verb Agreement: When Subjects and Verbs Do Not Match."
Classroom Activities: Discuss, plan, and draft comparison/contrast essay. Review homework exercises. Write draft of comparison/contrast essay in the computer. Ask students to print copies to take home for review and editing.
Writing Assignment: Comparison/contrast draft.

Week Seven
Reading Assignment: Ch. 36, "Commas."
Classroom Activities: Revise and edit comparison/contrast essay. Review homework exercises. Have students print copies of their comparison/contrast essays to exchange for peer editing, or have students trade computers and evaluate one another's essays on the computer screen. Run editing software on all essays.
Writing Assignment: Comparison/contrast essay.

Week Eight
Reading Assignment: Ch. 13, "Process Analysis: Writing That Explains How Things Happen."
Classroom Activities: Discuss, plan, write, and evaluate process analysis draft. Review homework exercises. Type process analysis essay into the computer. Run editing software. Edit and revise on the computer.
Writing Assignment: Process analysis draft.

Week Nine
Classroom Activities: Discuss connection between single paragraphs and body paragraphs of an essay. Review homework exercises. Introduce the format you want for the essay (margins, line spacing, headings, page numbers, titles, etc.). Have students begin revising draft of essay using the computer. Ask students to print copies to take home for review and editing.
Writing Assignment: Process analysis essay.

Week Ten

Reading Assignment: Ch. 17, "Cause and Effect: Writing That Explains Reasons or Results." Reread Ch. 5, "Finding and Exploring Your Topic: Choosing Something to Write About." Reread Ch. 6, "Making a Point: Writing Your Thesis Statement." Ch. 34, "Word Choice: Avoiding Language Pitfalls."

Classroom Activities: Organize ideas about cause/effect essays. Review homework exercises. On the computer, brainstorm a list of topics and their possible reasons or results.

Writing Assignment: Cause/effect draft.

Week Eleven

Reading Assignment: Reread Ch. 7, "Supporting Your Point: Finding Details, Examples, and Facts." Ch. 35, "Commonly Confused Words: Avoiding Mistakes with Sound-Alikes."

Classroom Activities: Gather details, examples, and facts on the computer. Review homework exercises.

Writing Assignment: Complete cause/effect essay.

Week Twelve

Reading Assignment: Ch. 20, "Finding and Evaluating Outside Sources: Preparing to Write a Research Essay." Ch. 21, "Writing the Research Essay: Using Outside Sources."

Classroom Activities: If your computers are connected to the college library system, use this week to introduce your students to research methods. Show them how to connect to the online catalog, how to do keyword searches, how to connect to online databases, and how to find articles and books in the library. If there is time, ask students to complete a library research worksheet.

Writing Assignment: Finish library research worksheet.

Week Thirteen

Reading Assignment: Ch. 18, "Argument: Writing That Persuades."

Classroom Activities: Discuss, plan, and draft argument essay. Do peer evaluations. Review homework exercises. Have students begin entering draft of essay into the computer. Ask students to print copies to take home for review and editing.

Writing Assignment: Argument essay draft.

Week Fourteen

Classroom Activities: Run editing software on all argument drafts. Have students print copies of their drafts to exchange for peer editing, or have students trade computers and evaluate one another's drafts on the computer screen.

Note: If you decide to incorporate research into the argument essay, now is the time to see if students are successfully integrating sources into their writing.

Writing Assignment: Argument essay.

Week Fifteen
Reading Assignment: Ch. 19, "Writing under Pressure: Tests and Essay Exams."
Classroom Activities: Review homework exercises. Have students complete their essay drafts, run the editing software, and print copies for evaluations. Practice planning answers to essay exams.
Writing Assignment: Sample essay exam.

Week Sixteen
Classroom Activities: Comprehensive grammar final.
Writing Assignment: In-class essay as final.

Using the Ancillary Package

Real Essays is accompanied by a wealth of resources designed to make your life easier and to make students' time in the developmental writing course more productive. Complete descriptions and examples of these resources are included on the first few pages of the *Instructor's Annotated Edition for Real Essays,* so I won't repeat that information here. But I would like to offer a few comments and suggestions for how you can use these resources in your course.

Instructor Resources

INSTRUCTOR'S ANNOTATED EDITION FOR REAL ESSAYS

The *Instructor's Annotated Edition* (IAE) is unique in that it was carefully designed as a teaching tool for instructors who all too often have less time than they would like for class preparation. It contains not only the answers to all exercises in the student text but also a series of teaching tips and references printed in the margins. (The IAE annotations are magenta.) In other words, as you page through a chapter, you'll find suggestions for presenting material in class, discussion prompts, options for collaborative learning, ideas for teaching in the computer lab, alternative assignments, ideas for teaching ESL students, and cross-references to other parts of the book and other parts of the *Real Essays* package. All are presented right where you need them, on the pages of the book itself. These aids make the IAE a true teaching text, a convenient resource that organizes the materials and ideas you need to teach a good class. You might want to highlight the ones you plan to use. And if you have teaching tips for specific topics or chapters that you would like to see in the IAE for the next edition of *Real Essays,* I urge you to send them to us at *Real Essays,* Bedford/St. Martin's, 75 Arlington Street, Boston, MA 02116.

The preface reviews the main features of the text and provides information on each of the ancillaries available with *Real Essays.* Immediately following the preface, a chart matches common course goals to the ancillary package. Take a look here to make sure you are taking full advantage of everything that *Real Essays* has to offer.

PRACTICAL SUGGESTIONS FOR TEACHING REAL ESSAYS

In *Practical Suggestions* (the instructor's manual that you are reading right now), you will find sample class schedules; suggestions for assignments and class activities; and advice on grading, dealing with developmental writing students, planning your course, and working with computers. In other words, this volume contains everything you ever wanted to know about teaching developmental writing but were afraid to ask.

Whether you are an old pro or a newcomer in the field of developmental writing, you should find the sample schedules (presented earlier in this chapter) beneficial in getting your course organized. Of course, what works for one instructor or one class may not work for another instructor or even for another class taught by the same instructor. However, the schedules and sample syllabi should give you a starting point for using *Real Essays* with your students.

If you are new to developmental writing, you should find the materials in *Practical Suggestions* especially helpful. I suggest that you pay particular attention to Chapter 2, Tips for New Instructors, which was written to give you a general feel for the developmental writing class. Not only does this chapter impart useful information, but it also provides emotional support.

As you progress into the semester and turn your attention to day-to-day concerns, you may want to consult the chapters on assessment, technology, critical thinking, and instructional approaches. Remember that the materials presented in this ancillary are just guidelines. As you become comfortable in the developmental writing classroom and familiar with *Real Essays,* you will probably adapt many of the suggestions and originate your own plans and assignments.

ADDITIONAL RESOURCES TO ACCOMPANY REAL ESSAYS

Welcome *Additional Resources* with open arms, for it includes materials that will make your job as an instructor easier. Here you will find diagnostic and chapter tests, additional exercises, and forms that you can reproduce as either transparencies or handouts: checklists, diagrams, planning forms, and so on. I always dreaded the arrival of a new text because I knew that I had to prepare new tests and perhaps new handouts or transparencies to match the terminology and content of the new book. Now, however, I can turn to *Additional Resources* for those materials and spend more time on actual class preparation, grading, and student conferences.

BEDFORD COURSEPACKS

These free resources let you integrate Bedford's most popular content into your course management systems.

TEACHING DEVELOPMENTAL WRITING: BACKGROUND READINGS Do you ever want confirmation that what you are thinking and doing is right or at least on track with other instructors? If so, then you will enjoy the selections in *Background Readings*. Chosen to help both new and experienced teachers, these readings cover a wide variety of topics that concern the developmental professional.

Even if your approach to developmental writing, grading, grammar instruction, or classroom activities has proved successful in the past, you may be ready for something new. If that's the case, the readings offer advice and suggestions from experts in the field and ordinary teachers in the trenches. Veteran teachers—those who have been there and not only survived the experience but enjoyed it—know best.

TESTING TOOL KIT: *A WRITING AND GRAMMAR TEST BANK CD-ROM* This CD, free to instructors using *Real Essays,* allows you to create secure, customized tests and quizzes from a pool of nearly 2,000 questions. Ideal for assessing students' writing and grammar competency, the test bank can also be used to create practices that are tailored to course goals. Ten ready-to-administer diagnostic tests are also included. See the inside back cover of this manual for a chart that correlates topics in *Testing Tool Kit* with chapters in *Real Essays.*

PORTFOLIO KEEPING: *A GUIDE FOR STUDENTS* AND PORTFOLIO TEACHING: *A GUIDE FOR INSTRUCTORS* Written by Nedra Reynolds and Rich Rice, these guides provide the practical information students, instructors, and writing program administrators need to use the portfolio method successfully in a writing course.

With an Access Package

REAL ESSAYS QUICK REFERENCE CARD This three-panel laminated Quick Reference card includes writing and editing advice, help with Web searches, and useful word processing tips. Have students stand it up next to their computer monitors for reference as they write.

FROM PRACTICE TO MASTERY If you teach in Florida, be aware that *From Practice to Mastery,* a study guide for the Florida Basic Skills Exit Tests, is also available with *Real Essays.*

WRITINGCLASS FOR REAL ESSAYS WITH READINGS AVAILABLE WITH ANY ACCESS PACKAGE *WritingClass for Real Essays* is a customizable course space that offers book-specific exercises, diagnostics, writing

and commenting tools, step-by-step multimedia lessons, and *LearningCurve,* an interactive learning tool that adapts to students' skill levels and helps build grammar proficiency. *WritingClass* provides students with a dynamic, interactive online course space that helps them stay focused and lets you see how your students are progressing.

Re:Writing Plus, now with *VideoCentral.* This resource, which can be purchased separately or packaged with *Real Essays* at a discount, gathers all of Bedford/St. Martin's premium digital content for the writing class into one online collection. It includes interactive help with writing a paragraph; tutorials and practices that show how writing works in students' real-world experience; *VideoCentral,* with over 140 brief videos for the writing classroom; the first-ever peer-review game, *Peer Factor; i-cite: visualizing sources;* plus hundreds of models of writing and hundreds of readings.

The Bedford/St. Martin's ESL Workbook. This workbook, free when packaged with the print text, includes many grammar exercises specifically for ESL and multilingual students, of varying language skills and backgrounds. Answers are at the back.

The Bedford/St. Martin's Planner. This planner is free when packaged with the print text. It includes many features to aid students in planning and using their time effectively. For example, it has advice on preparing schedules and to-do lists plus blank schedules and calendars (monthly and weekly). The planner is a handy size, so students can fit it in their backpacks or bags and take it with them.

MAKE-A-PARAGRAPH KIT WITH *EXERCISE CENTRAL TO GO* This fun, animated CD-ROM gives students everything they need to write successful paragraphs. First, students see a paragraph develop and undergo revision as part of an "Extreme Paragraph Makeover" "reality" program. Then, they write their own paragraphs based on a choice of six topics, getting advice and help along the way. Next, animated audiovisual tutorials show them how to find and fix the four most serious grammar errors (fragments, run-ons and comma splices, subject-verb agreement problems, and verb problems). Finally, students can build their own writing and revising checklist and get lots of grammar practice with *Exercise Central to Go,* the entire content of which is on this CD.

Student Resources

REAL ESSAYS STUDENT SITE AT BEDFORDSTMARTINS .COM/REALESSAYS This helpful, free site provides resources that help students with writing and research. Key features include annotated model essays, graphic organizers and peer review forms for all modes of writing, and exercises with immediate feedback. Instructors can find tools for teaching with *Real Essays,* including downloadable presentation slides for illustrating key grammar concepts, a downloadable version of *.Additional Resources for Teaching Real Essays,* and more. The site also provides links to *Re: Writing* online resources for instructors and students.

EXERCISE CENTRAL 3.0 AT BEDFORDSTMARTINS .COM/REALESSAYS *Exercise Central* is an online collection of exercises related to writing, grammar, punctuation, sentence style, word choice, ESL issues, and research. This collection is the largest available, with more than nine thousand items. It is thorough, simple to use, and convenient for you and your students. *Exercise Central* includes multiple exercise sets at a variety of levels as well as an interactive reporting feature. Students receive customized, immediate feedback for all their answers, usually including an explanation of why the answers are correct or incorrect—feedback that turns practice into a learning experience.

Before doing the practices on *Exercise Central,* students might want to take the diagnostic test on the *Real Essays* Web site. The test results are broken down by topic and include links to specific exercises on these topics.

When students enter *Exercise Central,* they will gain access to a Customized Lesson Plan based on the editing chapters in *Real Essays.* This lesson plan will help students make the connection between their online practice sessions and the content of the book and the writing course. In addition, the Customized Lesson Plan will help students keep track of which exercises they have completed and which topics they need more practice with.

Each editing chapter in *Real Essays* appears in the Customized Lesson Plan. Once students have found the chapter they want to practice with, they will immediately see a link to the primary exercises for this topic (in the first column). These are exercises that have been written especially to accompany *Real Essays;* the level and coverage match those in the text. You will probably want to direct

most students to start with the primary exercises. If students need additional practice, you might direct them to another exercise at the same level; links to other developmental exercises are included in the lesson plan. If students have done well on the first exercise, you might suggest that they practice further with another exercise at a higher level; links to more difficult exercises are also included in the lesson plan.

To simplify the task of course management, the reporting feature of *Exercise Central* allows you to monitor the progress of individual students or of the class as a whole; if you choose the latter option, you can see the results for a single exercise set or for all exercise sets at once. If you have several classes or sections, you can even create customized reports that will display results for each class or section separately.

The first time you sign in to *Exercise Central* as an instructor, you will be asked to register by supplying some information about yourself, your class, and your institution; you will also be asked to give your e-mail address. Once the registration process is complete, you will be sent a password by e-mail. When you sign in using this password, you will gain access to the instructor area of *Exercise Central.* If you want to see reports on your students' exercises, simply tell students to type in your e-mail address when they sign in. You will be able to view reports on all students who have supplied your e-mail address. Complete directions for using the standard reports and for creating customized reports are included in the Web site for *Exercise Central* itself.

E-Book Options

Real Essays is now available either as a CourseSmart e-book or in formats to use with computers, tablets, and e-readers. These can be good value options for your students.

For more information on any of these resources, contact your Bedford/St. Martin's sales representative, e-mail sales support at sales_support@bfwpub .com, or visit **bedfordstmartins.com/realessays /catalog.** You will find the offerings that will most suit your needs and help you and your students.

2

Tips for New Instructors

Where Am I and How Did I Get Here?

Like instructors at many other colleges, you may have been assigned a developmental writing course without any or much advance warning. You should realize that you are in for a semester of interesting challenges. Developmental students offer the instructor an opportunity for a great sense of accomplishment. Of course, right now you may be asking yourself the much more fundamental question "How do I prepare for this class?"

First, remember that many of your students did not ask to be in a developmental course. Some have learning disabilities, emotional problems, physical disabilities, or disadvantaged backgrounds. Usually, their problems are not of their own making; they don't need to be penalized again. They are adults, so treat them as adults. Respect their individuality.

Second, commit yourself to your students. Being committed doesn't mean you must spend every waking moment with your students. In fact, you will probably need to set limits (allow yourself a lunch break, for instance) or your students may take over all your office hours and more. Plus, if you are an adjunct, your time on campus may be extremely tight and you may be commuting between campuses. However, remember that you are teaching students, not a subject. Commit yourself to helping them learn, and make your classes as interesting and as varied as possible. If you can't cover as much content as you had planned, don't worry about it. You are the only one who will know. Your students will appreciate everything you do.

Third, have patience. If one student asks a question, two or three others will ask the same question. If you make an announcement in class, three or more students won't hear it. If you ask for

an assignment, several will claim that they didn't know you wanted it. If possible, protect yourself by limiting the consecutive hours you will teach developmental classes; they are demanding because the students require so much personal attention. Fortunately, however, most of your students will want to please, and most will want to learn.

Fourth, be realistic in your expectations. Don't ask your students to do any work you haven't tried beforehand. Work all the exercises yourself. That way, you not only discover which exercises to include and which to omit but also gain an idea of how long each assignment will take and how long you can maintain interest in it. If you get bored, your students certainly will. And if it takes you an hour to do the assignment, it will probably take them two to three hours, or more.

Fifth, find a supportive colleague. If you are teaching in a department where you are the only developmental instructor, find a colleague at a nearby college. Or find someone in your department who is sympathetic. You can always remind your colleagues that your developmental students will eventually move into their credit classes, so they need to take an interest in the developmental courses.

Sixth, find time for yourself and your professional growth. If at all possible, do not teach more than two-thirds of your load in developmental courses. Try to balance the levels of students you teach. (See Chapter 13, Surviving and Growing as a Professional, for more recommendations.)

Finally, take advantage of the instructional resources available and prepare thoroughly for class. *Real Essays* has a wealth of resources designed to make your life easier and your students' time in the developmental course more beneficial. (See Chapter 1 of this manual for more on *Real Essays'* ancillary package.) Use them to plan your semester and each day. Students appreciate an instructor who is organized and on top of things.

Anticipating a Successful First Week

The keys to surviving the first week are preparation and flexibility. Prepare as thoroughly as you can what you want to happen on each day, even plotting out how many minutes you expect to spend on each activity. (Plan to do too much rather than too little—it's much more disturbing to run out of things to do before class is over than to have class end before you finish.) But remain flexible: No matter how carefully you plan, anything can happen.

Chapter 1 of this manual contains a section titled "What to Do on Day One." Read it and use it as a guide in your planning. Here is an overview of what you should hope to accomplish in the first week of class.

GIVE AN OVERVIEW OF THE COURSE. Distribute the syllabus and discuss the course focus.

ESTABLISH RAPPORT WITH AND AMONG STUDENTS. Give them a little pep talk about how much they can learn this semester. Try to establish a feeling of comfort and openness from the very start. Always ask for questions. Try an icebreaking activity. (See Creating a Comfortable Environment, at right.)

ESTABLISH DEMEANOR. Let students know—either explicitly or through your own example—that you expect them to treat one another, themselves, and you with respect, and that you will do the same. Try to establish a sense of responsibility in the students and let them know that you are fair but serious about the class.

ESTABLISH ROUTINES AND POLICIES. Let students know the grading and attendance policies, tell them what textbooks and supplies they will need, and inform them of any daily routines (e.g., journal writing for the first ten minutes of class).

GET BASIC INFORMATION FROM STUDENTS. Have students fill out an information form that includes their addresses, phone numbers, class loads, and workloads. (See p. 3 for a sample form.)

ASSESS STUDENTS' NEEDS AND UNCOVER THEIR GOALS. Have students write a brief passage (150 words) so that you can assess their writing level and areas where improvement is needed. (See Chapter 1 of this manual for specific ideas about this first assignment.) Give them a diagnostic grammar test to evaluate their editing skills and needs. (*Exercise Central* for *Real Essays,* available on the book's companion Web site, includes a diagnostic test. The *Testing Tool Kit* CD with this book also includes diagnostics.)

HELP STUDENTS GET ORGANIZED AND PREPARED FOR SUCCESS. Distribute an assignment schedule and show students how to use it; let them know that they will be responsible for making sure that their assignments are handed in on time and that they are well prepared for tests. Have students set up class notebooks using three-ring binders or another system. Let students know how important being organized is to their own success and how you expect them to be organized. Many students may have taken a college success course, but walk them through the quick review of success strategies in Chapter 1.

Creating a Comfortable Environment

If you want students to learn, you need to make them feel comfortable in your classroom. Try to establish a sense of belonging. Make your classroom a place where students want to be and where they can feel free to participate. Let the students see that you want to be in that classroom with them and that you are there to help them.

Establishing a comfortable environment begins with the very first day. Many students appreciate a teacher who is not only friendly and open but also organized. Therefore, begin your first day with an overview of what you will study during the semester and how class will be conducted. Let them know when major assignments are due or when tests will be given. And, if you have an end-of-the-semester test that students have to take outside of class time, let them know when the tests are scheduled. When students know from the beginning what is expected of them and what to expect from you, they can relax and let the learning happen.

Beginning on the first day, you should also let students know that you are an understanding, although firm, teacher. Emphasize the importance of due dates and completed homework, but also convey that you know the unforeseen sometimes occurs. Encourage them to notify you in the event of an emergency so that you can work together to overcome any obstacles. Even if a particular student never experiences an emergency while in your class, he or she will appreciate your caring attitude and will be likely to open up about class problems.

Students need to feel comfortable not only with you but also with one another. Try some ice-breaking exercises at the beginning of the semester. For ideas, see p. 5 of this manual. And if you ask students to share information about themselves, you should be willing to do the same. Both students and teachers need reminders that we are all human beings with feelings and lives outside the classroom. Students also enjoy hearing personal anecdotes. I don't mean sharing life stories, because you will discover that most students truly want to learn and don't want to waste time in class. However, if you can talk about writing or grammar problems that you, former students, friends, or family members have had, or use yourself as the subject of a writing project that you are doing with the students, the class will learn to see you as a person rather than as an authority figure to be feared.

A sense of humor is imperative. Don't take yourself too seriously. If you can laugh at yourself, your students can relax and will be less afraid to make mistakes. If your tongue gets tangled, make a funny face, babble for a couple of seconds, shake your head, laugh, and start over again. Reveal your own problems with grammar or spelling or writing. Illustrate how you handle your writing problems or how you learned a particularly difficult grammatical point.

Help students feel comfortable speaking up. Students should never feel as though the teacher thinks they are dumb. This is especially important when going over exercises in class; remember that not all exercises have a single right answer. Take time to think about the student's response, then say whether it is okay or whether another answer would be better. Don't hesitate to tell a student you need time to think about that answer because it's not the one you had thought of.

Becoming involved with the students and their work will help you create an atmosphere that is conducive to learning. Develop awareness of your students. Try to read their faces to determine when someone is having problems. Do not hesitate to offer assistance if you think a student needs help. Students believe that teachers who provide individual attention are demonstrating that they want the student to learn the material, not just get a grade.

Believe it or not, a comfortable environment in the classroom can also depend on your accessibility outside the classroom. Have flexible office hours and an open-door policy. Remember that you have probably set up your office hours to accommodate your own schedule, but your students have work, home, and class schedules that may not coincide with yours. Also, like you, they may have problems, such as sick children or court dates, that may occur during your class time or office hours. Therefore, be willing to meet students early in the morning or to stay late in the afternoon if a student has to make up a test or needs assistance with a writing assignment. Or work out mutually convenient alternatives such as a prearranged phone conference. This alternative works well, especially for adjunct faculty. You might also encourage students to find a buddy to share phone numbers with; then, if they are absent or don't understand an assignment, they will have someone to call if you cannot be reached.

Encouraging Class Participation

Someone could earn a million dollars by coming up with a formula for making students participate in all classes. Unfortunately, what works in some classes won't work in others. You may want to refer to the sections on active learning and varying the pedagogy in Chapter 9 of this manual. Also, remember that your attitude does more to encourage or discourage class participation than you might think. Whether you are grading, lecturing, or going over homework, remain positive. Many of your developmental students will have low self-esteem and need positive reinforcement, so provide lots of verbal praise and encouragement. Here are some other ideas.

Give Credit for Participation

Even if your college uses the pass/fail system for developmental courses, most of your students will want to earn good grades and will strive for an A. So give credit for work other than tests or papers whenever you can.

Give homework checks. When students complete an assignment—answering questions, preparing an outline, writing a rough draft, or completing grammar exercises—put a check in your grade book. The checks can be tabulated as points for a certain percentage of the student's final average. One way to encourage attendance is to have a firm policy not to accept late homework; therefore, the grade could encourage students to attend class prepared. (You will probably want to make such a statement in your syllabus and/or on your daily schedule.) The more often students come to class with completed homework, the higher their homework grade. When they realize they will get credit only when they attend class with their homework ready, many will make a greater effort to get to school. But also encourage students to show up whether or not their homework is complete. Tell them that they can still benefit from being in class.

Plan In-Class Activities

Go over assignments in class. If the assignment will lead to a test, comment on how the exercises or rules will apply to the test, or point out which exercises resemble items that will be on the test. If students realize that they will get help toward a test or help with their problems during class, they may be more likely to attend and participate.

Also while going over assignments, ask students to provide answers (allowing them plenty of time, if needed). (For more on the need for "wait time," see p. 73.) You can go around the room and have each student answer a question. You can also call on individual students. Don't always rely on volunteers; often, the same students will be the first to respond. When the class expects a particular student to have the right answer to every question, others will stop trying.

Plan in-class work days that allow students to get one-on-one assistance from you without a grade. When individuals know that you are willing to help them find the solution to a grammar exercise or to a problem sentence, they will be more willing to speak up during whole-class discussions.

Although some students complain about small-group work, many believe that it offers them a chance to learn a lot and to establish a bond with other classmates. Some students enjoy small-group work because they find it less threatening or intimidating than participating in whole-class discussions. Others may enjoy being chosen as the spokesperson who will give an oral summary or report of the group's activity.

Managing the Classroom

Encouraging student participation and varying the class activities are probably the two most helpful classroom management techniques. When students are actively engaged in learning, both they and you will be happier and more productive. The following are some recommendations for channeling the energy of your students and handling occasional disruptions. Also see Chapter 9's discussion on varying the pedagogy.

LET STUDENTS KNOW THE COURSE REQUIREMENTS AND YOUR EXPECTATIONS. Make it clear that students are responsible for meeting them both. Students should know that you expect them to be on time and to remain until dismissed. In signing up for a course, they have agreed to meet at the specified hours; if they do not hold up their end of this agreement, they should be counted tardy or absent. Let students know that you will penalize late papers and missed tests. Also establish a deadline for accepting late work or makeup work (for example, one week past the original due date). Clearly outlining your expectations in the syllabus will help prevent students from misunderstanding what you require from them.

You may want to prepare a "student responsibilities" page so that students can read and keep an outline of their commitments; they should return a signed note to you agreeing to those terms. On page 37 is a sample Acknowledgment of Student Responsibilities that includes reference to the Texas Higher Education Assessment (THEA); you can adapt the statement to fit your own course requirements.

Acknowledgment of Student Responsibilities

As a student in Developmental Writing, I know that I need to take the responsibility for my own success. Therefore, I will

- attend class regularly,
- do assigned work,
- ask for assistance when I need it,
- participate in class activities,
- notify my instructor of any emergencies or problems.

Furthermore, I realize that if I entered this course because of THEA [Texas Higher Education Assessment] scores, I must attend class and participate or I will be dropped from not only this class but also all classes in which I am enrolled. In addition, state law dictates that I must remain in remediation until I pass THEA.

If I am THEA-exempt or do not take THEA during the semester, I will be bound by the end-of-the-semester essay, which I will take in the Testing Center. That essay will serve as my final exam as well as placement out of remediation.

If I take THEA during the semester, I will notify my instructor. When I receive my scores, I will take them to my instructor immediately. If I pass the Writing section of THEA and have been attending my developmental class, my instructor will record my THEA scores in the grade book and give me credit for the class. At that point, I have the option of remaining in class throughout the semester or not returning to class (with no penalty).

Please sign the statement at the bottom; tear it off, and return it to your instructor.

- -

I have read the Acknowledgment of Student Responsibilities and understand my options and responsibilities.

Signed: _____

Date:_____

Class Time: _____

REWARD TIME SPENT ON TASK. Homework and in-class activities are important factors in learning. If you ask students to do an assignment, show them that it's important by taking class time to discuss the correct responses and to answer questions they may have. Depending on the exercise, you can have students give an oral group response, go around the room and have each student answer one question, or divide the class into small groups to work with assignments. However, don't feel obligated to grade each piece of work. You can give homework checks for completed, ungraded work and in-class activities.

BE PREPARED TO DEAL WITH PLAGIARISM. Your colleagues have occasionally encountered student papers that borrow either language or ideas or both, and so will you. If you suspect plagiarism, try to pinpoint specific words or sections that you are concerned about. Then decide if the plagiarism is the result of inadequate documentation or of an outright attempt to submit the writing of someone else. If you think that a student has copied from another source, you might ask a colleague or a librarian if the piece sounds familiar. You might also enter key phrases from the paper into a search engine to see if you turn up any sources that use identical language. (See the sections in Chapter 8 of this manual on addressing plagiarism and on problems with plagiarism detection services.) Don't confront a student unless you are prepared to back up your accusation. Even when I have found the original piece, I have given the student the opportunity to confess by asking how he or she arrived at the final version or where he or she got the information. By requiring in-class writing and keeping some of a student's original work in a file, you can guard against plagiarism. In addition, by requiring that all drafts and research notes (if appropriate) be included with the final copy, you can see how the student's writing has evolved from the initial draft. However, if you worry about the possibility of plagiarism, you can develop and distribute a policy similar to the one on page 39.

Plagiarism Policy

The *Random House Dictionary* defines plagiarism as follows: "The appropriation or imitation of the language, ideas, and thoughts of another author, and representation of them as one's original work." The most obvious form of plagiarism is copying directly from printed or Web-based materials without using quotation marks. A less obvious form, but equally serious, is summarizing or paraphrasing the *ideas* of an author without citing the author as a source. Additionally, a third type of plagiarism that students must be aware of is using an editor—whether a friend, family member, or tutor—beyond a reasonable level. In this instance, the student's paper does not reflect the knowledge, voice, and/or style of the student author.

Improper or inadequate documentation will often lower a paper's score. In the case of plagiarism, however, no credit is given for a paper. In order to protect both students and faculty members, the following procedures may be followed when an instructor suspects plagiarism:

1. The instructor will indicate to the student that the paper is plagiarized and gets no credit.

2. The student may appeal the instructor's decision to the English Department Chair.

3. The Department will have the student write a similar paper under supervision. (In cases of works of literature, the topic assigned will be from the same work that the student explored in the first paper.)

4. The Department's designated readers will determine if the second paper parallels the first in sophistication of ideas, knowledge, syntax, punctuation, voice, diction, and style.

5. If designated readers agree that the paper does not reflect the work of the student, the first paper will not be accepted. On the other hand, if the designated readers agree that the two papers are written by the same person, the instructor will award credit for the first paper.

Sample Writing Assignments

Real Essays is filled with writing assignments for essays. However, every instructor appreciates having a handy compendium of all-purpose writing prompts, useful for filling a sudden gap in the class schedule. The following are a few that have worked for me. (For journal writing prompts, please see the section on journals in Chapter 9, Other Useful Instructional Approaches.)

Essay Topics

NARRATION:

Take a story that is well known in your family and interview at least three people about the incident. Write a paper that gives each person's perspective on the events.

Write a story about what you have been told about your birth. Include the reason for your name, people's anticipation of your birth, and anecdotes about the birth itself.

ILLUSTRATION:

Ways a college education will improve my life

Three changes I would make if I could start my life over

The worst job I ever had

The biggest challenge I ever faced

My proudest accomplishment

DESCRIPTION:

The most relaxing place I have ever been

My favorite holiday

PROCESS ANALYSIS:

How to make a good impression on a first date

How to give up a bad habit

CLASSIFICATION:

Types of students

Types of music or movies

Ways of handling a problem

DEFINITION:

A good or bad student, teacher, parent, or friend

Happiness

Success

COMPARISON/CONTRAST:

Two ways parents can handle their teenagers' problems

Two different jobs I have held or hope to hold

My mother's or father's childhood and my own childhood

The different styles or techniques of two athletes or teachers

CAUSE/EFFECT:

The effect of pressure on students to get good grades

The effects of sibling rivalry

The effects of wearing a uniform

ARGUMENT:

Colleges should (should not) require admission tests.

Colleges should (should not) provide a day-care center.

High schools should (should not) teach sex education.

The government should (should not) provide free higher education for everyone.

Crime in my city or at my school

Power and the police department

Drug usage in my community or school

Words of Advice

Everyone you talk to will have a different piece of advice on how to handle a class. My advice on how to survive emotionally is that when you first walk into a developmental classroom, you should realize that you don't have and won't have complete control over your students. You must understand that many factors influence your students, and their outside activities and obligations take them away from class and study time. An important task is to teach a student that he or she is someone you care about helping. When you do that, you're well on your way to success in the developmental classroom. Even if you think you aren't making a difference, one student can let you know you have succeeded. Sometimes, one student is all it takes.

What follows are some words of advice from experienced instructors across the country. If you have your own words of advice that you would like us to include in the next edition of *Practical Suggestions*, please send them to us at *Real Essays*, Bedford/St. Martin's, 75 Arlington Street, Boston, MA 02116.

> Students neither live nor learn in a vacuum; we must help them integrate what they learn in the academy and what they bring from their lives. They then complete the cycle of real learning by letting their academic discoveries inform their life choices. We can give them voices in the classroom by evoking what they bring with them; we give them voices in the real world as we nurture essential critical reading, writing, and thinking skills. We want those at risk to become active, successful students as we help them develop the skills needed to be active, successful citizens. Many at-risk students give themselves only one chance to succeed in the academy; it is up to us to make that chance count!
>
> —Sandra M. Carey
> *Lexington Community College, Kentucky*

> Be open to the lessons hidden in all that comes your way.
>
> —James F. Rice
> *Quinsigamond Community College, Massachusetts*

> I suggest that teachers who are new to developmental writing and to developmental students should read Mina Shaughnessy's *Errors and Expectations* for some sound thinking about developmental writing, Mike Rose's *Lives on the Boundary* for insight into developmental writers and readers, and Frank Smith's writings on the writing–reading connection. Smith's ideas about the "literary club" are very important. These three books give a lot of background and argue for hope and enthusiasm in teaching developmental writers. Good luck!
>
> —Jack O'Keefe
> *Daley College, Illinois*

> First make sure you understand why you want students to do a particular assignment, then make sure you articulate the "why" to your students. If you are fuzzy, then your students will produce fuzzy responses. Also, make sure you have figured out how the assignment could be done—if you have done the proper "fiddling" with the "ins" and "outs" and "ways" and "means," you can provide a clearer road map for your students. This is crucial.
>
> —Beverly Ann Butler
> *Shippensburg University, Pennsylvania*

> Really know what the developmental writing course objectives and outcomes are. Also know the writing expectations in the next-level writing courses and in content area courses.
>
> Do intensive diagnostic work with your students. Investigate their attitude toward writing, their interests, their goals as well as their mechanical problems. Address more than just the misplaced comma; deal with the whole student.
>
> Enjoy! Create a classroom environment that stimulates real discussion about topics and writing. Be creative; be excited about what you are teaching and what you are writing. Write with your students.
>
> —Patricia A. Malinowski
> *Finger Lakes Community College, New York*

> "Passive" student behavior often indicates resistance to the syllabus rather than indifference. Read Ira Shor's "The First Day of Class" in *Background Readings* (excerpted from *Empowering Education*) for suggestions about working with resistance. Better yet, read and discuss Shor's essay with your students. Solicit student ideas for improving the course. I've made important changes to the syllabus based on student suggestions. Students have provided feedback during class discussions, as part of written assignments, in e-mail postings, and in anonymous letters written in class. I welcome this exchange as an opportunity to research student concerns—and my own teaching practices.
>
> —Susan Naomi Bernstein
> *University of Cincinnati*

> Be wary of all the new technology that purports to offer solutions that will solve education's perceived woes. Teaching is still a human covenant between student and teacher. A reassuring smile or an encouraging pat on the back will often accomplish more than any of the "bells and whistles."
>
> —Steve Whiting
> *Sinclair Community College, Ohio*

> Creating a climate of trust, respect, and awareness of differences and cultures is crucial for students' (and an instructor's) success in the developmental writing classroom. From day one, you, as leader, need to be proactive in setting the tone. Figure out where students are in the writing process . . . what they already

know . . . what they feel confident about, and build from that point. Praise the positives, and give them tools to "fix" what they need to work on to reach competency in standard academic English writing.

Vary assignments and readings, if you use them, to appeal to different ages and cultural or language backgrounds. Especially for second-language students or internationals, be aware of cultural differences in writing styles and openly acknowledge them. "Your way of writing has worked for you in the past, but your professors will expect _____. Here's how to produce _____." Approach grammar, spelling, and punctuation as part of an editing and proofreading task that you always do before completing a manuscript. Don't make them a first-draft nightmare.

Avoid putting people on the spot. At the same time, give shy students a turn at being leader in a small group, or ask them to be "secretary" at the board, taking board notes on class discussion. Share leadership. One strategy that works well is to randomly pick a student and ask him or her to demonstrate at the board (for the benefit of absentees) a point you covered in the previous class. As the student "teaches" the class, take a chair and listen attentively. Have students in small groups photocopy their notes and share with others.

Use (and believe in) the idea that we're all here to learn more about writing—you, too. Take advantage of resources: listservs, online writing labs, e-mail. Some of your students may know more about computers and the Internet than you do, and you can learn from one another.

—Jan Bone
Roosevelt University, Illinois

Don't be intimidated by quiet classes. Enable students to explore their own personal experiences through their writing, knowing that every writer has at least one story that he or she can relate better than anyone else, and you may be the only person given the privilege to read it.

—H. L. Phillips
Collin County Community College, Texas

Although collaborative work in the writing classroom is very popular and often quite successful, teachers should be careful in assessing group projects. Particularly, teachers should never give "group grades" for group writing projects. Teachers can reward collaboration and individual effort by having each group member assign the other group members a grade based upon a set of criteria established before the project begins. Students should write their rationale for the grades they assign to their fellow students and should submit their grade suggestions in sealed envelopes. This method produces more accountable students and less resentment toward students who fail to do their part in the collaborative process.

—Lisa Windham
College of the Mainland, Texas

Developmental writers need to understand that they have all the words they need to express themselves well. What we as teachers can give them is the confidence to express these words honestly, as close to their thinking as possible. And confidence comes with something to say, knowing what it is that we think or believe and why. Many students have definite opinions; not all of them realize the power that comes with evidence, the evidence of personal or researched reading material. So my advice to new instructors of writing is to enliven your writing classes with reading materials you love or respect, engage students in lively discussions of them, discussions that encourage the students to relate their own experiences, and then make them write and write and write some more.

—Francine L. DeFrance
Cerritos College, California

Sometimes we just have to shut up. Not an easy thing to do. Especially for English teachers. And yet silence can be a highly effective tool, especially in writing conferences. As we sit with students, going over their writing, we often ask students questions, hoping that they'll see the sentence problem or the need for a transition or a supporting detail. We ask leading questions, questions like, "Hmm, something seems to be missing here. What do you think is missing?" And the student, knowing full well from past experience that questions asked by teachers are often rhetorical questions, waits for the teacher to answer. Which we usually do if a response isn't immediately forthcoming. Because we feel uncomfortable with the silence that hangs there. And because there are usually more students queued up waiting their turn. It's not easy playing the waiting game. But it is essential, for the student eventually becomes uncomfortable with silence, and then the student begins to think about the situation, to look at the writing, to venture a response. The student thus becomes a participant in a discussion, not simply a listener. The trick is to let the student know that you do expect a response and that if it takes a little time to think things through, well, that's okay. Our primary goal as writing teachers is to help students see for themselves—not to correct their writing or edit their papers. In order to help them see, sometimes we just have to be quiet.

—Tim McLaughlin
Bunker Hill Community College, Massachusetts

When I teach developmental writing classes, I see myself as a role model for students learning to be college students and participants in an academic community. As such, I try to teach them how to be college students: how to speak and write, yes, but also how to apply for financial aid, how to avoid test anxiety, how to work with other students, how to use a word processor, and so on. I believe that anything I can do to elevate their self-esteem by making them feel a part of the college is immensely valuable to their success.

—Elizabeth Boote Griffey
Florida Community College
at Jacksonville, Florida

One of the challenges of teaching an introductory writing course is that it is usually a requirement—students have to take it and instructors have to teach it. I try to subvert the "have to" atmosphere of the course right away by telling students how excited I am to teach the course. Before they even look at a syllabus, I let them know that this is an important thing for me to do, that I enjoy immensely the task of working with beginning writers, and that writing is something that I love and want other people to love. I find this approach is effective in clearing out any preconceptions about the drudgery of the course.

—Anne Aronson
Metropolitan State University, Minnesota

3

Working with Developmental Writers

The Typical Student

What kind of students will you face when you walk into a developmental classroom? To borrow from an old saying, every kind under the sun. That's what makes teaching a developmental writing class so exciting. Every student is unique, yet many share similar experiences, frustrations, and problems. Perhaps the best introduction to a typical student is through the words of some students themselves. Read how April, a twenty-year-old high school graduate, describes her experiences:

> My first semester in college has been wonderful. I started out scared, but suddenly things changed for the better. I had never attended college, so when I was told that I had to take a placement test, I really became annoyed and terrified more than ever. I've never done very well on tests. And when I failed that test, I was ashamed to call home and tell my parents that I was taking resource classes for the dumb. But after attending and participating in the classes, I discovered that the class was not for the resource people but for the ones who lacked knowledge in certain areas. I had never liked English, but as I started to pay more attention to the teacher and what she was saying, my feelings for English started to change. I can truly say that my teacher taught me something that I will carry on with me throughout life: I can do anything if I just work at it. I appreciate my teacher for showing and teaching me that I can do the work without feeling like I am in a remedial class.

Consider also the experiences of an older student who had feelings similar to April's. At age thirty-five, Anthony found himself in a developmental English class, but that didn't seem to bother him. After two weeks of school, he wrote the following journal entry.

> School is fun. I haven't been in a classroom in seventeen years, so I'm excited about being a student. I am enrolled in twelve hours, which makes me a full-time student. My first day was a disaster because I slept through most of my English class. I hated myself for doing that, and the next day I apologized and explained to my teacher that I hadn't been in school for seventeen years. She told me not to worry because she would make sure she'd bring me up to college level. To some, maybe that means nothing, but to me that took a load off. For, you see, that was my first class, and her encouragement made me feel I could make it.

You probably became a teacher because you wanted to reach students, to change a life or two. Developmental writing classes give you that opportunity every semester. In order to help your students, you need to understand them. These students may not be the same kinds of students that you have previously taught. Teaching a developmental course may be challenging, frustrating, yet it can also be rewarding because of the mixed population. For instance, in a class of twenty-five students, five may have goofed off and not taken the placement test seriously; three may be nonnative speakers; three may have enrolled to increase self-confidence; three to five may have serious learning disabilities and have little chance of completing the course in one semester (or two); three may be repeating the course; and the remainder may recognize that their skills are lacking and that they need the remedial instruction that the course offers. Some students start asking questions the minute they walk in the door, interrupt class to ask the same questions repeatedly, and remain after class to ask more questions. Other students resent being in a developmental class and may offer great resistance and a surly attitude. Some may be recent high school graduates, whereas others may have dropped out of high school or college years before and are trying again. With so many personal and academic needs, it is a constant struggle to keep all students interested and progressing.

In addition to recognizing the variety of reasons students have for enrolling in your class, you need to understand their academic styles and attitudes toward learning. Many may have one or more of the following characteristics:

- Genuine desire to understand

- Hope for a better life through education

- Enthusiastic approach to learning

- Low self-esteem or lack of self-confidence

- Little motivation

- Procrastination

- Few organizational skills

- Avoidance of challenges

- Erratic attendance

- Tendency to make excuses for poor performances

- Little practice with reading and therefore with using written models for writing

Although the variety may seem impossible to deal with in one class, you can find some common ground. In certain ways, developmental writers share common needs. No matter what category a given student falls into, these developmental writers need:

- Instruction in basic grammar, punctuation, and syntax.

- Help in thinking.

- Help in organizing thoughts.

- Patterns, formulas, or models to follow when they start to write.

- Assistance in learning how to study and to complete assignments.

- Lots of encouragement and positive reinforcement.

- Assistance in learning how to read critically, assimilate information, and respond to ideas.

- Revision techniques that work.

You probably will find it easy to teach motivated, focused students. Perhaps the biggest and most rewarding challenges of teaching developmental writers, however, come from those students who have experienced years of failure and frustration owing to conditions beyond their control. Many of your students have a history of learning disabilities, school transfers, family obligations, or personal problems that caused them to drop out or underachieve. Yet each is an individual who deserves the best education you can offer. As a teacher of developmental writers, you need to recognize the various backgrounds and remain sensitive to the individual needs of all students.

Students with Special Needs

Although most of *Practical Suggestions* discusses developmental students in general terms, you may benefit from a more in-depth look at certain special needs students. Suggestions for teaching ESL students are found in Chapter 10.

Learning-Disabled Students

A learning disability is a permanent disorder that affects the way people take in, retain, and express information. The incoming or outgoing information may become scrambled between the eye or ear and the brain. Learning-disabled (LD) adults often have deficits in one or more of the following areas: reading comprehension, spelling, written expression, math comprehension, and problem solving. Occasionally, they also experience problems with organizational skills, time management, and social skills. Many LD adults may have language-based and/or perception problems. Some studies report that two out of every ten people have some form of learning dysfunction; other studies indicate that four or more out of every ten people may have a learning disability.[1]

In LD students' writing, you will probably notice problems with sentence structure (fragments, run-ons, poor grammar) and spelling (omissions, substitutions, transpositions). LD students may write slowly, have poor penmanship, or copy incorrectly from a book or a blackboard. Orally, they may have

[1]*Sources:* Levinson, Harold N., *Smart but Feeling Dumb* (New York: Warner, 1984), and Ross-Gordon, Jovita M., "Adults with Learning Disabilities: An Overview for the Adult Educator," Information Series, no. 337 (Columbus: ERIC Clearinghouse on Adult, Career, and Vocational Education, Center on Education and Training for Employment, The Ohio State University, 1989) [ERIC no. ED 315 664].

difficulty expressing ideas (even those they seem to understand), speak incorrect English, or have trouble concentrating on and comprehending spoken language. They may have difficulty following oral and written directions, demonstrate a short attention span during lectures, be slow to start and complete tasks, and need help in time management.

When teaching writing, emphasize and practice the connection between listening, speaking, reading, and writing. Use the Suggestions for Discussion printed in the margins of the *Instructor's Annotated Edition for Real Essays,* encourage class discussion, and have students talk in complete, grammatically correct sentences. Teaching writing as a process helps the LD students monitor their progress through an assignment and keeps the assignment from becoming overwhelming. Break the written assignments into stages, assessing and responding to each stage (e.g., brainstorming, outlining, drafting, peer editing, revising). Encourage students to use the checklists in the Writing Guides in Part 2 of *Real Essays*; these show the process for each type of writing as a series of steps that can be completed and checked off. Although you may think that a formal structure is too limiting for writers, LD students find that, rather than constraining them, structure or format helps them generate a paper. Try having them use the planning forms provided for essays in *Additional Resources*. Once they learn the form, they will become more comfortable with writing and can branch out beyond that model.

In addition, you can help LD students—and all students, for that matter—by using the following suggestions:

- Provide a detailed course syllabus that outlines expectations, grading, material to be covered, due dates, and major tests.

- Start each class with an outline of what you plan to cover, and end each class with a summary of key points.

- Give assignments both orally and in writing to avoid confusion.

- Allow students to tape-record lectures.

- Announce reading assignments well in advance so that students who are using taped texts will have time to obtain the tapes.

- Provide study questions for exams that demonstrate the exam's format as well as its content.

- If necessary, allow LD students to demonstrate mastery of course material by means of alternative methods (e.g., extended time limits for testing, individually proctored exams in a separate room).

- Provide adequate opportunities for questions and answers.

- Write important information on the blackboard, use transparencies, or prepare handouts to help students identify and remember key points. (See *Additional Resources* for transparency and handout masters.)

- Teach study skills and foster organization by requiring a class notebook.

- Use a variety of approaches to appeal to various learning styles.

- Be patient.

By law, schools must provide auxiliary aids for students who identify themselves as having learning disabilities, as well as for students with physical disabilities. It is the student's responsibility to notify the college about his or her specific situation and the appropriate or required aids. The school must provide such services as taped texts, note takers, interpreters, readers, or student tutors. As the teacher, you might need to allow extended time for reading assignments, testing in another location, tape-recording of lectures, printed notes so students can read along as you talk, or other such accommodations. If your college has a special department that deals with students with special needs, contact it for assistance. That department will likely provide the services your students need and help you with testing. However, the greatest success will come when you and the student sit down together to determine what will work best for that student in your course. The results can be rewarding for both you and your student.

Dyslexic Students

Some studies estimate that as many as one in every seven students suffers from dyslexia to some degree, with approximately ten million Americans affected. Primarily, dyslexia is the inability to break down a word into its parts, with the reader/listener having difficulty distinguishing the individual sounds that letters and/or combinations of letters represent.

Historically, educational systems have relied on reading and writing to convey information and to test achievement; as a result, dyslexics are often viewed as having low intelligence. However, dyslexics often perceive more and formulate mental concepts more rapidly than other people. In fact, dyslexics often excel on the job, even if they are functionally challenged. They may be visual, multidimensional thinkers who are intuitive and highly creative and who often excel at hands-on learning. They merely have difficulty processing letters, symbols, and words. In addition, students with dyslexia may have short-term memory difficulties; therefore, new information needs to be given more than once and those students need to concentrate much more than other students.

Develop a holistic approach when teaching dyslexics. First, present an overview of the unit or explain why you are doing a particular activity. Once they know the whole picture, they generally will approach the parts willingly. The Understand section at the beginning of each chapter in *Real Essays* may be especially useful to these students. When you break down processes into steps, allow time for feedback to check understanding. Avoid reinforcing failure by using dictation exercises or forcing students to copy words they cannot see correctly. Encourage the use of technology, such as spelling dictionaries, computers, and grammar checkers. Remind your students of spelling strategies or memory aids. Many dyslexics learn by talking, so set up group activities in which students can explain concepts to one another; use the suggestions for discussion and teamwork printed in the margins of the *Instructor's Annotated Edition for Real Essays*.

When making writing assignments, be specific and write everything down; don't expect students to remember your oral instructions. Also, provide samples of the assignment and offer help with planning, structure, and organization. Focus on following set patterns (e.g., introduction, body, conclusion), identifying main points, distinguishing relevant from irrelevant details, and ordering points. In other words, give your students as many structural aids and formulas as you can.

Remember that dyslexics may be easily distracted by noise, activity, or visual clutter. They may need more time than other students do to absorb information and to work through the outside distractions. If you use a blackboard during your discussion, erase the board before presenting a new idea so that students can concentrate on one point at a time. In addition, try to break up learning sessions and discussions to give students enough time to process the information.

Usually, by the time the dyslexic student appears in your college class, his or her self-esteem has become greatly eroded. Restoring a student's self-esteem will probably be the best and most important technique you can use to help your dyslexic students (or students with any learning problems) succeed.

Students with Attention Deficit Hyperactivity Disorder

Although many people think of small children when they hear the term *attention deficit hyperactivity disorder* (ADHD), teenagers and adults can also suffer from this syndrome. In fact, some of your troublemakers might suffer from ADHD and not know it. Don't think that ADHD indicates a lack of intelligence. Quite the contrary—ADHD students often show signs of creativity and high intelligence. The following characteristics can help you identify an ADHD student:

- **A sense of underachievement.** Many ADHD students believe they are failures because they have trouble reaching their goals. This lack of self-esteem often results from years of being told they are lazy or different, or from frustrations caused by lack of success in projects.

- **Restlessness.** Although teenagers and adults don't always have the pronounced inability to stay still that we see in ADHD children, they can display fidgetiness through drumming fingers, swinging legs, shifting positions, or repeatedly getting up from the desk.

- **Difficulty getting organized.** ADHD students are easily overwhelmed by the tasks of daily living and are chronically late or chronically in a hurry. They can succeed if someone helps them get organized.

- **Chronic procrastination or trouble getting started.** Because they fear doing something incorrectly, ADHD students may become anxious and put off tasks numerous times. Similarly, some ADHD students exhibit enthusiastic beginnings but cannot follow through and thus have poor endings. Either of these traits leads to inconsistent work performance.

- **Impulsive behavior.** ADHD students have a tendency to say what comes to mind without necessarily considering the timing or appropriateness of the remark. Tied closely to impulsiveness is impatience, with a low tolerance for frustration. This frustration with not being able to do things the "right" way can manifest itself in an inability to follow proper procedure or go through established channels.

- **A tendency to become easily bored or distracted.** Because they have trouble focusing attention, ADHD students have a tendency to mentally drift away or tune out. The ADHD student exhibits poor listening skills and, when reading, may skip around or go to the end first.

- **A tendency to worry.** ADHD students seem to worry endlessly and experience a sense of impending doom, partly as a result of frustrations and previous failures.

If you know or suspect a student has ADHD, you can do the following: in one-on-one talk, make sure the student has comprehended the assignment; allow for reasonable freedom of movement within the classroom; vary the activities for the day; and constantly offer feedback and encouragement.

Adult Learners

Unlike some of their younger counterparts, adult students have often gone to great effort to enroll in college courses and are highly motivated to learn. They generally view learning as a means to an end, not an end in itself, though they may also want to do well in college to increase or maintain a sense of self-esteem.

When designing the curriculum, keep in mind that adults are usually goal oriented. They desire a course that is organized into clearly defined elements, and they prefer content presented in a straightforward, "how-to" approach. Also, adults have a wealth of life experiences and want to integrate new ideas with what they already know; in fact, such integration helps them retain and use the new information. Integrating the real world into the classroom comes naturally to these students and is one of the strategies most likely to ensure their success. (See Chapter 4, Bringing the Real World into the Classroom.) Most adults prefer self-directed learning over group learning experiences because self-direction gives them control over the pace. However, self-direction doesn't mean total isolation. Adult learners want other people as resources or guides. Therefore, one-on-one sessions work well with these students. Teachers can serve as facilitators while encouraging them to assume responsibility for their learning.

Within the classroom, remember that adult learners' self-esteem is constantly on the line. They tend to take errors personally, so stress that they will learn from their mistakes. To help them build self-

confidence in the learning experience, clarify all expectations before getting into the actual lesson. Let these students know where you are heading with the assignments and how the class will help them reach their own goals. Adult students usually prefer to participate actively in the learning process. Many adult learners will tell you that they are irritated by long lectures that leave no time for practice. In sum, remember that adults want learning to be problem oriented, personalized, and self-directed.

Some of the best ways to motivate adult learners are to align the course content with their reasons for enrolling, decrease any barriers, and create a comfortable learning environment. Should problems arise, you need to discover what is keeping your students from learning. Because people learn at different speeds, it is natural for them to be anxious or nervous when faced with a timed learning situation. Positive reinforcement can enhance learning, as can specific feedback.

Creating a Productive Environment and Motivating Students

Whether your students are traditional freshmen, non-native speakers, individuals with learning disabilities, or adult learners, they can all benefit from a classroom environment that encourages productivity and motivation. The following strategies will help foster students' ability—and their willingness—to learn.

SIMPLIFY OBJECTIVES AND LEARNING. Make sure instructions are clear and written down for students to check. Be clear in your own communications by making handouts easily comprehensible. Be explicit in your expectations. You may want to write main points and goals for the day on the board. You could divide the board into two sections. On the left, write what you hope to accomplish that day; on the right, remind students of the next assignment. That way, students know when they arrive in class what to expect and what you expect of them.

Also, remember to include oral assistance as well as written assistance. You can tape-record important class lectures or respond orally to certain texts. In addition, some computer programs have sound, allowing students to hear instructions and even lessons.

HELP STUDENTS FEEL COMFORTABLE WITH THE PHYSICAL ACT OF WRITING. Students who have difficulty writing may feel more confident using an erasable pencil than permanent ink. One instructor has had great success with the erasable pen because it helps her introduce the importance of a professional-looking product while giving her students the ability to erase. Given that many developmental students have poor handwriting skills, you might want to ask your class to skip every other line as they write—this can improve readability not only for you but also for the students themselves as they edit and revise. Using computers can also relieve stress, so you may want to encourage students to type their assignments. Not only does learning to operate a computer offer a lifelong skill, but word processors enable many students to see more clearly what they have written, eliminate the drudgery of handwriting, help with organization, and aid in spelling and punctuation.

REINFORCE GOOD STUDY SKILLS. Help your students learn to budget time by giving them an estimate on how long a particular assignment will take or giving them clues regarding progress stages on longer assignments. Give them a daily schedule that details reading assignments, homework, tests, and due dates for writing assignments. Encourage your students to prioritize their responsibilities, and work with them to establish goals.

MAINTAIN A SUPPORTIVE ENVIRONMENT. Help students feel satisfaction when they are successful. Sometimes just a few encouraging words or actions are sufficient; at other times you may need to work more closely with a particular student on his or her unique problems. Remember that if the student's self-esteem is not maintained or renewed, optimum learning will not occur. Try to boost your students' self-image by letting them know that they have capabilities and, when writing, that they have something to say worth reading. Showing that you care goes a long way toward motivating appropriate behavior. If you can get to know your students through their journals, do so. (For a discussion of journals in the developmental writing course, see Chapter 9, Other Useful Instructional Approaches.) Remember unique things, such as a child's name, a pet, an upcoming birthday, or a particularly stressful situation the student has described. Besides merely writing notes to the students in their journals, casually ask about the child, pet, or situation. Knowing that you are truly interested in them can motivate students to attend class and do their assignments.

BE ORGANIZED. All developmental students appreciate and need an organized teacher. Whether or not you distribute a daily plan for the semester, you need to operate from one. Of course, you can always make changes, but having a schedule keeps you focused and keeps students aware of homework, writing assignments, and due dates. Students are more willing to attend classes when the instructors seem to know what they are doing and what they want to do.

EMPHASIZE THE COURSE'S BENEFITS. If, as is the case in many schools, your developmental course does not carry college credit, the students may decide that your class is not as important as, say, history or science. You may discover that students are skipping your class and neglecting your assignments to study for tests in other classes. When you know that students do so, talk to them and point out that the information and skills they will acquire in your class will help them in their credit classes. Begin the semester by illustrating how important writing is to success in history, psychology, science, and English classes—and in the students' future careers. If you can provide advice from your former students, do so. Call attention to the Profiles of Success included in *Real Essays*. Incorporate real-world writing into your assignments. Once students can see connections among building their skills, the help that your course can offer, and their futures, you have a stronger chance of motivating them.

DO NOT GRADE EVERY ASSIGNMENT. One method of motivating students to revise papers is to avoid assigning a grade. A weak student may be satisfied with a low C, but if you put "Rewrite" at the top of the page instead of a grade, the student will feel obligated to revise and resubmit the paper. After students have done this for an assignment or two, they usually realize that it's easier to revise and edit on their own before they are instructed to do so by a teacher. You might also use red ink (the color most likely to get students' attention) to point out the paper's strengths.

ASK STUDENTS TO SET THEIR OWN GOALS. Another form of motivation requires the student's involvement in and commitment to his or her learning process. To encourage such active involvement, have students establish their own goals for the course and share them with you early in the term. Help students generate and articulate their goals. At midterm have the students look at those goals and write a note to you about why they are or are not reaching them. Respond to each note in order to let the students know if they are on target and to offer advice if they aren't.

As you attempt to motivate your students, keep in mind that a teacher can open the door but the student must go through alone; for the first thing that education should teach someone is how to walk alone. Thus, remember that no matter what motivational techniques you use, they will not always work. If the student is overwhelmed by other classes, work, family problems, or other distractions, what you do may not matter. As teachers we have to realize that we are not responsible for our students' total successes or failures; too many factors are beyond our (or sometimes their) control.

Handling Rude and Disruptive Students

Nothing is more disconcerting than having to reprimand students who should act like and be treated as adults. Sometimes classmates will handle rudeness or disruption for you by asking those who are out of line to be quiet or telling them to "grow up." However, if you can keep the situation from reaching that point, everyone will be happier.

Keeping students busy probably does the best job of prevention. If you have the class constantly doing something different, then the potential troublemakers don't have as much time to act up. If you are going over exercises and you have talkers, keep calling on those talkers. Merely rotate through the group, calling one name after another. Usually, the remainder of the class catches on before they do, but when they discover what you are doing, they will generally calm down and cooperate to keep from being singled out for answers. Humor sometimes works, but be sure to keep things light; sarcasm can be counterproductive.

If the problem isn't solved by any of the techniques suggested above, take the offenders aside and talk to them privately. Explain to them that even if they believe the material being covered in class is too easy or not important, most of their classmates believe otherwise. Emphasize that they are disturbing their classmates and keeping them from learning. Most of the time, students will react favorably if they realize they are disturbing their peers rather than their teacher.

Rudeness must be dealt with swiftly before it ruins the class atmosphere. At the first sign of rudeness, stop the class immediately; make it clear—the first time—that you will not tolerate such behavior.

Then, in a one-on-one conversation, try to discover why the student was acting rudely. Some students are rude and disruptive because they do not believe they belong in a developmental English class. If that is the case, calmly explain the school's placement policy and tell them how better prepared they will be for Freshman Composition after taking your developmental class.

If students are rude to you, tell them that you will all be happier and they will learn more if you treat one another with respect. If they are rude to students who are progressing slowly, ask them to be patient. Explain that everyone in the class has his or her own problems. You might even preempt or subvert rudeness by asking students to assist their classmates, pointing out that because there is only one of you, you would certainly appreciate any help they can give you.

Latecomers are a totally different issue. Some teachers exhibit a low tolerance for tardiness, whereas others don't let latecomers disturb them outwardly. Many developmental students have so many personal problems and obligations that they have difficulty arriving at school on time. Weather conditions, road construction, traffic accidents, and car trouble may affect anyone. However, you must make your standards known at the beginning of the semester, checking to make sure that your school will stand behind whatever you propose. For instance, some teachers lock the door when it is time for class to begin, but some schools do not allow students to be locked out of their classrooms. If your school has an attendance policy, you may be able to count a certain number of tardinesses as an absence. You could also give a brief in-class activity or test at the beginning of each period. If the student is on time, he or she gets credit. If the student is late, his or her grade suffers. Personally, although I want students to be on time, I prefer late arrivals to total absences.

When handling rude or disruptive students, be aware of your own attitudes or misconceptions. We often dismiss difficult behavior and weak performance as stemming from the student's poor attitude. However, we must consider the possibility that many students have lived through years of failure and frustration arising from conditions beyond their control. Some have serious emotional or learning disabilities. Such students have difficulty with reading, writing, spelling, organizing their thoughts and their lives, following instructions, or staying on task for a reasonable length of time. In addition, they often cause us frustration because they can perform well on occasion. By talking to students one-on-one, you may discover individuals who want to learn but don't know how, or who are afraid to try for fear of more failure.

Final Word

Teaching developmental students is a challenge, but the challenge is definitely worth it. Remember Anthony, the student who slept through his first class? He is the type of student who makes all the frustrations disappear, the kind who gears you up for the next semester. Three months after missing his first class, Anthony wrote his last journal entry of the semester:

> This is my last entry, and I really want to thank you for being a swell teacher. You are very good at your job. I think you go out of your way for us. In fact, I know you do. You've helped me a lot and what I've learned will be a benefit to my life. I promise I won't give up or quit. I want something out of life, a future to contribute to my family and to my people so someone can see there is hope. I know if I apply myself I can make it. You let me know at the first day of school that I could do it. So thank you for your support and teaching.

4

Bringing the Real World into the Classroom

All learners learn best when they can see connections between the material to be mastered and their own goals, needs, and interests. By bringing the real world—whether that means college, work, or everyday life—into the developmental writing course, you will be demonstrating such connections. Students will see that writing is important to real life and necessary to what they want to accomplish in their own lives. This strategy will prove especially effective with older students, who are typically pragmatic and goal oriented and who have already been immersed in the real world outside the classroom.

That students often think of the writing course as a strictly academic subject is ironic, given the status of writing as an essential workplace skill. There is no professional occupation that does not require writing skills and almost no employer who would not be eager to promote someone with good analytical and communications skills. As stated in *Workplace Basics*, a summary of research conducted under a two-year joint project of the American Society for Training and Development and the U.S. Department of Labor, "Basic academic skills—reading, writing, and computation—have long been revered as the keys to success in society and the workplace. . . . [W]riting is frequently the first step in communicating with customers, interacting with machines, documenting competitive transactions, or successfully moving new ideas into the workplace."

The importance of the real world to students and the importance of writing in the real world are central assumptions at work on every page of *Real Essays*.

As Susan Anker states in her preface, *Real Essays* shares an overarching purpose with its companions, *Real Skills: Sentences and Paragraphs for College, Work, and Everyday Life* and *Real Writing: Paragraphs and Essays for College, Work, and Everyday Life,* to put writing in a real-world context. This three-book series links writing skills to students' own goals in and beyond college. What's more, these books motivate students with photographs, quotes, profiles, and advice from current and former students—"people who have struggled with writing, have wondered why it is important, and are learning that good writing is not a mysterious, elusive gift but a skill than can be learned by anyone who is willing to pay attention and practice" (from the preface to the third edition of *Real Writing*). Together, these books form a foundation for success in the real world based on skills learned in the writing classroom.

The following sections present some ways that you can integrate the real world into your course and some hints for using the corresponding features and sections in *Real Essays*.

Allow Students to See Themselves in the Course

Incorporating the real world into your classroom doesn't necessarily mean focusing on politics or writing-across-the-curriculum topics. The first and perhaps most important connection to the real world is the connection to each student. Students should see themselves reflected in course materials, content, assignments, and policies. They should know that the course is about them. Consider making your students' first essay assignment the continuing writing assignment that runs throughout Part 1 of *Real Essays*; it asks students to choose a topic for their essays with which they are familiar, so it both helps them focus on their goals and lets them see that the course is about them.

Whenever possible, encourage students to interject information about their own lives and experiences into discussions and activities. Ask them to write about things that they find useful or interesting. (You may want to use the Survey of Interests form in Chapter 6 of this instructor's manual to learn more about your students' interests.) Ask them to make connections between a rhetorical concept and their lives outside the classroom. Also, let students know that you value and respect them as developing writers. Display samples of their writing in the classroom, or assemble finished pieces in a class publication. Share the works of other student writers with them.

Student voices are heard throughout *Real Essays*. Student-written paragraphs and essays appear in each of the writing chapters (Parts 1 and 2). In Part 8 Readings for Writers, many of the readings are by students. Suggest to students they too submit their papers for consideration.

Use Content from the Real World

Whether selecting content for reading, writing, or grammar practice, consider how well it reflects the world that your students experience outside the classroom. *Real Essays* is filled with examples intended to remind students of their real lives, whether that means college, work, or everyday life. Once you get into the habit, it's fairly easy to maintain this focus, but here are a few ideas to get you started.

COLLEGE

- Content related to the majors your students are studying, such as

  — Business

  — Accounting

  — Nursing

  — Health and human services

  — Medical technician/dental technician

  — Education

  — Computers

  — Manufacturing

  — Automotive technician

  — Agriculture

- Financial aid

- Racism and sexism on campus: discrimination, assault, official policies (including affirmative action)

- Smoking policies

- Drinking on campus

- Parking on campus

- Day care on campus

- Academic advising and other support systems for students

- Student lounge, other hangouts: how they should be changed, why they are good, why they are a waste of space or money

- The registration process

- What's a good student? What kind of student do they want to be?

- Study aids: how to study, how to get an A, how to juggle course commitments

- Access to computers and other electronic technology

WORK

- Finding a promising job

- Writing a résumé

- Preparing for interviews

- Interacting with boss and colleagues

- Learning new skills

- Developing a career plan/career goals

- Negotiating a promotion or salary increase

- Exploring content related to the occupations your students typically have or go into

EVERYDAY LIFE

- Parenting

- Relationships

- Friends

- Drinking/drugs

- Self-improvement

- Planning, goal setting
- Breaking bad habits
- Juggling home, school, and work
- Hobbies
- Crime
- Consumer goods
- Local industries
- Setting and managing a family budget
- Health threats
- Technology
- Terrorism

Whenever possible, you might want to find examples from the local newspaper or from magazines that your students are most interested in to illustrate points you are making. You can find examples of rhetorical strategies or of different grammatical or stylistic approaches. Better yet, you can have your students search for the examples. It is especially informative when they find mistakes or examples that don't follow your rules. Such examples provide excellent opportunities for discussions of different styles and different interpretations of rules.

Use Real-World Assignments

Be sure to introduce real-world writing topics of your own. Use situations straight from the news for writing topics. Have students find classified ads for jobs that they might want and write letters of application. Or ask them to write a letter to another teacher asking for a change of grade.

You can also create more full-blown real-world scenarios. Choose a current issue, local or national, that your students should be aware of. Gather statistics, newspaper articles, brochures, pie charts, photographs, and any other materials that can help students understand the situation. Create players or groups of players, assign roles, and let students work in groups to plan their strategy. Then you can spend one class period having the class act out the situation.

For instance, you can use the issue of threats against abortion clinics and even the murders of some of their personnel. Locally, you may have experienced protests and minor conflicts. Therefore, your question for consideration might be "What can we do locally to try to prevent the possibility of violence?" For groups, you could identify pro-life advocates, pro-choice advocates (such as Planned Parenthood personnel), local law enforcement officials, medical professionals (doctors and nurses), and representatives of the local governing body. Groups of students would need to examine the data and decide on a position statement. Then they would develop logical arguments to present their viewpoints. One group will be responsible for calling a meeting, determining how the meeting will be conducted, and appointing a moderator to direct the meeting and bring it to a close. During the meeting, the various groups will present their arguments so that everyone has a chance to speak and to hear all sides of the issue. The class should try to come to a logical conclusion.

The following writing assignments can be derived from such an activity:

- One journal entry on topic before assignment is given, a second during the process, and a third to determine if attitudes have changed

- A position statement with logical arguments from each group

- A letter to the editor stating the student's opinion on the issue

- A response to a letter to the editor that was sympathetic to the violent protesters

- A journal entry from the perspective of a doctor or nurse who was threatened

- A journal entry from the perspective of a woman who has had an abortion

- A journal entry from the perspective of a protester who was arrested

- A proposal to the town's governing body recommending certain actions

- An editorial examining how far someone should take a moral commitment

- An essay detailing the government's role in mediating or defusing such situations

Another interesting situation would be a proposal to legalize casino gambling. Students could represent churches, politicians, social service organizations, residents, businesses that cater to tourists, law enforcement officials, and casino operators. Other controversial topics include allowing cities or towns to fly the Confederate flag; planning an AIDS hospice in a residential neighborhood; building a Wal-Mart next to an upscale residential area; reforming welfare; finding ways to prevent violence in schools; beach erosion; or terrorism. The list of topics for simulation games is unlimited.

Use the Profiles of Success

At the beginning of each of the chapters in Part 2 of *Real Essays,* you'll find a Profile of Success: an interview with and photograph of a former developmental student who has gone on to be successful in the real world. In their own candid words, these people describe how difficult writing was for them in college, how important it is to their current careers, and what helped them turn their lives around. These profiles will go a long way toward motivating students by showing them that success at writing is both possible and important.

The profiles were designed to be visually engaging, so your students will most likely read them before anything else in the chapter. However, many students ignore anything that is not specifically assigned, so you may want to build specific activities around the profiles.

The profiles all contain references to the chapters in which they appear. For example, in Chapter 14, Classification: Writing That Puts Things into Groups, Rebeka Mazzone explains how she classifies financial strategies for her accounting clients. The profiles make wonderful lead-ins to the writing assignments in the chapters: You can ask students to discuss the type and quantity of writing the person profiled has to do on the job. Students may be surprised to discover the important role that writing plays in these people's careers.

In each chapter in Part 2, the Read and Analyze section contains a piece by the person featured in that chapter's Profile of Success. For instance, Chapter 14 contains a presentation that CPA Rebeka Mazzone wrote to give at a conference of her professional organization. Other chapters include samples of (or excerpts from) memos, summaries, instructions, articles, or personal writing. These samples give students a clear view of writing required in the real world. Like the other selections in the Read and Analyze section, these pieces are followed by a set of comprehension and analysis questions.

In addition or as an alternative to reading the work-related samples in the text, you could have students research the amounts of and types of writing people in their own chosen careers must do. For example, nursing students working on Part 2's chapter on illustration could brainstorm and research to find out how much illustration-type writing nurses typically must do.

You may want your students to write their own profiles of success: they can identify someone they consider successful (whether or not this means a successful career), conduct an interview, and give either an oral or written presentation about the person.

Similarly, you might want to have students write about themselves as profiles of success. They could write about themselves either in the present (focusing on some aspect of their lives in which they feel particularly successful) or in the future (imagining what they will be doing in two years, or five, or ten). You might want to ask students to expand on the goals they listed on the Writing Questionnaire that you may have had them fill out at the beginning of the semester.

If you have former students of your own whom you would like to see represented in the next edition of *Real Essays'* Profiles of Success, I urge you to send a letter about them to *Real Essays,* Bedford/St. Martin's, 75 Arlington Street, Boston, MA 02116. The author would love to consider them for inclusion.

Send Students Out of the Classroom

Create assignments that take your students outside the classroom and help them see how important writing is to success in the real world. You might have them write to an audience other than you, especially if their writing will help them accomplish something that they authentically want. For example, the class could collaborate in writing and sending (to the appropriate person on campus) a proposal for better parking facilities, improved curriculum standards, or more support services.

Another idea is to have students use their developing writing skills to help someone else. Investigate whether there are social service organizations in your community that need reporters or letter writers, and see if you can arrange for students to get credit for this work.

Students can also benefit from learning more about how writing is used in the careers they are looking forward to—as well as learning more about these careers in general. Ask students to interview someone who has a job they themselves would like to have. (They can use the sample Interview Guide on p. 57.)

Interview Guide for an Informational Interview

Use your interview guide to ask questions. Take notes on the person's answers, but do not forget to listen. Ask additional questions that occur to you during the interview.

Date of interview:

Name of person:

Company:

Position:

1. What are the major job responsibilities? (You may also want to ask for specific examples of tasks.)

   _____

   _____

   _____

   _____

2. What skills are necessary to do the job?

   _____

   _____

3. What prior experience is necessary or useful?

   _____

   _____

4. Describe an average day on the job.

   _____

   _____

   _____

5. What have you learned on the job?

_____

_____

6. What kind of person does well in the job?

_____

_____

7. What do people find interesting or like about the job?

_____

_____

8. What do people dislike or find frustrating about the job?

_____

_____

9. What kind of writing do you do in an average week? How important is writing to your job?

_____

_____

_____

_____

10. What advice would you give to someone who is interested in this type of work?

_____

_____

One interesting writing situation is to pair your class with a class from a local middle or junior high school. A class of sixth- or seventh-graders would benefit from knowing about the life experiences and challenges of many of your remedial students, and your students will have real-life readers.

Bring the Real World into the Classroom

Consider inviting a speaker into your class. A guest can provide a nice change of pace as well as give students a glimpse into life outside the classroom. (See Chapter 9 of this manual for more ideas about varying the pedagogy.) Think about the kind of information your students need. If you teach at a two-year college, invite a counselor or the registrar to talk about transferring to a four-year school. Ask the financial aid director to discuss grants and scholarships. Arrange for a librarian to give your class an orientation to the library and to library research. Other college personnel can let your students know what kinds of services are available to students.

Perhaps some of your colleagues could talk about career opportunities in their fields. You could also invite local businesspeople to visit. They can offer advice on applying for jobs and writing résumés, or they could describe what they look for in an employee. Better yet, ask some former students to visit. They can tell your current students about the kind of writing they are doing in upper-level courses or on the job. Every visit can be followed by some type of writing assignment, either for a grade or for practice.

5

Building Community in the English Class

Susan Anker

Rationale

We already have too much to do in a writing class; how can we justify incorporating the notion of community, however valuable an idea it might be? A good question, with lots of possible, layered answers. There are two overriding and pragmatic reasons for doing so:

1. It will help student retention.

2. It will give students something real to write about.

Improving Retention

I do not need to tell any educator that we need to help students stay in school, almost before we can help them thrive, though the two goals are intertwined. So many of our students have lives that are overflowing with responsibilities and demands, and they are taking only one or two courses in college. When some other part of their lives becomes difficult, as so often seems to happen, students may let go of their college course or courses. Doing so may seem the easiest route in part because many students just drop in, take a course, and leave, without forming connections of any sort. When they decide to leave, no one knows, and therefore no one can dissuade them. They are not part of the college community.

Over the many years that I have been involved in developmental writing, I have become convinced that the students who have the best chance of persisting and graduating are those who form strong connections to the college community. Certainly I am not alone in this conviction. Many reports (some of which are noted at the end of this chapter) substantiate the direct relevance of connectedness to student engagement, retention, and eventual graduation. One of the most extensive studies is the Community College Survey of Student Engagement (CCSSE, www.ccsse.org), which starts with the premise that engagement is a predictor of success and presents six principles that promote engagement and retention. The first principle is "personal connections." The report states that "to retain entering students, the earlier and more frequently that engaged learning experiences occur, the better." Often, these connections are with individual faculty members, but the report gives numerous other examples of effective practices, ranging from required student success courses, to clubs like the ping-pong club at Santa Fe Community College, to service learning.

Another of the six principles is "engaged learning," encouraging active, collaborative learning in the students' day-to-day experiences, in the form of group work, a community service component, and "other hands-on experiences" built into coursework. Research concerning a third principle, "an integrated network of financial, social, and academic support," reports that more than a third of entering students do not know about academic advising and planning services, face-to-face tutoring, skills labs, financial aid advising, or computer labs. Among the two-thirds of students who do know about campus resources, few seek them out, even when they could use the help.

Clearly, even though our priority is helping our students develop their writing skills, we need to work with the whole student, not just the piece of him or her that spends a few hours a week with us trying to become a better writer. Like anything else, working to incorporate elements of student success and connectedness into the already overloaded tower of goals we have takes some up-front time. Just as clearly, the results more than justify the time we take. Later, I will have some students write about how getting involved in community service benefited them. For now, I will let Christine Wright, a student at Durham Technical Community College, lay the groundwork for this chapter. "Getting involved helps you stay connected and broadens your experience as a student," Wright says. "You're not just coming to class and then leaving." Wright encourages students to "pick an activity and get involved." We can start that involvement from the first day of class.

Getting Started

Most of you probably have favorite ways to start your class, and I am always impressed when I am giving workshops how many wonderful activities instructors have to break the ice on the first day of class. Those icebreakers are essential (and often fun), and I am not suggesting that anyone replace those favorites with ones that build community. Many of the activities you use on the first day are in fact building community.

What I am suggesting, however, is that we make community building an explicit underlying goal of the course. By explicit, I mean that from day one, you talk about the importance of becoming a learning community in your class. Tell the students that it is a fact: Students who are part of the college community, who establish connections within that community, are much more likely to stay and succeed in college. The habits begin in your classroom.

Icebreakers

If your icebreaker involves having students introduce themselves, do something in small groups, or meet one another in some other way, perhaps preface the activity with a statement that this is the beginning of the class learning community. Whatever else you do, have students exchange contact information with at least two other students.

You might also distribute (or include as part of your syllabus) a list of community-building steps.

For example, you might tell students that each person in the class needs to find a learning partner for the semester who will do the following: (1) Take notes when one partner is absent and contact the absent partner, providing what he or she missed; (2) contact an absent partner who has missed two or more consecutive classes; (3) talk with each other with writing or reading assignments; (4) talk about and study for upcoming tests; (5) read each other's drafts; and (6) talk about problems either partner is having in class.

Beyond Icebreakers

The first chapter of *Real Essays,* Succeeding in College: What You Need to Know, starts with advice from students who have recently passed their first college writing course. These students offer practical, concrete advice to students who are just beginning it. Assign students to read this section (pp. 4–9) in the chapter, and ask them to write down three pieces of advice they found useful and why, along with a plan for how, specifically, they will act on the advice. Then, have the students discuss what they wrote, preferably in a small group of other students, or with a partner or the whole class, with you leading the discussion.

Then, move to the section in Chapter 1 on Use All Resources (pp. 13–18). Ask students if they have gone to their college's Web site and, if so, why. Assign Activity 1: Find Your Resources, either in class and working in partners or small groups, if you are working in a computer lab, or as homework. Make sure to go over the findings in class. In doing this activity, students become comfortable with the process of checking their helpful college Web site and familiar with what they will find there. They learn about particular resources available to them and get to write about the Web site, reinforcing relevant aspects of what they have learned. Students will also have information with which they can participate in a class discussion.

The other part of Chapter 1 that lays the foundation for student connection to the college community is Connect to the College. Have a student read aloud Why Join the Club? (p. 16), and then ask what they think about joining a club or getting involved. Many may feel reluctant to engage in a sustained commitment to any activity that makes more demands on their already full lives. You can explain that nine other students have profiles in *Real Essays* (see the Writing about Connections assignments in Chapters 10–18 in Part 2), and all these students also had pressing, competing outside responsibilities.

All of them made a connection very tentatively at first. They never expected to become as involved as they did, and they were shocked to find that (1) they enjoyed it a great deal; (2) they were somehow able to squeeze their activity into their lives; (3) they benefited academically, not just socially. In other words, they became highly engaged in precisely the ways that the CCSSE advocated. Assure students that they can start by completing Activity 3: Find the Clubs, which they can do on their own, with their learning partner, or in a small group.

As a follow-up, assign writing assignments 1, 2, or 3 in Chapter 1. Then have students read them aloud and discuss their responses.

Finally, have your students go to our Web site **bedfordstmartins.com/realessays** and take the VARK Questionnaire to determine their learning styles. Break them into small groups, either by putting like learning styles together or by mixing up learning styles. Then, have them discuss their reactions to knowing their learning style and brainstorm ways to use it effectively in college. If you want, keep these groups together to form a course-long learning community.

With these opening activities, you will have laid good ground for student engagement and connections to the college community.

Giving Students Something Real to Write about and Engage In

As the course progresses, you will be able to promote community in ways that will give students something "real" to write about. When students do join a club or take part in a campus or community activity, they can use their new experiences as the basis for writing assignments in Part 1, which takes students through the basics of critical thinking (Chapter 2), critical reading (Chapter 3), and the stages of the writing process (Chapters 4–9).

For reading, have students find an article on something they are interested in that is not specifically academic (a club, a local issue, a campus issue, a community problem). This activity also starts to engage them, in a nonintimidating way, in the practice of research. Then have them practice the steps of the reading process that are in Chapter 3. If you are met with blank looks when you ask students to find and read about something that interests them, you could direct them to browse among the following Web sites. Some of these sites might pique their interest.

I. A Selection of General Interest Sites

- **www.about.com, www.associatedcontent.com, www.ehow.com, www.helium.com, www.plinky.com, www.squidoo.com** provide places for people to share advice on all kinds of subjects in the form of articles, videos, recipes, step-by-step tutorials, and more.

- **thisibelieve.org**, from National Public Radio, archives short statements written by people from all over the world and all walks of life about the core values that guide their lives.

- *This American Life*, **www.thisamericanlife.org/favorites**, from National Public Radio, offers audio shows with interesting and unusual stories.

- *The Nutrition Source*, **www.hsph.harvard.edu/nutritionsource**, from the Harvard School of Public Health, provides articles and information on diet and nutrition.

- *The High School Graduate*, at **www.thehighschoolgraduate.com/editorial/DE/financial.htm**, discusses paying for college, among other things.

- **www.snopes.com** collects and discusses classic urban legends.

- *The Responsibility Project*, at **www.responsibilityproject.com**, offers a collection of short films that ponder the idea of responsibility.

- **www.postsecret.com** showcases anonymous, homemade postcards in which people reveal their secrets.

II. Selection of Sites Relating to Community Service

The following are just a few of the many sites that can get students thinking about community service. These sites offer ideas for getting involved in worthwhile organizations, many of which might already have ties to the college community. (More on that subject in a moment.)

- **volunteerguide.org** helps people find ways to volunteer, even when they have busy, unpredictable schedules.

- **www.coolpeoplecare.org** gives a range of ways to get involved and make a difference, starting with "5 Minutes of Caring."

- **www.idealist.org** is an interactive Web site where people can look for jobs and volunteer opportunities and talk to other people about making the world a better place.

- **www.rootsandshoots.org** helps search for local community service groups and projects.

- **www.idealbite.com** offers ideas for small lifestyle changes that can help the environment.

To work on the writing process with students (see Chapters 4–9), again have them choose a topic of their own based on what they find interesting. (If they cannot find a topic that interests them, they can choose one of the topics listed within the chapters themselves.) You are the most important influence on the direction that students take, and you may want to keep encouraging a connection to a college club or community organization. By connecting with a club or an organization of their choice, its other members and activities, students will gain a rich source of "real" topics to write about. When they are involved in what they are writing about, their writing tends to be much, much better, with fewer questions like "how many words does the paper have to be?" To build on the students' engagement and learning, you might ask a student who has connected with an organization to invite a speaker from that organization to give a presentation to the class, or you might invite the student to give a brief talk. The point is to use the students' engagement in the activity in the service of writing. In so doing, the writing improves, as does the students' sense of competence and self-esteem, all of which contribute to the students being more likely to stay in school, a place where, perhaps for the first time, they feel positive reinforcement and relevance.

Service Learning/Students in the Community

Student involvement in any activity associated with the college benefits them; student involvement with community service benefits them even more, and the two categories often overlap. For example, a nursing club or business club might sponsor a fundraiser for a local charitable organization or organize a clothing drive or clothing swap day. Many of the clubs by nature have at least one foot in the community beyond the college. In addition, more and more colleges have clubs that are explicitly devoted to service learning or community service. These clubs make it easy for instructors like you to expose students to community service without having to engage in a formalized service-learning course.

Many of the students I have met who have engaged in community service started with a simple writing assignment such as, "Choose an organization that you are interested in, commit to spend four to eight hours there over the (specify the number of weeks), and as you spend time there, think about what you want to write about." You can invite the adviser for the college service learning office or club to your class to talk about the club, its activities, and so on. Students can then follow up with the club to get a placement. Your role would be no more complicated than approving the student's topic and then working with the student as with any other writing assignment. This kind of assignment is also a great vehicle for students to discuss with learning partners or small groups. When instructors first see their students' writing about such activities, they are uniformly (and pleasantly) surprised by how rich the ideas are, how their students' voices come through, and how much better the writing is, not to mention how engaged the students are, both in the work and in the writing.

Beyond these substantial benefits, in fact there is an even greater one: growth in self-esteem and confidence. In the words of Dan Simonet (Simonet 2008), "When students connect the content of their learning with the challenge of a real situation their feeling of competence increases." (His report, listed in the resources at the end of this chapter, is well worth reading.) Because this positive effect is connected to the college experience, the students feel, perhaps for the first time, a positive reward associated with their academic experience. It was surprising to me how many of the students who were pushed or dragged grudgingly into their first experience of a college club or community service continued with their involvement. Many credit their involvement with their staying in college and doing better academically. Those who have graduated still volunteer: It is really amazing. As Simonet so aptly summarizes, "Service learning is a *process* that creates greater student engagement, which in turn results in the *product* of student retention."

Writing about Connections

All the chapters in Part 2 of *Real Essays* explicitly incorporate the theme of community, particularly in the fourth writing assignment in each of the chapters: Writing about Connections. Each of the students profiled as part of the writing assignment got "hooked" on the college and the community—often much to their surprise. They talk about what they did, and the assignments options allow for varying degrees of campus or community involvement. Neither you nor your students will have to do extra work, in either setting up the assignments or fulfilling them: The book provides a wide range of ideas and opportunities. And, of course, four other kinds of writing assignments appear in each of the chapters, providing a variety of approaches. Before leaving the subject of community, however, here are some words about community from a few of those students who are profiled in the Part 2 chapters.

AURELIUS TAYLOR (Chapter 10): "At first I wasn't comfortable being around smart people who got good grades. But my role in student government has made me a leader on campus, and now I help other students about to start college. I tell them it won't be easy, things will get bad at some point, but they need to make a commitment to education. Change is not easy, but it's worth every stressful moment."

LONZA FRUITREE (Chapter 11): "I have become a role model for others. I tell them, if I can do it, they can, too. I say, 'You can start, and you can finish. It's okay to stumble, but pick yourself up, and keep on pushing yourself. And if you are involved on campus, you have others who will help you when you need it."

TIFFANY EWIGLEBEN (Chapter 13): "My journey from high school dropout to confident and successful student leader began with a few hours of community service."

STACY GORDON WELCH (Chapter 17): "The more involved I am, the better I do in school."

These students display great passion when asked about their work, and they have no doubt that the connections they formed were fundamental to their academic, social, and professional success.

A Few Last Thoughts

Real Essays is not a book with an agenda other than to be a good tool for writing teachers. It began with a conviction that students need to understand that they will need writing in their future lives in order to achieve success in any field. As I have met and worked with more and more students over the years, I have, I suppose, been conducting field research on what makes at-risk students succeed in college. First, they have to be there, and so many leave that trying to find any way to staunch the loss is always on my mind. Like most complex problems,

there is no single answer. The best solutions are multipronged efforts that share these certainties:

- Engaged students are better students.

- Students write better when they are writing about "real" things.

- We need to show them ways to become engaged, and then coach them.

- When one thing doesn't work, try another.

- Keep trying.

In the concept of community, both in the classroom and beyond to the college and the larger community, I stumbled on one approach that seems to have engaged students in palpable ways. I know that many of you have been incorporating this kind of approach for many years, and I hope that seeing a matching approach in a writing textbook may make your jobs a bit easier. *Real Essays* is one of your tools; you are the real teacher and a major influence on your students.

Resources: Building Community

Articles

Bringle, Robert G., and Julie A. Hatcher. "Innovative Practices in Service Learning and Curricular Engagement." *New Directions of Higher Education* 147 (2009): 37–46. Print.

Duffy, Donna, et al. *Service Learning Course Design for Community Colleges.* Providence: Campus Compact, 2007. Print.

Elwell, M. D., and M. S. Bean. "The Efficacy of Service-Learning for Community College ESL Students." *Community College Review* 28.4 (2001): 47–61. Print.

Hathi, Sejal, and Bob Bhaerman. *Effective Practices for Engaging At-Risk Youth in Service.* Washington: Youth Service America, 2008. Print.

Hodge, G., et al. "Collaboration for Excellence: Engaged Scholarship at Collin County Community College." *Community College Journal of Research and Practice* 25 (2001): 675–90. Print.

Kinzie, Jillian. *Promoting Student Success: What Faculty Members Can Do.* (Occasional Paper No. 6). Bloomington: Indiana U Center for Postsecondary Research, 2005. *National Survey of Student Engagement.* Web. 11 Nov. 2011.

McClenney, Kay M. "Research Update: The Community College Survey of Student Engagement." *Community College Review* 35 (2007): 137–46. Print.

Mohr, K. A. "Planning for Productive College-Level Work: Using the Course Assignment Framework." *Community College Journal of Research and Practice* 26.6 (2002): 469–77. Print.

Simonet, Dan. *Service-Learning and Academic Success: The Links to Retention Research.* St. Paul: Minnesota Campus Compact, 2008. Print.

Web sites

Center for the Study of College Student Retention
www.cscsr.org

Community College National Center for Community Engagement
www.mesacc.edu/other/engagement
This site is a great resource, with syllabi, assistance setting up programs and assignments, funding sources, and information about the national conference.

Community College Survey of Student Engagement
www.ccsse.org

6

Integrating Critical Thinking into the Course

Chet Meyers, *Metropolitan State University*

Teaching writing and teaching critical thinking go hand in hand. *Real Essays* makes this partnership manageable. Even at the most fundamental level, the writing skills of sound paragraph and essay structure, organized and thoughtful presentation of support, and careful editing form the basis for more sophisticated critical thinking skills. You need not have two texts or two approaches in order to foster critical thinking in your developmental writing students. *Real Essays* encourages these students, who often have difficulty seeing themselves as thinkers and as writers, to *think like writers*. This section of *Practical Suggestions* offers you an overview of critical thinking (as educators have defined it in the past two decades) and gives some concrete applications and activities for the classroom.

Critical thinking begins with a strong foundation of skills, content/knowledge, and attitudes. Because the interplay of these three factors is so crucial, a general framework for thinking about critical thinking can help teachers examine their teaching practice and explore how to encourage sound thinking in the teaching of writing. The framework that follows summarizes some of the major themes and issues that have characterized the critical thinking movement during the past two decades.

Three Ways of Thinking about Critical Thinking

SKILLS. During the late 1970s and early 1980s, critical thinking in college and university teaching was generally associated with formal or informal logic, or with various approaches to problem solving.

The assumption was that if we could teach students generic critical thinking skills, they could then apply those skills to any discipline. To some extent that has proved true. The more or less commonsense tools of inference, deduction, and sound argumentation illustrate basic reasoning skills that cut across all disciplines. However, a student who masters a course in informal logic or problem solving may need further practice to apply those skills to, say, art appreciation or college algebra.

CONTENT/KNOWLEDGE. A second approach, advocated by John McPeck in *Critical Thinking and Education* (1981), suggests that we consider how critical thinking necessarily varies among different disciplines. It does seem obvious that an artist goes about critical thinking differently than does a physicist. Likewise, a physicist's critical thinking abilities differ somewhat from those of a historian. The differences are natural, given the different assumptions these disciplines make about the nature of reality and their different ways of knowing. Most of us can relate to this personally. We have the ability to think critically about some subjects and yet remain baffled by others. Training in critical thinking involves practice in asking critical questions so that the physics student learns to think like a physicist, the history student learns to think like a historian, and the writing student learns to think like a writer.

ATTITUDES. A third approach to critical thinking grew out of the combined work of developmental psychologists such as Jean Piaget, William Perry, and Carol Gilligan and educators such as Steven Brookfield and Mary Field Belenky. The argument here is that, in Piaget's terminology, our mental structures (the ways we organize our thinking processes) develop more or less naturally and become more sophisticated as we mature. As children encounter increasingly complex life problems, their mental structures become more sophisticated. Although there is still disagreement among developmental theorists and educators about the exact nature of these stages of development (particularly differences between men and women), there is overriding agreement that thinking skills are linked to ego development. And that suggests that cognitive skills are intimately tied to affective attitudes and, as Richard Paul wisely suggests in his book *Critical Thinking: What Every Person Needs to Survive in a Rapidly Changing World*, to moral development (255). Thus, students are more likely to advance intellectually in supportive and nurturing environments and where attitudes such as encouragement, open-mindedness, risk taking, appreciation of complexity, and collaborative learning are fostered.

If we consider these three approaches not as competing ideologies but as each having something worthwhile to contribute to the teaching of critical thinking, we can create a simple framework that can help us build a foundation for critical thinking in writing.

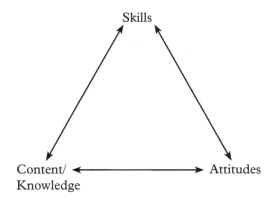

With this historical framework in mind, we can now consider the practical implications of these three different approaches to critical thinking and how we can use them to formulate an approach to teaching that will help students improve their thinking abilities.

Implications for Teaching and Learning

SKILLS. Students need to develop basic cognitive skills, some of which seem to come naturally and others of which need to be more explicitly taught. Teaching developmental writing should involve fostering students' analytical and evaluative skills as well. Many of the steps in the writing process for a paragraph or an essay—exploring and narrowing a topic, writing a topic sentence, organizing information and creating a structure, supporting a main point with details and evidence, and revising and editing for clarity and coherence—involve critical thinking. *Real Essays'* Critical Thinking boxes and Writing Guides encourage students to analyze and evaluate by asking them to focus on a particular skill or process, ask themselves key questions, and write or edit based on their answers.

CONTENT/KNOWLEDGE. Thinking skills do not exist in a vacuum. Students cannot write about a topic unless they know something about it. Good thinking grows out of a strong base of information and evidence. In teaching developmental writing, we cannot expect students to have extensive knowledge of any particular subject, but we are not starting from zero. We can begin by drawing on students' interests and life experiences, and then challenge them to explore those areas in more depth and with sophistication. Rather than assigning all students to write about the Declaration of Independence, begin with something that is already percolating in their minds. *Real Essays* helps you do this in a number of ways. All assignments, for example, allow students to choose from a broad range of general topics; real-world assignments throughout the writing chapters reflect familiar or interesting situations. Allowing variety in topic selection, variety that appeals to different student interests, is a good starting place. To that end, I have included a simple Survey of Interests form (see p. 69), which you may consider distributing at the beginning of the first class. Use this tool to discover what students really might want to write about and to collect an initial writing sample.

Survey of Interests

Please take a few minutes to complete this brief survey. The information you provide will help me to create assignments that draw on your experiences and interests, so that the writing you do in this course is connected to your life and your goals.

1. When you are not doing schoolwork, what kinds of magazines and books do you read?

2. What are two of your favorite hobbies and/or extracurricular activities? (Please be relatively serious here.)

3. What commitments and responsibilities do you have outside of school? (for example: work, child care, or other family responsibilities; membership in a group or organization)

4. What is your own assessment of your writing abilities, and what in particular would you like to learn from this writing class?

5. Turn this page over, and on the back side, write a two-paragraph letter to a friend, explaining to him or her how you *feel* about taking this writing course.

Thank you for taking the time to complete this survey.

ATTITUDES. Students will develop good thinking skills in an environment that both challenges and supports them. The best critical thinkers are individuals who have some sense of their own worth and who have experienced success in their undertakings. Open-mindedness, risk taking, persistence, inquisitiveness, the humility to admit mistakes, and the courage to start over do not develop in an oppressive and punitive atmosphere. I cannot stress strongly enough the role of the teacher as coach and cheerleader. The best teachers know how to combine discipline and rigor with support and encouragement. Indeed, the general atmosphere in the classroom is often one of the best indicators of whether or not critical thinking is being encouraged. If students are actively engaged—discussing, laughing, arguing, or even quietly pondering—it's a good bet they are developing sound thinking abilities. (See the *Instructor's Annotated Edition for Real Essays* for suggested collaborative activities and discussion tips.) In contrast, in those neatly ordered, rows-all-straight-and-tidy classrooms where the teacher is front and center presenting information and where students always sit passively jotting down a note or two, there is little encouragement for the development of good thinking abilities.

Tips for Fostering Active, Critical Learning

Teaching skills, content/knowledge, and attitudes in a developmental writing course may sound like heaping just so many more expectations on already burdened instructors. That need not be the case. But to alleviate the supposed burden, some of us do need to rethink what teaching is about and focus our attention on *learning*. Thirty years ago we knew much less about the exact nature of the learning process than we do today. The old model of teacher-as-lecturer and student-as-note-taker was firmly rooted in the assumption that the teacher's job was to *transmit* knowledge to the student. Students were regarded as empty vessels waiting to be filled by wise and knowledgeable teachers. Today we know that that old model has very limited efficacy. Indeed, most recent studies by educational psychologists and cognitive scientists argue that learning is less about receiving knowledge than it is about constructing knowledge. In the words of Jean Piaget, "children do not receive knowledge passively but rather discover and construct knowledge through activities" (119). That means we need to take more time

in our classes for students to engage in activities that will help them formulate new mental structures to serve as the building blocks for critical thinking (Meyers 13). Numerous studies have shown that when traditional lecturing is compared with more active forms of teaching and learning, in the context of general retention and practical learning outcomes, active learning almost always wins out—hands down (Erickson; Bransford; Kolb; Pollio).

So critical thinking and active learning are inextricably linked. The trick is to learn how to structure our classes so that active learning becomes a regular part of the teaching/learning process that both teachers and students can enjoy. What follows are four rather simple suggestions that can serve as a guide to creating a classroom that fosters critical thinking. (For additional suggestions, see Chapter 9 of this manual.)

ENCOURAGE STUDENT INTERACTION. When Fortune 500 executives spend hundreds of thousands of dollars for consultants to help them arrange office furniture in optimal ways to enhance employee interaction, you know American business is on to something. In the real world of work, a dynamic and flexible physical environment enhances employee productivity. It is unfortunate that some college classrooms—where students prepare for work—still have desks bolted to the floor. "Unbolting" the desks is the first step in encouraging shared inquiry, collaboration, and critical problem solving.

There are many different ways to arrange classroom furniture to encourage interaction. Desks can be placed in a horseshoe shape, with the opening toward the writing board. An ideal arrangement for a writing class is to place tables and chairs in a modified diamond shape, with four to five chairs at each table. One advantage of tables is that students can work in small groups. Many college writing programs stress a small-group approach to the teaching of developmental writing. A class might begin with a brief presentation by the teacher on paragraph construction, followed by illustrations from a few models. Next, students work individually on a paragraph and then meet as a group to share their writing and to receive helpful feedback. Of course, good small-group interaction needs to be modeled and ground rules for interaction must be laid down (see Chapter 7 in this manual), but the activity of students working with one another is a powerful stimulation to learning. The key here is to structure small-group activities for optimal productivity (see Johnson, Johnson, and Smith).

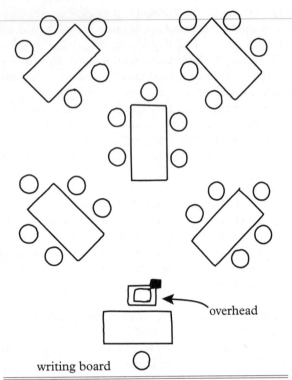

overhead

writing board

Modified diamond-shape arrangement facing the teacher and writing board

ALLOW MORE TIME FOR STUDENT–TEACHER AND STUDENT–STUDENT INTERACTION. Perhaps the most difficult aspect of helping students develop their own critical thinking skills is the need for teachers to move from center stage. The best teachers of critical thinking in any discipline are those who see their role as chief choreographer, not lead actor. There is very little that we lecture on that cannot be conveyed by means of some other, more engaging method.

Although brief mini-lectures provide a good way to focus attention and to set the agenda for the day, most time in class should be focused on student activities: sharing and critiquing papers, group editing, learning how to provide helpful feedback, or working on other small-group tasks. Once active learning becomes a regular part of the teaching–learning process, students remain focused, and instead of fidgeting ten minutes before class ends, they often have difficulty disengaging from their small-group activities. They will become more goal-oriented and less concerned with the clock.

TO GET CLASS STARTED, CONSIDER BRIEF ACTIVITIES. The key to sound classroom activities is inciting student interest. Presenting activities and content in a real-world, familiar context is a productive

start. You can design successful, interesting class openers around a short reading and problem-solving exercises that build basic reading and writing skills. Consider the following options, and see Chapter 9 of this manual for more suggestions for active learning.

Students enter class and sit at tables with four to five chairs. You direct them to read Barbara Huttmann's essay "A Crime of Compassion" in the Readings for Writers section of *Real Essays*. It will take about ten minutes to read the guiding question and the essay. Ask students to (1) summarize the main point of the essay in one or two sentences, (2) cite with a direct quote one of the consequences of treating a dying patient, (3) explain Huttmann's rationale, and (4) imagine, if terminally ill patients were granted "the right to die," what the implications might be. Students spend another ten minutes writing their individual responses to these questions, and then they collaborate to see if they can build a consensus answer. You then solicit a response from each group to build a classwide consensus. The entire exercise takes about twenty-five minutes and can provide a jump start for a longer writing assignment. Skills involved in this exercise include reading, reflecting, summarizing, seeking evidence, analyzing, drawing one's own conclusions, talking and listening to others, and synthesizing to build consensus. (You might refer students to the coverage of reading-based writing at the end of Chapter 2 of *Real Essays*.)

Second, consider circulating a short paragraph that needs editing. Each of the grammar chapters in *Real Essays* ends with paragraph-editing practice that you can use for this activity. Ask students to spend five minutes editing the piece individually and to work for another five or ten minutes in a small group to come up with their best editing suggestions. Then ask each group to report back while you use an overhead projector to explore options and illustrate the class's final editing suggestions.

Finally, you may want to use one or more of the critical thinking activities provided at the end of this chapter. Each of these provides a critical thinking warm-up for the rest of the day's activities and helps to promote active, critical learning. You may spend five or ten minutes discussing how the skills involved in the various critical thinking activities apply to the writing process.

ALLOW QUIET TIME FOR REFLECTION. The hustle and bustle of an active-learning classroom is contagious and does a lot to stimulate thinking abilities, but so does quiet time. Different students learn in different ways. Some are more reflective than others;

and no matter what their learning style, all students need some quiet time for the brain to process and incorporate new learning. In John Dewey's words, "All reflection involves at some point, stopping external observation and reactions so that an idea may mature" (210).

A problem here is that most teachers are very uncomfortable with silence in the classroom. Studies of what is referred to as "wait time"—the time between when a teacher asks a question and, seeing no response, either calls on a student or volunteers his or her own answer—suggest that teachers wait only about as long as it takes a butterfly to flap its wings once, or 0.9 seconds ("Slow Down, You Move Too Fast"). Time for reflection can be built into writing exercises and problem-solving exercises or made a part of the teacher's open queries to the class. "What do you think the main problem with this paragraph structure is?" PAUSE . . . PAUSE . . . and more PAUSE. When we do take time to slow down and allow our students the luxury of a few moments of silence in the classroom, some wonderful things can happen. Students who never spoke before might volunteer, or we might find a student's answer challenges our own interpretations, allowing us also to experience the gift of new learning. Our purpose is to foster an environment where students can think critically, not quickly.

Developing Writing Assignments That Promote Critical Thinking

It is important to remember that learning to think critically does not happen overnight. The nature of teaching critical thinking in writing requires a building-block process that starts with simple assignments and progresses to higher levels of thinking. Here are some tips you may find helpful in designing effective writing assignments.

SEQUENCE ASSIGNMENTS TO BUILD SKILLS. Sequencing assignments to build from basic to more sophisticated cognitive skills enables you to observe student progress and allows students the opportunity for practice and, in turn, increased confidence. *Real Essays* offers carefully sequenced assignments: Students move through the rhetorical methods from narration to argument, and within each chapter of Part 2 and Part 8, Readings for Writers, students read and analyze example essays before writing their own. Consider beginning with narration or illustration, which involve thinking abilities such as sorting through information, providing ex-

amples, organizing key details and events, and summarizing. Beyond that, ask students to spend some time writing comparison/contrast essays, which involve analytical thinking. You might then progress to argument essays, which require students to recognize and counter assumptions. Throughout the process of any writing assignment, encourage students to ask a series of critical questions. By sequencing assignments that build from basic cognitive skills to higher-level thinking, we can help students become more aware of the role that critical thinking plays in writing.

DRAW ON STUDENTS' REAL-LIFE AND WORK EXPERIENCES. Another consideration in creating writing assignments is to develop them on the basis of our students' real-world interactions. The deathly prose that too often characterizes student papers often results from the "already dead" subjects they are asked to write about. Consider using the form Survey of Interests provided in this chapter, or one that you create on your own. Nothing enlivens writing more than assigning topics that are already fermenting in students' minds. Providing a real-world context helps to build critical thinking and writing skills. Issues being debated on your campus—tuition hikes, placement testing, or student parking, for example—can all serve as grist for the writing mill. The assignments throughout *Real Essays* have been constructed to reflect as accurately as possible students' real academic, work, and personal experiences.

A note about giving instructions for writing assignments: I cannot overemphasize the importance of being clear and unambiguous. We may know what we mean when we ask students to summarize, evaluate, or analyze, but students don't always know. Analyze, perhaps the most overused word in college assignments, may have many different meanings for students: "compare similarities or differences," "respond to personally," or "debate." Be clear in your definition of words such as *summary, evaluation,* and *analysis.* You may want to ask students to define these words and describe what kind of thinking each requires. Then, measure their responses against your own expectations for individual writing assignments. Also, consider referring students to the discussion of these terms in Chapter 3 of *Real Essays.* See especially the chart on page 36. Carefully consider the types of thinking, as well as the types of rhetorical development, that you want students to practice in each writing assignment.

There are many ways writing teachers can help their students build a strong foundation for critical thinking. The challenge is to trust that students do, in fact, have the ability to begin thinking critically, if we will only provide a foundation and a context, and then get out of the way and allow them time in class to practice and develop those abilities. Stepping down from the podium does not mean relinquishing all control. But becoming a good choreographer for student learning will require us to rethink our role as teacher. There are some losses in no longer being the center of attention. The gains, however, are considerable when we see the progress our students make and know that we helped point them in the direction of active, critical learning.

Critical Thinking Activities

On the pages that follow are a variety of activities that promote critical and creative thinking:

- *Think Again* activities are logic puzzles that students must solve by abandoning conventional lines of thought and uncovering new possibilities.

- *Figure It Out* activities are visual puzzles that require students to deduce rules from a set of statements and then to articulate the rules in clear definitions.

- *Focus—and Refocus* activities are also visual, but as in the Think Again activities, students must solve them by reconsidering assumptions and finding unconventional perspectives.

- *Conundrums* are exercises in logical deduction—with a creative twist.

All activities but the Conundrums can be photocopied and distributed to students for either independent or group work. These activities work well as icebreakers or to introduce collaboration. The Conundrums are meant to be read aloud and worked on by the class as a whole (or by a smaller group) as a collaborative, in-class activity.

The solution for each Think Again, Figure It Out, and Focus—and Refocus activity is printed on the back of the page, so you can either copy and distribute these as well or simply let students know what the answers are. Encourage students to challenge answers they find faulty or to defend alternative solutions. By analyzing and discussing the assumptions and logic of each puzzle, students will greatly increase their abilities to think critically and creatively.

Set A

Sometimes you need to look at a problem from a new perspective to see the solution. Try some creative thinking to solve these puzzles.

1. Two plumbers were working together on a new apartment building. One of them was the father of the other one's son. How is this possible?

2. What five-letter word becomes shorter when you add two letters to it?

3. Tom has two younger sisters who each want him to take her to the movies. Tom also has a limited budget. Would it be cheaper for him to take his sisters to see a movie together, to take them each separately, or doesn't it matter?

4. A king has promised his kingdom to whichever of his two children has the *slower* horse, and he starts them on a race to the most distant city in the realm. Because neither of them wants to arrive first, the prince and the princess meander slowly around the kingdom for weeks. Finally, they meet an old villager who proposes a solution, and the prince and the princess are soon racing as fast as they can to the distant city. What is the villager's solution?

Answers for Set A

These are the answers that we had in mind. If you came up with something different, though, you might just have a different perspective.

Answer for 1. The plumbers were husband and wife.

Answer for 2. The word *short* becomes *shorter* when you add *e* and *r*.

Answer for 3. Tom should take them both together. Then he will only pay for three tickets altogether (one for him and one for each of his sisters) rather than four.

Answer for 4. The villager proposes that the prince and the princess trade horses. Now each of them wants to reach the city first, so that the horse that the other one is riding is shown to be slower.

Set B

Sometimes you need to look at a problem from a new perspective to see the solution. Try some creative thinking to solve these puzzles.

1. An airplane flying off the coast of Southern California has as its two passengers two men trying to settle a bet. One of them has bet the other that if he drops a one-pound brick out of the plane ten seconds after the other man has dropped a one-pound sack of cotton out of the plane, the brick will hit the ground first. Which of the two will actually hit the ground first?

2. A careless driver drove his truck under an overpass that was not quite high enough to let the truck through. He was stuck tight and could drive neither forward nor backward. Finally, he came up with a way to get his truck unstuck. How did he do it?

3. Two mothers and two daughters were fishing, and they each caught a fish. But only three fish were caught. How is this possible?

Answers for Set B

These are the answers that we had in mind. If you came up with something different, though, you might just have a different perspective.

Answer for 1. Neither. If the plane is flying off the coast of Southern California, they will both hit the water.

Answer for 2. The truck driver let some of the air out of his tires.

Answer for 3. There were only three people fishing: a grandmother, a mother, and a daughter. The mother is both a mother and a daughter.

Pringles

Imagine you are learning a new language and are shown the objects below. Some are called *pringles* and some are not, but it is difficult at first to figure out exactly what makes an object a pringle. Analyze the objects to find out what the pringles have in common; keep in mind that there may be other pringles than the ones you see here.

When you have figured out what makes an object a pringle, write a clear definition here:

To be a pringle, an object must _____

_____

_____

This is a pringle.

This is a pringle.

This is not a pringle.

This is a pringle.

This is not a pringle.

This is not a pringle.

Answer for Pringles

This is the answer that we had in mind. If you came up with something different, though, you might just have a different perspective.

To be a pringle, an object must _____ *be a shape with sides of equal length.*

Laracks

Imagine you are learning a new language and are shown the objects below. Some are called *laracks* and some are not, but it is difficult at first to figure out exactly what makes an object a larack. Analyze the objects to find out what the laracks have in common; keep in mind that there may be other laracks than the ones you see here.

When you have figured out what makes an object a larack, write a clear definition here:

To be a larack, an object must _____

_____

This is a larack.

This is not a larack.

This is not a larack.

This is a larack.

This is a larack.

This is not a larack.

Answer for Laracks

This is the answer that we had in mind. If you came up with something different, though, you might just have a different perspective.

To be a larack, an object must _____ *be an eating utensil intended to hold liquid.*

Squares

To figure something out, sometimes we need to look beyond the obvious answers—and sometimes we need to consider the answers that we thought were *too* obvious to be important. Be sure to explore all the possibilities.

How many squares are in this picture?

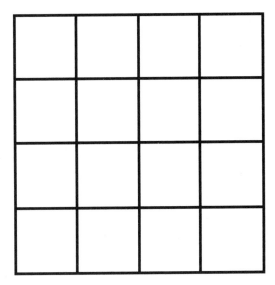

Answer for Squares

There are thirty squares.

Focus—and Refocus

Word Puns

To figure something out, sometimes we need to look beyond the obvious answers—and sometimes we need to consider the answers that we thought were *too* obvious to be important. Be sure to explore all the possibilities.

What does each of these mean?

1. $\dfrac{\text{STAND}}{\text{I}}$ = _____

2. /READING/ = _____

3. T = _____
   O
   U
   C
   H

4. $\dfrac{\text{MAN}}{\text{BOARD}}$ = _____

5. LIFE/THE = _____

6. ECNALG = _____

Answers for Word Puns

1. $\dfrac{\text{STAND}}{\text{I}}$ = _____ *I understand* _____

2. /READING/ = _____ *reading between the lines* _____

3. $\begin{array}{l}\text{T} \\ \text{O} \\ \text{U} \\ \text{C} \\ \text{H}\end{array}$ = _____ *touchdown* _____

4. $\dfrac{\text{MAN}}{\text{BOARD}}$ = _____ *man overboard* _____

5. LIFE/THE = _____ *the afterlife* _____

6. ECNALG = _____ *backwards glance* _____

Lines

To figure something out, sometimes we need to look beyond the obvious answers—and sometimes we need to consider the answers that we thought were *too* obvious to be important. Be sure to explore all the possibilities.

Can you draw a line through each of these dots, without lifting your pencil and by making only three turns (for a total of four straight segments)? You can only go through each dot once.

Answer for Lines

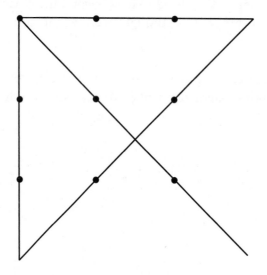

Conundrums

Note to Instructor: These are meant to be used for collaborative in-class activities, not treated as handouts. You (or a student) should act as the presenter and read a scenario out loud; the presenter should know what the solution is. The students listening should take on the role of detectives and work together to find the solution. The detectives can ask the presenter any question that can be answered with a yes or a no, and the presenter must answer truthfully.

SCENARIO 1
A woman walks into a restaurant and asks for a drink. The waitress quickly pulls out a gun and points it at her. The woman says "thank you" and leaves. What happened?

SOLUTION 1
The woman had hiccups. The waitress frightened her and helped her get rid of them.

SCENARIO 2
A man is afraid to go home because there is a man with a mask there. What is going on?

SOLUTION 2
The man is playing baseball and is on third base; the man with the mask is the catcher, who has the ball.

SCENARIO 3
A guard walks in and finds a prisoner has hanged himself, using the fabric from his shirt to make a noose and stringing it over a hook in the ceiling. The man's feet dangle three feet off the floor, but there is no furniture in the cell and nothing but the floor to stand on. How did the man hang himself?

SOLUTION 3
There is a puddle of water on the floor. The man stood on a block of ice, which has now melted.

SCENARIO 4
In the middle of the Mediterranean Sea is a large yacht with several corpses floating nearby. What happened?

SOLUTION 4
The passengers decided to go swimming, so they all dove into the water. However, they neglected to set up a ladder, so they couldn't get back into the yacht.

SCENARIO 5
Jake comes home to find broken glass and Ginger lying in a pool of water and broken glass. Although Ginger looks fine, he knows immediately that she is dead of suffocation. Why?

SOLUTION 5
Ginger is Jake's goldfish and her bowl has broken.

References

Bransford, J. *Human Cognition.* Belmont: Wadsworth, 1979. Print.

Dewey, John. *How We Think.* 1910. Lexington: Heath, 1982. Print.

Erickson, S. C. *The Essence of Good Teaching: Helping Students Learn and Remember What They Learn.* San Francisco: Jossey-Bass, 1984. Print.

Johnson, D., R. Johnson, and K. A. Smith. *Active Learning: Cooperation in the College Classroom.* Edina: Interaction, 1991. Print.

Kolb, David A. *Experiential Learning: Experience as a Source of Learning and Development.* Englewood Cliffs: Prentice-Hall, 1984. Print.

McPeck, John. *Critical Thinking and Education.* New York: St. Martin's Press, 1981. Print.

Meyers, Chet. *Teaching Students to Think Critically.* San Francisco: Jossey-Bass, 1986. Print.

Meyers, Chet, and Thomas B. Jones. *Promoting Active Learning: Strategies for the College Classroom.* San Francisco: Jossey-Bass, 1993. Print.

Paul, Richard. *Critical Thinking: What Every Person Needs to Survive in a Rapidly Changing World.* Sonoma: Center for Critical Thinking, 1992. Print.

Piaget, Jean. *Psychology of Intelligence.* 1947. Totowa: Littlefield Adams, 1976. Print.

Pollio, H. R. *What Students Think about and Do in College Lectures Classes.* Knoxville: Learning Research Center, University of Tennessee, 1984. Teaching and Learning Issues 53. Print.

"Slow Down, You Move Too Fast." *Phi Delta Kappan* 69 (1987): 234. Print.

Whitehead, A. N. *The Aims of Education.* 1929. New York: Free Press, 1967. Print.

7

Facilitating Cooperative Learning

Marian L. Beaman, *Florida State College at Jacksonville*

In October 2010, thirty-three Chilean miners found themselves trapped nearly a half mile underground below 700,000 tons of rock. To survive the seventeen days prior to being discovered, the miners needed to cooperate. Fortunately, Luis Urzua, the shift foreman, effectively motivated and led the miners to devise and execute a plan for survival. Urzua divided the men into teams, one creating a map and digging for a latrine, another figuring out food rations, and other teams meeting the medical and spiritual needs of the miners (Rooshanak). Above ground, rescuers cooperated in teams as well to ensure the safe return of all the miners.

Under less dramatic circumstances, instructors can effectively devise cooperative activities that will facilitate their students' successful passage through the semester. Like Luis Urzua, good instructors elicit the best from their students by providing strategies that include *working in teams*. For students, this cooperative work in teams means (a) experiencing positive interdependence with their peers, as commonly occurs in the workplace, and (b) taking personal responsibility for learning and for the final outcome of their written work.

Benefits of the Cooperative Approach

Students today are used to communicating regularly with their friends—talking in person, phoning, and texting, and generally sending and receiving messages of all kinds in abundance. Clearly the texting and casual talking that students do is a different modality from the communication in an English class. Working in teams, however, involves students in the same varied mix of discussing, writing, and responding that they like and do well. The collaborative approach plays to their strengths, in other words. Working in teams promotes face-to-face interactions that enhance students' writing skills by giving them a tangible idea of *audience* for their written work. There are other advantages too.

- In a cooperative atmosphere, students learn to recognize the characteristics of excellent writing, brainstorm with others to develop topics, give and receive constructive feedback on their drafts, and even incorporate the ideas of other student writers into their work, crediting others' contributions.

- Students benefit by learning social skills, such as listening and reaching consensus.

- Instructors appreciate the dynamics of a cooperative classroom where knowledge is jointly constructed by both teachers and students. Instead of constantly functioning as the "sage on the stage," the instructor at times becomes a "guide on the side," focusing on a few students while others are interacting with their peers.

- The flexibility of the approach allows it to work well for developing both writing and grammar/usage skills.

- Finally, this approach blends the mastery of writing skills along with social skills, so that students learn to work well in the classroom—and also in the workplace. In the workplace, little is written in isolation, by one person alone, with no input from peers, so the cooperative approach is good preparation.

Exercises and activities in this chapter are inspired by and adapted from the cooperative learning theory and practice of educational researchers Dr. David W. Johnson, Dr. Roger T. Johnson of the Cooperative Learning Institute, and Dr. Karl A. Smith of Purdue University, West Lafayette, IN. See the references at the end of the chapter for more information on this approach and its benefits. As noted above, this paradigm of instruction is characterized by

- positive interdependence among group members and

- personal accountability of the student.

These two overarching benefits form the basis for the instructional suggestions that follow.

The Cooperative Learning Environment: How to Begin

A cooperative classroom is one in which a dynamic interaction is taking place—between you and the students and among the students themselves. To create this dynamic interaction, you will design lessons so that students work together to maximize their own and others' learning. Using this approach, students work in small, often heterogeneous groups. Students are more accountable in a group of two or three. Pairs are fair: *It's hard to be left out of a pair!*

Group members are evaluated by comparing performance to preset criteria. Everyone can strive for and achieve mastery whether it be learning a grammar skill such as proper subject-verb agreement or composing coherent, engaging paragraphs. To ensure accountability, each group member is responsible for the final outcome. And joint success is celebrated.

Set the tone for cooperation during your first class meeting. Make that first ten minutes count. Typically, instructors introduce themselves to the class and give a brief introduction to the course. If that type of first class meeting has been your pattern, consider trying something different this term: After your introduction, ask students to introduce themselves to someone sitting nearby whom they do not know. You might have them exchange with one another their career goals or interests as well. The hum of voices helps dispel the awkwardness students feel that first day of class.

Learning in groups is widely practiced in higher education, and most students will have encountered working in small groups in previous classes. Still, it is good practice to indicate verbally and in writing what students can expect. For instance, in the syllabus you hand out on the first day, use wording that communicates to students, particularly returning or nontraditional students, that your teaching method values and includes group work. For example, in your syllabus under the category of "Teaching Method," you might state something like, "You will have opportunities to confer individually with the instructor and your peers at major steps in the writing process. In addition, cooperative learning techniques will be used to create and critique your writing."

To provide additional rationale for your intention to use small learning groups, refer to the Learning Pyramid on student retention of content (see p. 114 in this manual).

Introductory "Ready-to-Go" Activity: Syllabus Search in Pairs

The syllabus can also provide an early opportunity for cooperation. Tell students they will be learning about this course with a partner. Organize students into pairs and distribute the syllabus to all students. To ensure positive interdependence, tell students to use only one sheet of paper for answers. Indicate also that you expect handwriting from both students to appear on the page. For example, Student A is to complete the answers for questions 2 to 5; Student B is to complete the answers for questions 6 to 10. Both students are to participate in finding the answers to all the questions. Give each pair a paper with the following questions or project the questions on an overhead, adapting them first to be relevant to details of your particular syllabus. Allow a specific amount of time for the activity, probably 20 to 25 minutes. (You should always assign a time limit to each activity before students begin. If students require more or less time, you can make a flexible adjustment as appropriate.)

1. Introduce yourself to your partner. Name? Career goals? Main interests?

2. What textbook(s) are required?

3. How many points can be accrued during the term?

4. What is the policy on (fill in something of import from your syllabus)?

5. What is the attendance policy?

6. What are the options for tardiness?

7. What paper is due on (fill in date from your course calendar)?

8. What pages in the text will help you write a summary?

9. Which course component is done online in (fill in BlackBoard or other course management system.)?

10. What syllabus item do you notice but think others may overlook?

After the allotted time is up, ask someone in each pair to volunteer at least one answer in a whole-class review. After all items are discussed, request each student to sign the answer sheet. Explain that the signature is significant for three reasons. It recognizes

- that the student participated in searching for the answers,

- that he or she agrees with the answer, and

- that he or she can explain the response in detail if necessary.

Return the papers with some notation during the next class period. Giving bonus points for each participant is always a crowd pleaser and recognizes early effort.

Forming Groups

Instructors often grapple with two big questions as they plan for group work: First, how many students shall I include in the group? Second, how will I form groups? The number of students you choose per group is related to the type and complexity of the assignment. Understand your goal for the activity and then choose a group size that matches it. For example, activities like brainstorming for writing topics require divergent thinking and can accommodate three to four students in a group. However, an activity like grammar quiz-taking works best with a pair. Generally, unless students are assigned roles like reader/writer, grammar checker, or summarizer as in a more formal group lesson, it is best to keep group size small to ensure individual accountability. The smaller the group, the more difficult it is for students to hide and not contribute their share of the work. Group work should not be seen as an invitation for students to slack off.

As you form small groups, take into account ability in writing, varied personality types, and diverse learning styles. Early in the term, students may take the Learning Styles questionnaire (at the book's companion Web site: **bedfordstmartins** .com/realessays). Generally, the more diverse the group members in personality, learning styles, and interests, the richer will be the student experience during the activity.

Ideas and Options for Forming Groups

INSTRUCTOR SELECTION—RANDOM. One effective way of assigning students to groups is to do so randomly, which usually results in a diverse group of students. Here are the steps:

- Divide the number of students in your class by the group size desired. If you have thirty students in your class, and you wish to have groups of three, divide thirty by three with a result of ten. That's the magic number: ten.

- Ask students to number off by tens and remember their own number. In this case, you will hear numbers one to ten three times as students individually call off numbers.

- Now it is time for students to move. Students with matching numbers find one another and sit together: All those who had called off "one" group together, all those who had called off "two" group together, and so forth.

- Explain *how* students should sit together. You want students to communicate face to face, so you might say, "Imagine you are meeting friends at Starbucks, Dunkin' Donuts, or a local gathering spot for coffee."

When arranging students into groups, the groups seldom come out perfectly evenly. If there are an uneven number of students in class, form a group of two (or possibly four) members.

During the first week of class, you may want to form small groups of twos or threes as names appear on the class roll, and then project group names on a screen. As you get to know students better, you can tweak group formation. If you are teaching an online writing class where the face-to-face component is missing, it is best to wait a few weeks to form writing groups, until you have had a chance to become more familiar with your students and they have had a chance to learn more about their peers.

INSTRUCTOR SELECTION—MODIFIED RANDOM. Students in your classes will have varying degrees of writing competency. Thus, using a modified random approach to group selection may be desirable.

For example, when groups are used during peer evaluation of writing, you want to ensure that one competent writer appears in each group and then form the groups accordingly.

SELF-SELECTION. Students gain a sense of autonomy when they select their own groups. However, self-selection predictably results in students choosing friends or those who seem most like them. One useful modification of this method is to have students list their preference for team or group partners and then place them in a learning group with one student on their list and one or more students the instructor selects.

SELF-SELECTION: CLOCK APPOINTMENTS—ROCK AROUND THE CLOCK. Using clock appointments is another self-selection method, but with a twist. The clock—a list of times on a page—is a device for students to interact with different people during the course of the term. It is effective when you want students to work in pairs. Here is how this method works.

- Before class, duplicate the blank form, Cooperative Digital Clock Planner. This form simulates a digital clock planner, with increments: 1:00, 2:00, 3:00, 4:00, and so on, depending on the number of times you plan to use pairs during the term. On this form, students will record their clock appointments "hour by hour." (These are not literal hours; the time slots are merely a way for students to make certain appointments for future cooperative activities, as explained in greater detail at right.) Print one blank clock appointment form for each student. See the two samples, one a blank form (below) and one showing this form filled out (at right).

- Explain to students that for each appointment line on the form, they will be selecting one other student to interact with for later quizzes or other cooperative activities that will be occurring during the term. (Each hour on the digital clock corresponds to one student-to-student interaction.)

- Demonstrate yourself how the process of getting appointments works, modeling a scenario yourself: Approach one of your students and invite him or her to work with you.

- Emphasize that students are *trading* names, by saying, "You write the name of the person who agrees to meet with you at a particular increment of time on the clock and your partner will write down your name on his or her clock." Then you go on to the next person for a new appointment.

- Some guidelines: All should start at the same time on the clock, for example, 1:00, and no one should use anyone's name more than once.

- After 10 to 12 minutes, students have chosen partners for multiple future cooperative activities. Then later, when you want students to work in pairs, just say something like this: "Today you will take a ten-question grammar quiz with someone you have previously chosen to be a partner. Take out your clock appointment page and pair up with the person you have named as your one o'clock appointment to take the quiz."

Again, this system may not work out perfectly, but if students end up lacking a partner for one of the times on the clock, explain that there may be others lacking partners on the day pairs are used, and they can then team up with one of those students.

COOPERATIVE DIGITAL CLOCK PLANNER

My Appointments: *Freshman Writing*

1:00   _____
2:00   _____
3:00   _____
4:00   _____
5:00   _____
6:00   _____

COOPERATIVE DIGITAL CLOCK PLANNER

My Appointments: *Freshman Writing*

1:00   Jacob _____
2:00   Molly _____
3:00   Max _____
4:00   Brittany _____
5:00   _____
6:00   _____

Organizing students into such groups requires a certain amount of bravery on your part, but there are huge rewards. Students are choosing their own partners. Shy students have a good excuse to meet others. And a sense of energy infuses the classroom. Using the clock appointment strategy is also a time-saver for you. Students will quickly become accustomed to it and go right to the right person, making the group formation process efficient, and the result will be that, by the end of the term, most students will have worked together, by means of this clock appointment method and by other group formation methods you employ.

Once you have groups formed or your method for making groups established, you will want to make sure you have many interesting and pedagogically effective ways to use these groups. The rest of this chapter is devoted to activities that are "ready to go." Some of these activities include informal questions to help students begin interaction. Others are academic exercises. As you will see, some academic exercises involve planning more structured cooperative elements, such as assigning of roles within student groups.

"Ready-to-Go" Cooperative Activities

1. Informal Questions to Begin

1. "Turn to your neighbor": This device can be used to focus attention on new or previously learned material. For example, probably on class meeting two (or any time after the Syllabus Search the first class meeting), have each student introduce him- or herself to someone new. Then ask them to take turns mentioning one item each remembers from the syllabus during the Syllabus Search.

2. "What is your favorite _____?" Blend the social with academic work, as students get to know each other: Before pairs or triads approach serious work during a class period, ask students to share something about themselves that you designate (of a not overly personal nature), for example, their favorite food, place, type of music, musical group, movie, or TV show. Have them make a note of the answer or memorize it, as something they may be asked about later, to encourage attentiveness and communication.

2. Brainstorming and Discussing: Methods for Exploring a Topic

Check out the *Instructor's Annotated Edition (IAE) of Real Essays,* which contains marginal notes labeled "Teamwork." These notes describe cooperative exercises, cooperative writing activities, and group writing projects. In particular, look at the IAE notes for Chapter 5 of *Real Essays,* Finding and Exploring Your Topic, and at this chapter itself. Chapter 5 of *Real Essays* describes two methods of exploring a topic—brainstorming and discussing—that are especially useful cooperative strategies. Both can be used as the basis for productive group work in the cooperative class.

3. Essay Reconstruction

Take a model essay and scramble the paragraphs. Then ask students to work in separate groups to arrange the paragraphs in logical order to conform to the original essay. You will monitor students' progress and probe for reasons for their particular arrangement of paragraphs. This activity helps students read more critically because they need to focus on transitions and other clues to solve the puzzle. Sometimes groups compete to see which group can complete the assignment first.

An important social benefit of this exercise is that students can learn to challenge one another in a polite manner, so they can finally reach consensus. Of course, the academic goal is that students will apply critical reading skills to their own writing.

MODIFICATION. Take a model essay and scramble the sentences within each paragraph. Then ask student groups to number the sentences in different paragraphs in logical order.

If your institution has published exemplary student writing, freshmen students are usually not aware of it and enjoy seeing essays from students who have completed the course they are now enrolled in. Besides, students have a high standard to aspire to. Also, their textbook *Real Essays* is rich with excellent student model essays throughout.

4. Sentence Combining

The exercise of sentence combining is a complement to essay reconstruction because students are required to focus on the syntax of each sentence and supply appropriate connectors to form coherent sentences.

DIRECTIONS. Use all the prompts in parentheses in the order in which they appear to compose a coherent sentence, using both coordinating and subordinating devices.

Example: Brandon left Ashley.
Brandon was aware of her cheating.
(because) (but)
Brandon went to Kim.
Kim was worse than Ashley was. (who)

The exercise can progress to more complex sentences of six discrete parts or more. The goal here is mastery of coordination and subordination techniques.

NOTE ON ASSIGNING ROLES. As described at the beginning of this chapter, the shift foreman in the Chilean mine disaster assigned miners various roles to boost everyone's chance for survival. So too, you, as instructor, can assign complementary roles for small groups to function smoothly. Assigning specific tasks or roles for each participant to achieve helps structure interactions among students. This structure, in turn, heightens a sense of responsibility, increasing the chance that each person will contribute to the final outcome and discouraging students from "hitchhiking" on the work of others.

Here are some sample roles you can assign:

- Monitor (ensures all contribute, serves as timekeeper)

- Checker (ensures all prompts are used, makes sure prompts are used in proper order)

- Punctuation editor (ensures the punctuation is impeccable)

PROCEDURE.

- Read questions silently.

- Discuss possibilities verbally.

- Come to a consensus about the best possible combination of words.

- All contribute to sentence construction; all take turns writing successive sentences.

- One sheet of paper per group.

- All must agree.

- All sign and turn in group effort for credit.

5. Pair-Written Essay: Process Analysis

Divide students into two-member teams and assign each team a hands-on process such as how to bathe a dog, how to buy a used car, how to clean a closet and dispose of any discarded clothes or items, or others of your own invention. The teams then talk through the process, outline the process step by step, and then draft the essay.

6. Writing about an Image

One suggested assignment for the various rhetorical types in your text is accompanied by a photo or other image in your text. For example, in Chapter 16, Comparison and Contrast, the Writing about Images assignment at the end of the chapter depicts a series of Ken dolls from different eras. In your class, pairs can examine the photos, brainstorm, and then build a response or an outline together. Creativity flows as one idea sparks another and different people notice different details. Then, after the pair constructs the "bones" of an essay through a word web (a one-page summary), they interact with one other group who offers suggestions for further developing the summary into a formal essay—for example, a narration essay, description essay, or, in the case of this example, a comparison and contrast essay.

7. Grammar Quizzes in Pairs

Using clock appointment pairs or other duos, students taking short grammar quizzes can experience success with a good score. They can see the wisdom of the expression "two heads are better than one." Students actually teach each other as they tackle the questions or even use the index of the main book to find and check the grammatical explanations in *Real Essays*. Taking a practice quiz in pairs often has the benefit of reducing students' anxiety on longer tests taken individually.

8. Peer Review

It is easier for students to spot inconsistencies in others' papers than in their own. Thus, peer review has value. Before beginning peer evaluation, refer students to a student paper of the same rhetorical type in the text or provide a model paper from a previous term.

PAIRS. Have pairs trade papers after consulting Chapter 9, Revising Your Draft: Improving Your Essay. In Chapter 9, direct your students to the Understand What Peer Review Is section and the questions there for peer reviewers. Students need to understand what peer review is and then refer to the set of criteria in the boxed Questions for Peer Reviews in the same section. Rule of thumb: If the reader needs to reread a sentence more than once, it probably needs revision. The topic of peer review recurs in every Writing Guide in Part 2, and these mentions also provide excellent junctures and opportunities for cooperative group work.

TRIADS. Groups of three can also be used for peer review if you clarify the role for each reader. In this configuration, each student reads and comments on two other essays. Students trade papers, and during the first wave of reading, each student performs the role of "writing coherence specialist," focusing on content and organization of ideas. In the second trade to a different writer, students use a different color of pen to perform the role of "squinty-eyed grammar checker," focusing on the punctuation and mechanics. This activity may extend over two consecutive classes, depending on length of class period. For optimum results, be sure one very competent writer is in the group. (See the Instructor Selection—Modified Random section under Ideas and Options for Forming Groups on p. 93.)

Peer-review guides for all Part 2 chapters are available online at **bedfordstmartins.com/realessays**.

9. Quick Questioning: Assessment

STUDENT TO INSTRUCTOR. This activity asks students to write a one-minute paper. At the end of class, especially early in the term, have students take out a sheet of paper and respond to these prompts in one to two sentences each, which you can read over and comment on during the following class period:

- One important thing I learned today

- One thing I have a question about

Address the responses either in writing before the next class period or verbally during class.

STUDENT TO STUDENT/STUDENT TO INSTRUCTOR. This activity involves having students do group processing, using the Likert Scale:

1. Rate yourself on the following involvement (e.g., brainstorming, writing activity)

    1 2 3 4 5 6 7 8 9 10 completely involved

2. Share your self-rating with the other members of your group and explain why you rated yourself as you did.

3. As a group, list three ways of increasing members' involvement in the next cooperative assignment.

Then have students turn all papers in to you.

Conclusion and References

Instructors who use cooperative learning strategies in their writing classes often see themselves as coaches who design a game plan in which students can experience higher achievement, greater retention of material, and positive interpersonal relationships, a skill highly prized in the workplace (Johnson, Johnson, and Smith, "State" 27). And they celebrate small and large successes with their students along the way.

References

Johnson, David W., Roger T. Johnson, and Karl A. Smith. *Active Learning: Cooperation in the College Classroom*. 8th ed. Edina: Interaction, 2008. Print.

This text provides a comprehensive view of the use of various types of cooperative groups in the college classroom. Numerous specific lesson structures are included.

———. "The State of Cooperative Learning in Postsecondary and Professional Settings." *Educational Psychology Review* 19.1 (2007): 15–29. Print.

The references above define and explain the learning theory and practice of Dr. David W. Johnson, Dr. Roger T. Johnson of the University of Minnesota–Minneapolis, and Dr. Karl Smith of Purdue University. Their techniques, substantiated by decades of research, are highly structured and applicable to all ethnic, cultural, ability, and gender groups. Research reflects higher achievement, greater retention of material, and an increase in critical thinking skills. According to the abstract in the source cited immediately above, "Cooperative learning is being used in postsecondary education in every part of the world."

Rooshanak, Mir. "Teamwork in Business: What to Learn from the Chilean Mine Rescue." *UPrinting.com*. 14 Oct. 2010. UPrinting Small Business Blog, Web. 11 Nov. 2011.

8

Teaching with Technology

Sharon Gerald, *Jones County Junior College*

We no longer ask *if* we are going to use technology in the classroom; we only ask how. Technology permeates academic, professional, and personal lives. The immense popularity of social networking sites such as Google+, Facebook, and Twitter, along with iPhones, Blackberries, Kindles, and other Internet gadgetry, means that writing via technology is simply a fact of life for one and all.

Regardless of major, regardless of the degree of academic preparation for college, all our students need basic technological communications skills. This need presents a conundrum for faculty who may not have a technological background and may not always feel comfortable teaching with newer technologies. You do not have to be an expert, however, to find effective ways to use computer technologies in the classroom. You can learn some skills at the same time that your students learn them. In fact, letting students know that a technology is new for you, and that you will be learning with them, helps them work past their own technological nervousness and gives them a cheerful model—we are all in this together—for working through technological questions.

Just because incorporating technology is important does not mean that every technological advance that comes along is vital for your classroom. Adopt technologies thoughtfully and selectively. They should complement the purpose of your course and your own teaching style. They should not distract from your interaction with students. Technology is rarely a good substitute for personal instruction. Rather, it should supplement and enhance your own best teaching.

As you sort out what technologies to use in your classroom, here are some ideas you might find helpful. You will also find ideas for computer use in the margins of the *Instructor's Annotated Edition for Real Essays*.

Word Processing

Not so long ago, we debated whether to have students type or handwrite. Those days are gone. Formal handwritten communication is a thing of the past. We assume students will use word processing as an integral part of writing.

The ability to create a typed, well-formatted paper is a basic literacy we expect students to achieve, and the word processor makes it easier to do. Any paper can at least look good humming out of the printer. But when we look past the word processors' formatting defaults to how this technology supports the writing process, we see ways students can begin to brainstorm, plan, and draft directly from their word processors, making computers into a rich writing tool. For example, most students will more willingly revise and edit when they do not have to rewrite laboriously by hand or retype. So, computers can both save students time and help them improve the quality of their writing. Word processing in itself does not improve writing, but word processors include tools that can improve both writing and editing if used properly, and even computer-savvy students need guided instruction in the use of these tools. So it helps to review a few basic concepts.

Spell Checkers

Spell checkers are useful writing aids. They can cut down on spelling errors significantly. Of course, spell checkers do not work for commonly confused words (*there, their, they're,* and so on; a list of these words is given in Chapter 35 of *Real Essays*). Spell checkers are also of limited value for students with a learning disability manifested in their spelling or who are particularly poor spellers. The spell checker might not give options for these students' extremely misspelled words, and when options do appear, the students might not know which to choose. And sometimes, a correctly spelled word might not be in the spell checker's dictionary, and so the checker might suggest an alternative that is wrong. Still, for most students (and for some faculty) a spell checker can help writers avoid spelling errors that significantly detract from the readability and polish of a piece of writing. But the thing to teach students about spell checkers is to look at the word that is being flagged, and to look at the choices, and to make the right decision about the spell checker's recommendation. If a word is correct, but is flagged as incorrect, for example, the student can add it to his or her dictionary.

Grammar Checkers

Grammar checkers are useful but more problematic. First, they isolate a sentence and put it in the grammar checker box, pulling it out of the context of the essay. They ask students to look at the sentences and consider them with a focus on some aspect of grammar. Which is all to the good. However, this is where grammar checkers can be problematic: Remind students that the computer can neither read nor reason. The grammar program looks for patterns or formulas in word order and then tells users where the program has found a passage that does not fit the formula. The students themselves must analyze the sentences to determine if there is a problem. Inevitably, grammar checkers have "false positives" that identify an error where there is none, and "false negatives" that fail to identify an error where there is one. Students who do not have great skill or confidence in their writing skill will find it difficult to evaluate the computer's advice, and, certainly, students do not learn or even guarantee their success by simply accepting what the computer suggests. You can ask students to use the word processor's highlighter to mark sentences that the grammar checker flagged, but that they remain unsure about revising, or where the grammar checker advice confuses them. Collect those sentences and build editing or grammar revision labs around them because those sentences will likely represent issues many of your students have. Remind students that a grammar checker is no substitute for their own sentence-by-sentence review and encourage them to consult their textbook—by looking up the grammar issue flagged in the table of contents or index—or to ask you or a writing center tutor for help.

Word Processing Tools

Word count and "find and replace" functions are other standard features of word processing programs that can be useful to developmental English students. The word count function can help both students and teachers keep track of the amount of development that occurs throughout the writing process. The "find and replace" function can aid writers in using stronger verbs and avoiding repetitive word choices. So for example, students might find variations of the verb "to be" (*is, was, were, are,* and so on) and replace those with ****; after replacing, the activity will be to reread the essay and to replace the *to be* verb with a stronger verb. This strategy might lead to sentence combining and other revision techniques. Another great use: Replace "it's" with "it is" to see where *its/it's* confusion might be occurring. If a sentence becomes "The cat chased it is tail," the student will know that "its" should replace "it's."

Files

Saving a file properly is also important. Students can use "File/Save As" to save files in a format that can be shared. Some students will have word processors that save in *.docx* format, which not everyone will be able to read if they share files. Problems may also arise between users of Macs and PCs. Have your students save to a standard file format such as *.rtf* in order to share documents with people working on other systems. Practicing these essential communication skills will help save students from future difficulties. In addition to saving their files in the correct format, students should use consistent file naming. This practice helps both you and the students stay organized. If you collect twenty-five papers per class from five classes, you will want students to follow some naming conventions. One strategy for naming files is to use the student's name along with an assignment indication: for example, *MariaTrujillo_draft2_illustrationessay1.* Advise students that it is best to save work at different stages. Instead of working in one computer file as they write and revise, they should save and label different drafts as separate files. They can follow these steps to set up a system of folders to keep their files organized:

- Create a folder with the name of the course.

- Within the course folder, create a folder named *Writing Assignments.*

- Within the *Writing Assignments* folder, create a new folder for each assignment. Save all writing for the assignment in this folder.

- Whenever they work on a draft, they should use the "Save As" feature under "File" to save a new version of the document with a new name: *Assign5Tuesdraft, Assign5Weddraft, Assign5Fridraft.*

Feedback on Student Papers

Instead of scribbling notes and suggestions in the side margins and a summary evaluation at the end of an essay, you can set up a computer file under the student's name, type of essay, and draft. For example, the file might be labeled *Trajillo, Maria Illustration Essay 1.* As you read the essay, use a simple number key to mark the places in the essay that correspond to your suggestions, or use the comments feature in the word processing program to insert comments. To find this feature in most word processing programs, go to "Insert." The "Insert" drop-down menu will list either "Comment" or "Note." This feature will allow you to mark any spot in the essay you want to address. Your comments will then show up in the margin or as a footnote, depending upon how your word processor is formatted. You can add summary comments at the end (perhaps in a different color font to attract attention to them), save the file, and return it to the student via e-mail.

Using a word processing program to review student essays has many advantages:

- **Neatness.** The computer provides a tidy alternative to messy notes, especially after long hours of writing feedback on students' papers. Word-processed comments model the orderliness and professionalism that we urge our students to use in their writing. Ironically, most instructors would not accept a paper written in the messy handwriting in which they give their feedback to students.

- **Archiving.** When reviewing later drafts, it is easy to access your past comments on early drafts, to see how a student is progressing.

- **Addressing common errors.** Certain errors recur in most students' papers, errors such as fragments, run-ons, misuse of commas in compound and complex sentences, informal word choice, incorrect formatting, and so on. With the computer, you can build a file of responses to these common errors. You can also put extra effort into providing more comprehensive feedback so that each type of error is discussed with greater depth and quality. This way, you do not have to reconstruct an excellent answer multiple times for each writing weakness, some-times repeating the same response many times per grading session over multiple grading sessions per semester.

Research

A student may now get a college degree without ever having set foot in a physical library. For faculty members who put in their time with the *Reader's Guide to Periodical Literature* and spent hours in the stacks as student researchers, the new reality can be hard to accept. Of course, students will benefit from knowing their way around the physical library stacks, and you may wish to offer or arrange a library tutorial. But you will also want to help students learn to navigate digital research tools effectively.

Databases

Library databases that make published information searchable are good sources to which to direct students. Materials referenced in these databases were most likely selected for publication through an editorial process conducted by a newspaper, magazine, journal, or newswire service. We can explain this vetting process to students, then concentrate on helping students understand related topics: how to differentiate between magazines and journals; how to determine what type of source might be more appropriate for the kind of research they are doing; and how to search effectively using Boolean search methods. (Many library databases come with instructions for Boolean searches. If not, those instructions and tutorials are easily found online.)

The Internet

The Internet at large also contains useful sources for your students' research papers. We might be tempted to avoid or limit our students' use of Internet sources, but we do them no favors if we do. Their lives are inundated with questionable information. They need to learn the importance of healthy skepticism and methods for evaluating the reliability of sources.

Source Evaluation

Evaluating sources is a crucial skill. You might introduce your students to Internet research by sending them to mainstream or established sites that you trust. Consider using a social bookmarking tool such as Delicious.com to share sources with students or to have them share sources with one another. Source sharing through a social bookmarking site gives you an opportunity to discuss which sources you trust and why, as well as which sources appear to be more helpful. Teach students to ask critical questions of their sources to determine reliability. You can point them to the Questions for Evaluating a Print or Electronic Source in Chapter 20 of *Real Essays,* or *The Bedford Research Room* at **bedfordstmartins.com/researchroom.** This site teaches students effective online research skills, and offers advice on finding, evaluating, and citing sources. Also, encourage students to check with you or a college librarian whenever they have doubts about an Internet source's reliability.

File Management

Teaching file management helps students to collect, store, and process information electronically. You have already addressed some file management issues if you taught students a draft saving/naming convention for class, how to put their writing into folders, and how to track their writing history. You might teach them the elements of keeping an electronic portfolio. (For more on e-portfolios, see *Portfolio Teaching* and *Portfolio Keeping* by Nedra Reynolds and Rich Rice; ask your Bedford/St. Martin's rep for exam copies of these great little books.)

Documentation Tools

Online tools for online documentation are becoming increasingly common. Students save time researching and will be less likely to make documentation errors if they develop a system of typing out notes and documentation as they find information. Note-taking can be done in a word processing file or in an online tool such as Google Notebook, Evernote, or another easy option, the *Bedford Bibliographer* at **bedfordstmartins.com/bibliographer,** which is free, includes citation creation, and offers advice from Mike Palmquist, author of *The Bedford Researcher.* If your campus supports Firefox, Zotero (**www .zotero.org**) is a free research tool that comes as an add-on to the Firefox browser.

You might suggest that students use a blog as a place for research notes. With this method, students track sources by linking to or citing the source in the post with notes about it. It can also help students think of links as a means of documenting. You will be able to talk about how and why informal ways of documenting take place online even as students are learning formal, academic documentation styles.

In addition to the *Bedford Bibliographer* site mentioned above, EasyBib (**www.easybib.com**) and CitationMachine (**www.citationmachine.net**) are examples of sites that help students format bibliographies: Students enter bibliographic elements into forms that then create a draft (not final) citation. So students still need to know how to cite a source and find the citation elements. The draft citations these sites provide are only as accurate as the information students enter. But they do help with initial formatting of the citation, and the forms prompt students about what information a citation needs.

Some library databases provide bibliographic citations in MLA, APA, and other styles that can simply be copied and pasted into a word processing file. These tools produce bibliographies that may or may not exactly match the latest versions of the style guides, and they may produce bibliographies with mistakes in them, if students type in incorrect information or type information into the wrong fields. They can, however, be useful as students learn to format bibliographies. If nothing else, you can use these online documentation tools to create sample bibliographies to critique in class. Have students review these draft citations for possible corrections.

E-Mail

E-mail is a highly efficient method for instructor-student communication. Students ask questions and you answer at times convenient to you both. Students reluctant to speak up in class or to visit during your office hours may feel more comfortable e-mailing questions. E-mail also saves paper, which has environmental and administrative advantages: Students can e-mail papers and assignments, and instructors can e-mail back suggestions and feedback. If used effectively, e-mail can significantly cut back on the substantial costs of paper, copying, and printing.

Consider, however, that while e-mail might be more convenient for students than having to call or come by during office hours, younger students tend to consider it a formal type of communication, while texting and chatting are both more informal and more immediate. It might be useful to make e-mail just one of a variety of ways students can contact you. Because e-mail is now considered the more formal choice for digital communications, discuss e-mail protocol and conventions of formal letter writing with students. One useful activity would be to work as a class on composing effective and appropriate e-mails.

Computer Projectors

Projectors and Smart Boards have become relatively common in college classrooms. If your room is equipped with projection technology, use it effectively. Educators tend to think of PowerPoint when computers and projectors are mentioned, but while PowerPoint may be ubiquitous, it is not always the best choice.

"DEATH BY POWERPOINT" (also the title of a book by Michael Flocker) has found its way into the education vernacular as a tongue-in-cheek description of the pervasiveness of poorly designed, boring PowerPoint lectures. Technology used in the classroom should not distract from the interaction between teacher and student.

DO NOT USE POWERPOINT JUST TO SHARE LECTURE NOTES. This approach risks students writing instead of listening while you speak. Reading to students what they see on the PowerPoint and waiting for them to write it down is not effective lecturing. Many instructors give examples and elaborate on the information while students are writing, but the students still, for the most part, just write what is on the screen, and the instructor still just walks through bullet points. With a truly vibrant, engaging lecturer, the "walking-through-bullet-points" approach might spark some great classroom interactions. In many cases, however, it deters natural classroom discussion.

PROVIDE STUDY GUIDES AND LECTURE NOTES IN WAYS THAT WILL NOT SLOW YOU DOWN IN CLASS. Can the information in your PowerPoint slides be distributed more efficiently through PDF files posted to a class Web site or by some other means? Make podcasts or videocasts. Post notes to blogs or to a course management system. Distributing study guides and notes using these methods frees you to use PowerPoint as visual stimulation and discussion prompt rather than as a static method conveying detailed information. Presentation software is not designed to share large amounts of text: Look at it as a way to share one concept or one prompt at a time.

If you use PowerPoint often, read some books on presentation design. Sometimes simple tweaks can make a slide more appealing and effective. (One excellent book on the topic is *Presentation Zen* by Garr Reynolds.)

With or without PowerPoint, here are some examples of ways you can use computer projectors or Smart Boards to facilitate classroom instruction:

- **Prewriting.** Some prewriting activities, such as brainstorming, adapt beautifully to computer projectors. Project a prompt and have students brainstorm topics while you type them onscreen. You could also project a topic and have students brainstorm thesis statements, or project a thesis statement and have students come up with supporting points and examples.

- **Thesis Statements.** Project draft thesis statements onscreen and have students work together to improve them.

- **Grammar.** Sentences with grammar mistakes (fragments, run-ons, comma errors, and so on) can be projected onscreen, and students can work together to identify and correct the errors.

- **Sentence Style.** Display text with one or more of the following grammar and style problems: short, choppy sentences; wordy sentences; phrases without parallel structure; misplaced modifiers; pronouns with unclear reference; and so on. Students then identify and correct the errors and make appropriate revisions.

- **Technological Demonstrations.** If students will be required to work through some technological processes on their own (Blackboard logins, accessing class wikis or blogs, using quiz sites), the projector provides an excellent way to show students what they are supposed to do. (This demonstration means more to the visual learners than any written instructions they might be given.)

- **Group Activities.** If you use a class discussion board, blog, wiki, or another type of online tool, you can project in class what students have done online. Doing so can prompt discussion or help the class as a group assess what they are accomplishing online.

One advantage of using projectors and Smart Boards is that you start to build your own repository of files for classroom use. Those files can make it easier to share information with students who have missed class or to help slower note-takers keep up. The projectors can also be used to engage the digital natives in classroom activities. The world of digital media is highly visual. Students who have grown up with video games, the Internet, and the general gadgetry of the past couple of decades often want visual stimulation and visual clarification of information.

If you have access to computer projection, use it. You will find what works best for you and your students, and avoid the "death by PowerPoint" trap.

New Media

The explosion of new media tools in recent years has created a chaos of choice, and it is often difficult to know where to start changing classroom approaches and adopting new technologies. You cannot change everything at once, and use every technological tool that comes along, but you can start somewhere.

Privacy Issues

As you explore classroom uses for new media, keep in mind that you also have to address the new issues created by these technologies. Will you require your students to engage in public writing on a blog, wiki, or social media site? Do you believe there is an ethical dilemma in requiring public writing? Can you incorporate social media while still protecting students' privacy? Discuss issues of privacy with students. Give them the option of determining how much information they want to share about themselves online, and talk to them about both the security issues involved and the kind of impression they want to make with their online presence.

Many social media sites allow settings to be marked "private," where only approved subscribers or members can view the information. If required public writing is an issue for your classroom, you can choose "private" settings. Either way, make informed, deliberate decisions, and be sure students understand who has access to their writing.

Here are a few ideas for ways to incorporate new media into the classroom.

FACEBOOK / GOOGLE+. Though Facebook and Google+ are often seen as distractions to schoolwork, they are effective communications tools. You might be surprised by what students accomplish when given room to be creative with social networking. One good way to start might be to hold office hours on Facebook. Students can contact you by posting public messages on your wall, engaging in real-time chat sessions, or sending private messages to your inbox. Friending students through a designated class account could also give you the opportunity to make class announcements in a space that students might be more motivated to check than e-mail or Blackboard. Students could also use a social networking site as the framework for a class project. The notes or blog feature could be useful for posting portfolio items, for example. Students may also want to use the links-sharing feature for research. For class projects, you might want to insist that students create new accounts separate from the ones they use socially.

TWITTER. Microblogging sites such as Twitter are great places to interact with students. The short posts are akin to text messages, which is now the primary means of communication for the younger generations. You can use Twitter for class announcements and class discussions. Students can access posts via cell phone or computer. Twitter can also be used to facilitate discussion in face-to-face classes. If your class Twitter stream is projected in the room as you ask questions, and your students are able to answer with their cell phones or computers, you might get interesting real-time feedback.

NING. Ning is a site that allows you to create your own social network. It is a good option for teachers who want to avoid Facebook or Google+. On Ning, you interact with only one network at a time (as opposed to Facebook where your students might have many friends from many other contexts on the same account they are using for class). Ning will create one primary newsfeed that everyone can see. At the same time, it provides individual blogs and ways for students to share links, videos, and pictures. It can be used as a discussion forum that looks more like the type students might be accustomed to from their experiences on other social networking sites. If course management tools like Blackboard are not generating the kind of class discussion you want, consider going to Ning.

BLOGS. Blogs have many possibilities in the classroom. They can be used as class journals or as individual project-management tools. A student could blog through a research project, for example. Blogs can also be used for group projects or for class discussions, or simply as a means for the instructor to communicate with students by posting announcements, handouts, and instructions. Free sites such as Blogger and WordPress offer easy ways to get started.

WIKIS. Wikis, or multi-authored Web sites, are good ways to manage group or class projects. Some classes have even created their own textbooks using wikis. If students are doing group writing assignments, consider using a wiki. Each group can create its own pages, and the collective work of the class will produce the Web site as a whole. Another use for wikis might be a class research project. If your research has a theme around which all the students have chosen topics, the wiki might be used for sharing information found by individual students with the class. Or maybe you want to make a grammar wiki with students themselves creating lessons and examples. Once you familiarize yourself with a wiki platform such as Wet Paint, PB Wiki, or Google Sites, you will find any number of uses for it.

THE GOOGLE SUITE. With a free gmail account, you gain access to a whole suite of Google products. With Google Sites, you can make an individual or a group Web site. With Google Docs, you can make individual or collaborative word processing, presentation, or spreadsheet files which can be shared selectively or published to the Web. With Google Groups, you can create e-mail lists or discussion forums. Blogger is also included in a gmail account. Other products by other companies accomplish many of these same things, but Google does offer free accounts and collaborative features that make their products very useful for the classroom.

SOCIAL BOOKMARKING. Delicious, Citeulike, Blackboard Scholar, and Zotero are examples of social bookmarking tools. These sites allow you to gather and share links to useful resources, and to also tag or label bookmarks by topic. These are useful ways for teachers to share links with students, for students to share, and for teachers to track student research progress.

AUDIOCASTING. If you communicate online with your students, you might consider making audio recordings to share; after all, the spoken word is a powerful teaching tool. You only need a computer and a microphone to get started. Download a free audio recording program such as Audacity to produce mp3 files or check with your school's tech support to find out if they subscribe to Wimba or other podcasting software for Blackboard. You can also do a search for a Web site that will allow you to make online recordings. AudioBoo, for example, allows iPhone users to simply call in audio recordings, and no computer or microphone is required.

In addition to creating your own audio recordings, you can find and share helpful audio programs. Mignon Fogarty's *Grammar Girl* podcast is one of the most popular shows on iTunes, and it is free. Your students might truly benefit from it or other educational podcasts. And because they can download podcasts to listen to while they are doing other things, this is a form of education that complements students' mobile, multitasking lifestyles.

VIDEOCASTING. Like audiocasting, videocasting is increasingly common and useful for education. Many digital cameras now have video capabilities, and laptops often come with built-in Web cams. Digital video cameras have also become much more affordable. Additionally, screencasting software for creating video tutorials is now available in free versions such as Jing. Videocasting is a good option for both online and face-to-face teachers. Try posting videos to YouTube or TeacherTube, or create video lectures on a site such as Seesmic using your Web cam. Also like audiocasting, plenty of educational videos are available online, so you do not always have to create your own. Search YouTube or other social video sites for clips useful to your students.

E-Portfolios

E-portfolios, or electronic portfolios, are more and more important to the writing classroom. They can be assigned as project portfolios, class portfolios, or career portfolios. In any of these variations, they offer a chance to write with and through technology that is essential to basic literacy in the digital age.

Some schools purchase e-portfolio platforms that provide ways to grade, record, and track student progress in addition to the tools for creating portfolios. Others adopt e-portfolio building blocks for Blackboard or other course management systems. If your school has access to one of these options, consider using it. If not, there are plenty of free options.

VISUALCV.COM. VisualCV is a free site that allows for online CV building. It also provides space for uploading text files and linking to other sites, making it a perfect place to build a career portfolio.

WIKIS. Wet Paint, PB Wiki, and other wiki sites can be used for project, class, or career portfolios. Because wikis are designed for collaborative work, they are great for group projects and portfolios. They do not have to be used collaboratively, however, and make for easy ways to create Web sites. They could easily be adapted for the purpose of a career portfolio.

BLOGS. Blogger and WordPress are just two of the many free blogging sites available. Blogs are an interesting way to create portfolios. One approach might be to publish portfolio items in blog posts, saving the last post (the one that will show at the top) for the portfolio introduction. Another method is to link to portfolio items in the sidebar and have only one post that serves as an introduction. If this approach is used, consider publishing portfolio artifacts as Google Docs. This approach provides an easy, free way to link to text files.

GOOGLE DOCS + PRESENTATION. Presentation slides can be used as introductions to individual portfolio artifacts. Publishing items in Google Docs to then link to Google Presentation works well. This also invites the opportunity to work with presentation design as part of the project. Another advantage is that Google Presentations can be either published to the Web or shared with select viewers. The latter option might be an answer for students reluctant to make their writing public.

Regardless of which e-portfolio option you choose, from those discussed above or another, you will help students create something they can be proud of when you assign an e-portfolio. You will also help them learn some of the basic delivery methods of twenty-first century literacy. (For more on using writing portfolios, see Chapter 12 in this manual.)

Addressing Plagiarism

Preventing plagiarism is hard work. Fears that cheating is more common in the digital age may be well founded. It is as tempting for instructors to turn to electronic plagiarism-detection services such as Turnitin.com or SafeAssign (a plagiarism-detection option that comes free with Blackboard 6.0 or higher) as it is for students to copy and paste parts of their writing assignments from online sources. There is no single answer to preventing plagiarism, however. Plagiarism-detection services should not be considered the only way to address the issue, nor even the primary way.

The biggest deterrents to plagiarism, regardless of the digital tools involved, are student engagement in the assignment and instructor involvement in the student writing process. Students might cheat for a variety of reasons: they care about the grade but not the assignment; they feel overwhelmed and underconfident; their attention has been on other things; cheating is easy enough to be tempting. We might not guess exactly why a student has cheated, but we do know he or she is less likely to cheat (1) if the assignment itself matters to the student as much as the grade, (2) if cheating is more trouble than doing the assignment, and (3) if the assignment is stepped out in drafts, evolving from class discussions or freewriting or brainstorming that you assign. We also know that not all

plagiarism is deliberate. For more on addressing plagiarism, including additional handouts to use in your course, visit **bedfordstmartins.com /plagiarism** for the Bedford/St. Martin's Workshop on Plagiarism.

Before deciding whether or not to use a plagiarism detection service, consider other ways to prevent plagiarism:

- **Make sure students understand plagiarism and your policies regarding plagiarism.** Remember that some skills, such as proper paraphrasing and documentation, are difficult to master even after they have been covered in class. These skills can be difficult even for upper level students and professionals, so they certainly could pose problems for the new and struggling college student. Assume that initial mistakes in documentation, even to the extent of copying too much text from sources, are learning opportunities rather than deliberate academic dishonesty.

- **Give unique assignments and assignments applicable to the students' lives where possible.** Using the same topics as other instructors or the same topics from previous semesters can be an invitation to recycle past papers. A plagiarism-detection service is of limited use to detect this cheating, as it can only find friends sharing work if both essays were uploaded to the same database. Make it more difficult from the start for students to borrow from friends or from Web sites by changing assignments often.

- **Spend time responding to early drafts.** Consider assigning portfolios that require multiple drafts with significant revision. This technique makes you more aware of students' writing styles even as it becomes more difficult for them to find papers to copy elsewhere.

- **Walk your students through the entire writing process.** Talk to them about their writing even in prewriting stages. Get to know their ideas and thinking on the subject. Find out if they feel overwhelmed or if they need extra help coming up with ideas. Challenge them to move beyond vague, general ideas that might leave room later for copying from others.

All these strategies for avoiding plagiarism are practices of good writing instruction whether technological tools are involved or not. No tool is a substitute for what the teacher does.

Problems with Plagiarism-Detection Services

Plagiarism-detection services have been as controversial as they are popular. If your school or department has adopted Turnitin or another service, you may decide to use it with your students, but first make yourself aware of the controversy.

Many complaints have been made against Turnitin and services like it falling into three main categories: (1) problematizing instructor/student relations; (2) infringing on the students' intellectual property rights; and (3) questionable reliability.

INSTRUCTOR/STUDENT RELATIONS. Use of a plagiarism-detection service could send the message that the instructor assumes the students are cheating, which is not a healthy attitude for good working relations. In addition, there is the risk that the tool might be used for punitive measures rather than instruction. If the plagiarism-detection service is only used to catch students doing something wrong, then we should question what instructional value it really has and whether its value is worth the potentially damaged trust between instructor and student.

INTELLECTUAL PROPERTY RIGHTS. When your students upload writing to Turnitin, their work goes into a database where it is compared with other items in the Turnitin databases. Turnitin then keeps your students' writing in its databases, in order to compare other essays to it in the future. A school can discover if students are sharing essays by building its own repository in a plagiarism-detection service database. This presents an ethical issue, however, in that Turnitin then profits from its large database of student writing while the students themselves receive no compensation. In addition, the students do not voluntarily submit their work to the database; they are compelled to do so in class. Because of this use of students' intellectual property, some instructors choose to avoid Turnitin.

RELIABILITY. A plagiarism-detection service is simply an electronic tool. It runs on a formula like spell check. It does not have human intuition or reasoning skills, and is accurate no more often than a grammar checker. The question for the instructor then is whether the reliability level is worth the cost, since students usually pay for the use of this service. The instructor should always question whether students are getting their money's worth.

If you decide not to use Turnitin or SafeAssign, you can also try free online sites such as **www.articlechecker** .com and **www.plagiarismchecker.com**. These are useful for quick checks of suspicious materials. Whole passages can be copied in, and then the programs run searches for Web matches. These programs search only the Web: They have no databases of their own and cannot check subscription library databases. They will work, however, to locate blatant cases of Internet copying and pasting. A simple Google search on a suspicious title, phrase, or sentence can also often yield faster and more accurate results than paid services.

If you do decide to use Turnitin or another plagiarism-detection service, think about how to use it as an instructional rather than a punitive tool. Remember that the percentage identified as unoriginal in the reports does not necessarily mean that exact percentage is plagiarized. It is also possible that *none* of the writing is plagiarized. For example, Turnitin might mark something like "In our society today, we often think . . ." as unoriginal. It is indeed unoriginal, but it is not plagiarism. Also, Turnitin.com and SafeAssign both support calling an assignment a draft, which lets you and students run a check to see if there is matching text. After the check, students can revise the draft to address any matching text not properly cited that should be.

Practice some of these techniques to avoid compromising student/instructor relations when using a plagiarism-detection service:

- Make sure students understand what the plagiarism-detection service is and what it does before assignments are uploaded.

- Make sure students are aware of your plagiarism policy before assignments are uploaded.

- Give students full access to their own originality reports.

- Allow students to upload rough drafts to the plagiarism-detection service so that they have a chance to make corrections if unintentional plagiarism is found.

- Go over a sample originality report with students (perhaps on a piece of your own writing) so that you can talk about which items marked would be considered plagiarism, which would be correctly documented quotations, and which would be simply unoriginal language and not actual plagiarism.

- Use instances of unoriginality in writing as opportunities to learn how to be more original. Do not use the reports simply to find and punish wrongdoing.

- Understand that the number given as the percent plagiarized in the report means little, given that some of the items marked might be acts of deliberate plagiarism, some might be acts of unintentional plagiarism, and some might not be plagiarism at all.

- Do not expect the originality reports to be infallible. Just as they will sometimes mark sentences that are clichéd but not plagiarized, they will also sometimes miss passages that are plagiarized. Work from your own judgment just as you would without the plagiarism-detection service.

Using Course Management Tools

Course Management Systems (CMS)

Using programs such as Blackboard or WebCT, you can develop custom Web sites tailored to your courses' individual needs. Check your college Web site or ask your IT department which systems might be available to you. You can also use Bedford/St. Martin's online course space *WritingClass*, which has instructional material, activities, and simple writing tools, helping students keep up with assignments and letting them work when they have time, and where they have Web access. (For more on *WritingClass,* see the Using the Ancillary Package section in Chapter 1 of this manual.) Many schools now require instructors to use course management systems to some degree, so becoming familiar with these tools is important. Here is some basic information to help you get started.

What Course Management Tools Are

Course management tools allow you to post syllabi announcements, assignments, and other course materials to a Web site that your students can access. They might also provide communication tools such as chat rooms and discussion boards. These tools can be used as an aid to traditional face-to-face classes, or may be a key part of distance-learning courses.

How to Get Started

If your school requires you to use a course management system, chances are good that the school also provides training. Take advantage of any available training.

Your school's technology staff should set you up with an account, password, and basic shell for your course content. They should also be able to answer any further questions you might have. Additionally, your course management system may come with training or support tools to access any time you need help. Or you can search YouTube or the company site for the CMS platform provider for possible video tutorials.

If you are using a CMS for the first time, leave yourself plenty of time before the first class to become familiar with the system. Understand what types of information you can post, and decide what content makes the most sense for your class. Also, before the first class, post sample content and check links. You might want to work with another instructor teaching the same or a similar course to test each other's content and determine best practices.

How to Build Your Site

Major course management systems like Blackboard and WebCT include features like course information, course documents, external links, and discussion boards. In the course information area, you can include such items as the course syllabus and schedule, the school's plagiarism policy, and any other documents that spell out policies and procedures.

The course documents section can be used to post handouts on course content, additional readings, and other materials. Perhaps you can post assignments here, removing them as needed so that students are not overwhelmed or confused. Organize course documents by week or topic, whatever works best for you.

In the external links section, provide links to all kinds of online writing help, including the *Real Writing Student Center* at **bedfordstmartins .com/realessays** or *Re:Writing Basics,* a collection of writing resources at **bedfordstmartins.com /rewritingbasics.** You might also include a link to your school library's Web site or to sites recommended by a librarian or colleagues.

Discussion boards allow you to set up discussions on concepts, assignments, or readings covered in class, or post open-ended questions or prompts for response. Many instructors find that students who freeze up when told they must write a paper write freely in online discussion forums; in fact, they may do some of their best writing on discussion boards and truly become engaged in communicating with their peers. For this reason, online discussion can serve as prewriting for longer, more polished papers.

Decide how involved you want to be in online discussions. Some instructors add to or comment on their students' discussions frequently, while others mostly stay out of the conversation, maintaining the discussion board as a "student space." Whatever level of involvement, go over the ground rules for online discussion early in the semester. For instance, encourage students to stay on topic when possible, and explain that profanity and personal attacks will not be tolerated.

Another good approach early in the semester is to ask students to introduce themselves in a brief posting. They can write about their children or families, their reasons for going to college, their current jobs or jobs they want, or their interests outside of work and school. Students might then comment on one another's postings.

For First Timers

If you are teaching in a computer classroom for the first time, the following advice should help you feel more in control:

- Arrive early. It takes time to turn computers on and check peripherals.

- If you have a networked area, do not just position yourself in front of the computer and not budge. Developmental students need one-on-one reinforcement from their instructor. Move around the room, from board to overhead to student stations. Your moving also allows all students to hear you clearly above the hum of the computers.

- When you lecture and give instructions to be followed later, have students darken their screens so they will listen to you. Otherwise, they may pay more attention to the computer.

- Help students by providing detailed handouts on assignments. Include specifics on what you want: type of writing, acceptable topics, due dates for drafts, peer editing, final copy, and materials to be submitted with final drafts.

- Be patient with students who may need special orientation and reminders about using the computers. If your computer and software has a built-in tutorial, use it with your students, so they can progress at their own speed without feeling either rushed or held back. You may want to prepare a worksheet for students to complete as they work through a tutorial. Whether using a prepared tutorial or walking students through an introduction, devote at least one class session to learning how to use the computers before you give a writing assignment.

- Go slowly. Blend writing and computer instruction. Introduce a little bit of information at a time. Make sure students are comfortable with basic word processing before starting in on editing features.

- When introducing a new task on the computer, keep the class together. Be sure each student is with you, and do not let students work ahead. Have students who finish early help their classmates.

- Prepare simple handouts that students can take with them to the labs detailing all the tasks they need to perform with the various software programs. Even if the computer or software manuals are available, few people want to read them. (If they are frustrating to you, imagine how the developmental student would feel trying to make sense out of one.)

Possible Problems and Solutions

When incorporating computers into the developmental curriculum, expect the unexpected and remain flexible. However, because we normally want to be prepared, here are a few possible situations that could occur and some ideas for handling them.

Computerphobic Students

Though we now expect students to have prior experience with computers, they do not always come to our classes feeling comfortable in their computer skills. Some, especially older or returning students, may actually have had little exposure to computers. For those students, keep up the encouragement by assuring them they will enjoy writing with the computer. In addition, be extremely patient with their questions. Usually, the light dawns, and they finally grasp what to do. Refrain from doing any task yourself that students need to learn how to do. If a student asks how to save or quit for the day, for example, stand behind the student and verbally walk him or her through the process. But keep your hands off the mouse or keyboard. The student will learn only from firsthand experience.

Computerphilic Students

On the opposite end of the spectrum are the computer whizzes (or at least they think they are). These students create a different set of problems because they do not wait for instructions. In addition, they get frustrated with slower classmates, or they cause disruptions because they finish an assignment early and want to play around or visit with other classmates (even if those classmates have not finished). Alleviate some of these problems by asking at the beginning of the semester who has experience with the computers you are using in class. Then ask those students who respond to be your assistants. Explain that alone, you cannot quickly get to all students with computer or printer problems, and you could use their help. Also, when you introduce a new program or assignment, ask everyone to *stay with you*. Point out that the computer-savvy students may understand the computer, but they do not know exactly what you want. Again, privately ask a stronger computer user to keep an alert eye toward a student who sits close by who appears to have problems with the directions.

Note that some computerphilic students will want to surf the Internet, e-mail friends, check their Google+ or Facebook pages, or play games during class. As with cell phone use, during the first class state your policy regarding non-class-related computer activities. If you do not want students on Facebook during class, make your policy clear.

Difficulty Adjusting to Writing on a Computer

Even a computer-literate student may have a bad writing day and sit staring at the screen. These situations are easily handled when you move around the room as your students work. If you notice a student just sitting, stop and chat. Try to determine what the problem is. Sometimes, students merely zone out for a few moments because they are tired, thinking about a test in another class, or trying to figure out what to say next. If the student is struggling for words during the writing of a first draft, offer suggestions on how to continue: typing the first word that comes to mind, or entering a string of question marks to indicate a word problem. Remind the student that the draft is not a final version. He or she will have plenty of time to revise and find that perfect word. If the student has not done the assigned preparation, recommend starting at that point and suggest that he or she visit the lab after class to catch up. You can also take the time to talk through the writing with the student. Often, students know what they want to write, but they cannot think of a way to write it. If you have them tell you, you can then say, "Okay, type what you just told me." Or, suggest that the student just start typing—doing

freewriting to see where the subject will go (freewriting and other prewriting strategies are discussed in Chapter 4 of *Real Essays*).

If students do not ask you for help, ask yourself why. Do you isolate yourself from students by staying at your own computer? If so, walk around and perhaps read over a few shoulders. By making yourself more accessible, you make students more comfortable about asking for assistance. Also, remember that some students do not need help. They are self-motivated and have done the homework, and get to class ready to begin writing. These students will come to you when they hit a rough spot. In addition, some students prefer to ask another student rather than the teacher. (Remember that when one student helps another, both can benefit.) However, some students have been rejected by teachers in the past or may feel intimidated by a teacher. Your friendliness and frequent offers of assistance may eventually turn some of those students around, but others may never feel comfortable asking for help.

Mechanical Problems

Mechanical problems may be harder to deal with. You will be more comfortable in the classroom and save a tremendous amount of time if you learn everything you can about the computers. Work with your college's IT support staff to find out solutions to problems you might face (or read the computer manual's troubleshooting guide). Then, ask for guidance on quickly correcting the problem. Some problems with nonworking computers or printers are simple to solve:

- Check the power switch.
- Check cable connections (cords can come loose).
- Make sure the student is using the correct printer (some students print three copies of a document because they thought the computer was connected to a different printer).

Sometimes computers overload and freeze up, which can be frustrating. A frozen computer can often simply be restarted: The safest way to restart a PC is to press down the *ctrl, alt,* and *delete* keys (*option + command + escape* for Macs). This keystroke combination will usually allow you to close any programs that are running but not responding. It is amazing how often this relatively simple solution does the job.

Unfortunately, not all problems are simply solved. If a computer crashes because of a power surge or momentary power outage, then the computer will usually start working again as soon as the power comes back on. However, anything students have done since they last saved will be lost. Therefore, remind students often to save their documents every few minutes. Tell them that the few seconds the process requires can save them the frustration of reconstructing an hour's worth of work after a power outage. (Microsoft Word can be adjusted for frequent "saves": Under the "Word" drop-down menu, click on "Preferences," then "Save.")

If a classroom computer has a problem you cannot fix, request help from your school's computer support staff. (Familiarize yourself with the procedure for requesting assistance so you know what to do when the occasion arises.) Since some problems will not be fixed during class, always have a backup plan so that you can continue teaching without the computer or computers.

9

Other Useful Instructional Approaches

Every instructor makes use of a different set of pedagogical tools—and we can all benefit from learning about the tools that other people use. This chapter is a compendium of useful instructional approaches, classroom techniques that other instructors and I have used over the years and have found to be useful to our students. Some topics that you might expect to see covered here (e.g., collaboration, critical thinking, and bringing the real world into the classroom) are treated in depth in other chapters. This chapter is more of a grab-bag, with briefer suggestions for a wider variety of approaches, all of which are supported by the pedagogy and resources of *Real Essays*. I hope you find at least a couple of ideas that you want to try out in your next semester.

Vary the Pedagogy

"Varying the pedagogy" means taking a break from the traditional instructional format of instructor lectures and independent in-class writing by students. This traditional model assumes a learner who has a particular learning style (linear and abstract), but few developmental classrooms (or few classrooms of any stripe) are filled exclusively with such students. Your class will probably consist of students who have a variety of learning styles: visual, verbal, auditory, hands-on, and interpersonal, as well as linear. There are a variety of methods of classifying learning styles, but the exact details of the scheme matter less than recognizing that the students in your class are tuned to a variety of different frequencies. If you broadcast your message on a single frequency (with linear, abstract lectures), you will connect with some people but miss others. Varying the pedagogy is a way to reach more students. Students typically learn more, enjoy the class, and pay closer attention when you vary the classroom activities.

A varied pedagogy can also help by breaking things up—it's difficult for anyone to concentrate on a single voice talking in a single format for forty-five minutes, and it's especially difficult for students with attention-deficit hyperactivity disorder (ADHD) or other learning disabilities (see Chapter 3 of this manual for an overview of teaching students with ADHD or other learning disabilities). Almost anything that departs from the normal pace or format can be useful: Small-group instruction, group work, one-on-one conferences, student presentations, independent study, and discussions are just a few of the possibilities.

One View of Learning Styles

VERBAL LEARNERS RESPOND WELL TO . . .

- Exploring ideas in words
- Journal writing
- Imaginative writing
- Instructions given orally
- Storytelling
- Debate

LINEAR/ABSTRACT LEARNERS RESPOND WELL TO . . .

- Complex systems reduced to underlying principles
- Processes presented as a sequence of discrete skills
- Lists and outlines
- Logic and problem solving
- Quantitative information
- Symbolic equations

VISUAL/SPATIAL LEARNERS RESPOND WELL TO . . .

- Information presented as pictures

- Colors

- Diagrams

- Overviews

- Mapping and clustering

INTERPERSONAL LEARNERS RESPOND WELL TO . . .

- Developing an understanding by interacting with others

- Informal person-to-person communication

- Collaborative projects

- Peer editing

- Acknowledgment of motivations and feelings

- Seeing someone else's point of view

INTRAPERSONAL LEARNERS RESPOND WELL TO . . .

- Silent reflection

- Metacognition techniques

- Focusing and centering exercises

- Awareness and expression of feelings

If, like most teachers, you are a linear learner, you should experiment with instructional approaches that seem almost counterintuitive to you. For instance, a step-by-step progression with drill and review may be great for students who learn sequentially, but visual/spatial learners are systems thinkers. They learn holistically rather than in a step-by-step fashion. They need to see the whole picture before they can understand the parts. They often get confused by all the individual sections if they can't see where you are heading. Thus, if you begin your presentation with an overview of the entire unit and relate previous lessons to the current one, these learners will be better prepared to move into your step-by-step approach. Some teachers misinterpret a student's difficulty by applying the standards of their own learning styles: When a visual-style student fumbles with drill-type instruction, a sequential-style instructor may believe the student simply needs more drilling when, in fact, a better strategy may be to change the instructional approach.

One of the essential underpinnings of *Real Essays'* own approach is the assumption that different learners have different learning styles and that a change of pace is good for everyone. For example, the design of the book is intended to highlight important information in interesting ways and to present a variety of visual textures instead of a monotonous gray page that intimidates everyone but the most solid of linear thinkers. Features throughout the book appeal to different learning styles; here are just a few:

REAL ESSAYS FEATURES THAT WILL APPEAL TO VERBAL LEARNERS

- Opportunities for writing throughout

- Models of student and professional writing

REAL ESSAYS FEATURES THAT WILL APPEAL TO LINEAR/ ABSTRACT LEARNERS

- Treatment of writing as a series of discrete, masterable skills

- Writing Guides in Part 2 chapters

REAL ESSAYS FEATURES THAT WILL APPEAL TO VISUAL/ SPATIAL LEARNERS

- Visuals near the start of Part 2 chapters and in the Writing about an Image assignments in these chapters

- Quick review charts in Parts 4 and 5 that map chapter content

- Diagrams of challenging concepts

- Chapter overviews in the Understand section of chapter

- Information in marginal notes

REAL ESSAYS FEATURES THAT WILL APPEAL TO INTER- PERSONAL LEARNERS

- Profiles of Success in Part 2

- Opportunities for discussion and teamwork (primarily in *Instructor's Annotated Edition* marginal annotations)

REAL ESSAYS FEATURES THAT WILL APPEAL TO INTRA- PERSONAL LEARNERS

- Critical Thinking guides

- Writing Guides

Here are some other suggestions for varying the pedagogy in your classroom.

- **Have students introduce themselves.** Ask students to introduce themselves to the class, using no more than one minute. You might suggest that they mention the other courses they are taking, their feelings about writing (or English), and/or their goals for the semester. Begin by introducing yourself to serve as a model.

- **Use spoken instructions and feedback.** Try to incorporate an oral component into the classroom. The spoken discourse can be as simple as oral responses to homework exercises or small-group work. As students improve their ability to process and generate spoken language, they also improve their ability to process and generate written language.

- **Use class discussion.** To create a community of writers, encourage discussion of topics and strategies. When introducing a new assignment, have the class brainstorm out loud. Write their responses on the board, on a computer projecting onto a screen, or onto a transparency. Then let the class orally evaluate their brainstorming and organize the information. Depending on class time, you can have them work together to write an outline, a paragraph, an introductory paragraph, or an entire essay. For summary, review, and instant feedback have the entire class respond orally, ask class members to raise their hands to agree with certain responses, or give short multiple choice tests.

- **Use debate.** When you are ready to begin a persuasion unit, have students form groups depending on which side of an issue they support. After the groups have had time to organize their thoughts, instruct the class to argue its points. When you teach students to anticipate and acknowledge opposing points of view, you may try grouping students so that each one is encouraged to argue the side of an issue that he or she doesn't personally support.

- **Use of guest speakers.** Your students may appreciate the opportunity to hear someone else occasionally. Keep a watchful eye for guest lecturers who are coming to your campus and see if you can work those presentations into your schedule. Perhaps you can give your students extra credit for attending a lecture on campus, or if the presentation coincides with your class time, take the class on an on-campus field trip. Students can write a journal entry, paragraph, or essay on what they learned or how they reacted to the guest speaker. If your college isn't having an appropriate speaker, invite someone

to your class. Think about the kind of information your students need. (See Chapter 4 of this manual for specific suggestions.) Every visit can be followed by some type of writing assignment, either for a grade or for practice.

- **Have a treasure hunt for people.** Make up a list of characteristics to hand out to your class. For example, ask students to "Find someone who loves to write" or "Find someone who can speak another language." Then give students a certain amount of time to find a different person to fit each category. You may want to give a prize to the person who finishes first or to the person who gets the most names. This can be done in the first class as an icebreaker (see p. 5 of this manual) or later on as a prelude to a specific assignment or a collaborative exercise.

- **Assign a biography talk.** Ask students to find someone in the class whom they don't already know. Give the students fifteen to twenty minutes to chat with each other to discover interesting information. Then ask them to spend about five minutes preparing a brief introduction of their partners to present to the class. You may want to put a one- to two-minute time limit on the introductions.

- **Assign a group talk.** Divide the class into groups of three to five people. Put a transparency on the overhead that gives the students questions or topics to discuss. The discussions can be about grammar, writing, school in general, or personal interests.

Encourage Active Learning

A Chinese philosopher once said, "What I hear, I forget. What I see, I remember. What I do, I understand." This quotation provides an excellent motto for teaching. Experience shows that students learn by doing their own active and interactive processing over time. As the Learning Pyramid on page 114 illustrates, the more actively involved people become with their own learning, the more they will retain. With active learning, students make the course content their own—both by processing it in a way that makes sense to them and by investing their own energy in it. The students take charge of the learning; we merely facilitate. Or as one of my colleagues says, "In active learning, the teacher is the band master who directs but never plays an instrument during the performance."

LEARNING PYRAMID
Average Retention Rate

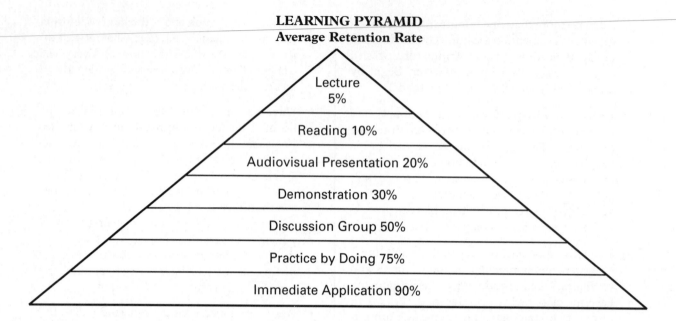

Active learning does not mean that instructors relinquish control of the class to students. If anything, it requires a more challenging type of preparation in order to create the best possible context—and then the fortitude to sit back while students forge their own way within that context. For active learning to work, tasks must

- have a built-in motivation,

- be relevant to students' needs and goals,

- be attainable,

- be satisfying.

Much of the pedagogy of *Real Essays* is based on the model of active learning. The entire real world component is based on the assumption that succeeding in the worlds of college, work, and everyday life is a primary motivating factor for students—so, students will be more motivated to tackle writing tasks if they can see the immediate relevance and applicability to these arenas. Similarly, the Profiles of Success are intended to motivate students by showing that effective writing is a necessary and attainable skill. The instructional focus is on whole-paper assignments (whether for paragraphs or for essays) rather than unconnected drills, so that writing tasks are satisfying and create a sense of closure and accomplishment. In Part 2, Writing Different Kinds of Essays, students are given an overview of the lesson in the Understand section, then practice their skills in the Read and Analyze and Write sections. The editing chapters also begin with an Understand section; then students move on to a Practice section to work on common grammar errors, and an Edit section in which they learn how to self-edit. In other words, students move from being passive recipients of knowledge to active participants who apply skills to tasks that mean something to them, from the top of the Learning Pyramid to the base.

Active learning can happen within many contexts, including individual work, small-group work, one-on-one conferences, large-group work, reading, writing, talking, listening, or reflecting. Journal writing, peer evaluations, and collaboration are forms of active learning that we use frequently (these are discussed in detail in other sections). Here are some other suggestions.

- Ask specific prediscussion questions, and let your students know that you'll call on anyone in the class. In class, build on their homework. Discuss and use the questions in either small or large groups.

- Place a suggestion box in the room and encourage students to make written comments every time the class meets. Give them a few minutes during class to do so.

- Before a test, pair students so that they can quiz each other or write sample sentences illustrating a particular rule of grammar or punctuation.

- Encourage study partners—this format not only helps students interact but also places more of the responsibility for learning on their shoulders.

- Ask students to paraphrase in two or three sentences, either orally or in their journals, what you've discussed during that day's class.

- Have students use the Learning Journal prompts in *Real Essays*. These ask students to reflect on and evaluate their own progress, one of the most important elements in becoming responsible for one's own learning.

- Assign a quick-response paper (sometimes referred to as a one-minute paper). Ask the class to answer two questions in one sentence each: (1) What was the most useful/meaningful thing you learned during this session? (2) What question(s) remains uppermost in your mind as we end this session?

- Use the RSQC2 Technique in which students **R**ecall the most interesting or significant points of the previous class; **S**ummarize important points in one sentence; Raise any **Q**uestions that they still have about the topic; **C**omment in a word or phrase on how they felt about the discussion during that class; and **C**onnect what they learned during the last class with previous classes or with the next assignment.

- Encourage students to become active readers: Have them read, discuss, and practice the suggestions for active, critical reading in Chapter 3 of *Real Essays*. You might also have them work through the Close-Reading Questions in the margins of the essays at the end of the book.

- Use the ideas for self-assessment included in Chapter 11 of this manual. Placing students in the role of evaluator helps them to see the big picture and take responsibility for their own progress.

To encourage active learning, you may need to reevaluate your approach to certain activities or assignments. Too often, our typical behavior reflects and maintains a notion of learners as passive recipients rather than active participants. Give students the time and space to be active.

- Allow sufficient wait time when you ask a question. Too often, we answer the questions ourselves before students really have a chance.

- Move around the room as students are writing, and answer questions they may have as they work.

- Encourage students to ask a question whenever they have one. Remind them that the best time to ask a question is when they think of it.

Instead of giving pat answers, probe student comments and ask follow-up questions.

- Offer students the chance to voice their opinions about what you are doing in class, the topics you've assigned, the homework, or even the course itself.

- Remember that when you place students in groups for the first time, they may be shy and uncomfortable. (You may want to consider cultural tensions as well. Muslim women, for example, may feel uncomfortable in a group with men.) Therefore, allow some get-acquainted time and try not to move the discussion along too rapidly. Suggest that students introduce themselves to one another and that they briefly discuss what they hope to get out of the day's activity.

Active-learning techniques serve many purposes. Aside from the most important aspect of making the student more accountable for his or her learning, they can also relieve some stress for the teacher. Increased participation can lead to more interesting classes and less need for lectures. Active-learning techniques can also help your students interact with one another and with you. Some activities can help you and your students to get to know one another or to break the ice. In addition, some activities give you an opportunity to assess understanding without the actual grading. Active learning can help everyone get the fullest benefit more from the class.

Getting Students to Do the Readings
Linda B. Nilson, *Clemson University*

Why Students Skip the Readings

Students have a lot going on these days: part-time and even full-time jobs, "real lives" with family and household responsibilities, homework for multiple courses, community service commitments, and physical fitness routines—not to mention less noble activities like parties, football games, hobbies, "obligatory" television programs, Internet entertainment, and other forms of fun. Who has time for reading assignments?

Besides, as students reason, not doing the readings has no consequences. The next test is weeks away, and what good will the readings do anyway? They didn't do them in high school and still got good enough grades to get this far. Certainly, skipping the readings in college won't hurt their chances of landing that lucrative first job they aspire to and expect. Bottom line: The professor will lecture the *Reader's Digest* version of the chapters during the next class anyway.

With little practice in "book learning," it's not surprising that few students are proficient in reading academic material. Most read passively, superficially, and rather slowly, averaging 100–250 words per minute, depending on the technical density of the text.

At this speed, reading fifty 500-word pages would take students from 100 minutes to over four hours. Of course, these estimates assume that they can focus their attention on the text for so long. But many can't focus for even five minutes, so they give up after a few pages.

What can faculty do to help students and push them to finish their reading?

It may seem too obvious to mention, but the first thing you must do if you want your students to do the readings for your class is to get your students to buy the required books. At the first class meeting, tell them that they will have to read and possibly even mark up the books daily for a chance at a passing final grade. If they can't or won't buy the books, they should drop your course.

Be realistic in selecting the books, articles, Web pages, and other materials that you assign. Don't choose a reading because you like it. As an expert in the field, you've internalized all the cognitive shortcuts that make it easy reading for you. Consider that your average student's reading ability is probably marginal at best, and his or her love of sophisticated nonfiction less than passionate. Look for readings with graphics and pictures that reinforce the text, and pare down the required pages to the essentials. The less reading assigned, the more likely students will do it. If you're uncertain about the reading level of an assignment, get a quick analysis at www.harrymclaughlin.com/SMOG.htm.

SELL STUDENTS ON THE READINGS

Everyone else is trying to sell our students something. Why aren't we? Do not assume that your students think you have their best interests at heart. Explain why you chose the readings you did, as well as their purpose, value, and relevance to the course. Students see this as a sign of respect. Make explicit connections between the readings and in-class activities, written assignments, and exams. Preview and promote the next reading assignment in class, and help students over the hump by letting them start reading key pieces in class. Finally, stop lecturing the readings in class. Extend or update the material in the readings, or clarify what you know students won't grasp on their own. But you can't expect rational people to do the reading if the knowledge will be spoon-fed to them in class the next day.

TEACH READING STRATEGIES

Chances are your students are not familiar with how textbooks and academic publications are structured, so take a little class time for them to peruse the table of contents, the introduction, and the chapter/section layout. Have them identify "road signs" such as headings, subheadings, and bold and italicized text. Why send them into foreign territory without a map?

Teach students how an expert reads—and it's not from the first word to the last. In order to anticipate the content of a particular reading, we often preview it, skimming through the subheadings, graphics, and italicized words on our way to the conclusion, which we typically read first. Thus, we start at the beginning of a piece already knowing its destination and a bit about how it gets there. Why not share this cognitively efficient reading strategy with our students?

Further, expert readers read with a purpose. As a rule, we're looking for something that's useful and important to our work. Students often tackle assigned readings with no purpose at all, so we have to give them one: study questions to answer, for example, or problems to solve (end-of-chapter or our own).

This type of assignment cues students as to what we consider important, something they desperately want to know. We should have them write out and turn in their answers or solutions and give them points for a good faith effort. Additionally, we should have them write out or concept-map a summary of the readings.

Another expert reading method to teach your students is marginalia, which is actually teaching them how to recognize "the main point" of a passage.

Lead an in-class exercise on a few pages of an assigned reading in which the students write three to five words next to each paragraph either summarizing or reacting to the material (your choice). Also have them underline a few key words and phrases—no more than 10 percent of the text. Then have them justify their marginalia and underlining choices and compare their choices against yours.

In a similar way, you can teach your students a related reading strategy: highlighting with discernment. In Weimer's (2005) two-class technique, she builds highlighting into the first two reading assignments and moderates two class discussions about what her students highlighted versus what she highlighted. In this way, students learn what an expert's reasons are for distinguishing some text as central and other text as support or elaboration.

HOLD STUDENTS ACCOUNTABLE FOR THE READINGS

If we don't grade students on an assignment, they think we regard it as unimportant. So to communicate to students the value of the readings, we have to assign reading-related activities that are worth points—enough throughout the semester to total at least 20 percent of the final grade.

Since you're grading on a good faith effort, you needn't commit or correct. Just allocate points for students' meeting the reasonable length requirement you set and demonstrating familiarity with the readings. You can grade these activities as complexly as a 3/2/1/0 points system or as simply 1/0. Best of all, grading these efforts not only motivates students to read but also enhances their learning and retention.

One accountability option is written homework, like having students respond in writing to the study questions or problems mentioned above. Students now average only three hours of homework per week for each course, so it's not unreasonable to expect that they can do more. Further, you can extend the homework into in-class activities.

Another effective alternative is the daily quiz on the readings' major points. For online, pre-class administration, many faculty rely on electronic test banks for basic-level multiple-choice items, which essentially grade themselves. If you print out items for an in-class quiz, you can first have students take it individually and turn it in, then have small groups retake it as a unit. This second step allows for students to talk about the readings. For higher-level quizzing that requires thinking beyond recall, you can compose an in-class mini-essay question. To save time, you can dictate it or display it on a slide. Judging a good faith effort will take you only seconds.

Once you stop lecturing the readings, you will have abundant class time for the third possible activity—in-class written exercises that have students restate, apply, summarize, examine, and/or assess the readings. For instance, students can work on problem solutions to turn in or to present to the class, or they can do any number of writing-to-learn exercises, such as freewriting on the main points in the readings. The key is to make most or all the task an individual one, so that a nonreader can't hide behind a reader, then to grade the product on a good faith effort.

Finally, you can hold your class accountable with some kind of in-class oral activity on the readings, preferably where you cold-call on students and, again, grade their answer on a good faith effort. You can start with recitation (recall) questions and move into thought-inducing discussion questions, or even simulations and role plays that require the knowledge in the readings. To ensure "random" cold-calling, put each of your students' names on an index card and shuffle the deck. Mark the good-faith "grade" on the card, return the card to the deck, and shuffle again. Don't let anyone feel too safe or get too comfortable!

Students Will Do the Readings

After attending one of my workshops, Clemson University English instructor Skye Suttie instituted daily quizzes in her classes. Each day she had her students write an answer to a general, open-ended question on the readings. She found "they worked like a charm! . . . I noticed a huge change in the grade as the semester progressed. They were actually sometimes disappointed on days when I opted not to give them quizzes!"

Mick Lalopa, associate professor of Hospitality and Tourism Management at Purdue University, witnessed a similar transformation in his students. For years most of them hadn't been doing the readings and, as a result, were gleaning little from his PowerPoint-studded lectures. Then, after perusing the literature on increasing reading compliance, he started requiring his students to write "detailed study notes" on the assigned readings, which they turned in for a grade.

"The technique has worked wonders," Lalopa claims. He opens the discussion with the broad question "What did you learn about _____ in chapter _____?" With this and a few follow-up questions, most of the class participates in articulating the key points. "Best of all," he continues, "the students indicated that they were HAPPY that they were being required to prepare study notes because it forced them to read the chapter . . ."

Use Journals

To encourage students to write abundantly and freely, consider journal writing as a requirement in your course. Journals provide practice in thinking on paper, and journal entries can later be revised and refined for a formal writing assignment. They also encourage self-growth and exploration and give you some insight into your students' lives and thoughts.

I find three entries per week (one-half to one page each) a reasonable requirement. Ask students to number and/or date each entry, and encourage them to set aside certain times each week to write. Some students enjoy arriving in class early, taking out their journals, and writing for ten minutes before class begins. If you want to emphasize the importance of regular writing even more, you can devote five to ten minutes of every class to journal writing. If you are in a computer classroom, you might want to try an online journal.

Suggest that students either write their journal entries on regular notebook paper or type them into the computer and then print them out. Then they can keep their entries in a special section of their three-ring notebooks. When you collect them throughout the semester, students can remove the newest entries, staple them together, and turn in merely a few pages. This practice will save you the hassle and strain of having to collect and carry seventy spiral notebooks at a time.

Journals can be read in different ways. You might want to use a highlighter to mark journal passages that you particularly like or use a bright-colored pen to make brief comments periodically. By writing comments, you let your students know that you are reading every word, and they become more serious about the assignment. When you assign a grade, do so only on promptness and completeness, not on grammar, spelling, punctuation, sentence structure, or paragraph organization. Journals are a form of freewriting, and students should be assured that the assignment is an exercise in putting words on paper, not editing and creating polished prose.

If you collect journals throughout the semester (perhaps three times), the reading isn't quite as laborious. Besides, you will discover a wealth of information about your students that will help you understand their frustrations, their motivations, and their other responsibilities. If you are afraid of burnout on journal reading, you can ask students to turn down the corners of a certain number of entries that they would like for you to read and comment on. The remainder of the entries can be skimmed and noted for credit.

Another alternative is to collect journals only at the end of the semester. Ask students to add page numbers, a title for each entry, a table of contents, and an evaluative conclusion. In this way, students can analyze their own work for the semester and observe their growth as writers throughout the semester.

You can establish criteria for format and content, but the best journals are those for which the student has free rein to select the topic. Prepare a handout that explains the journal assignment (several samples are included on pp. 119–23) and offer suggestions. Have students read the section on journals in Chapter 5 of *Real Essays*. This section focuses on journals as an idea-generating strategy. Another type of journal is the reading journal in which students keep a running record of what they are reading and write responses to it. Frank Smith and Mike Rose, among others, point to the value of summarizing, digesting, and recasting something a student has read in his or her own words. When students can process a selection in this way, they have a certain hold on it—as well as a memory aid for recall and review at exam time. Ideally, students make reading-journal entries before, during, and after the actual reading. Before reading, students should write predictions based either on the title and a quick skim or on the first paragraph. During reading, students should note sentences or thoughts that may lead to more writing or that simply interest them. After finishing the reading, students should somehow process the piece as a whole in a response of their own that takes off where the selection ended. (Later in this chapter, see the Reading Response Guidelines, by Jack O'Keefe at Daley College in Chicago.) The apparatus in *Real Essays'* Part 8, Readings for Writers, meshes well with this approach. The Guiding Question that appears at the beginning of every selection can be used to make a prediction about the work. Questions in the margins of readings encourage further prediction, as well as reflection on the writer's ideas and identification of main points, support, and so on. The follow-up apparatus asks students to summarize and respond to the selection, and includes ideas for essay writing.

Journal Writing Tips

A journal is a place to save what you think and feel by recording your reactions, motives, insights, and important ideas. Keeping a journal will not only develop your self-expression but also help you grow as a person. Then, too, it may serve another purpose: it can provide a bank of ideas from which to draw for writing assignments. Professional writers often keep journals for saving details about unusual events they see and interesting conversations they hear. Later they may use the items in articles or novels, because they know that true-to-life details give depth and authenticity to writing.

In a journal, you can describe your ideas and emotions without worrying about punctuation, grammar, audience, or evaluation. Your goal is to discover what you really think and feel, to dig down into your mind and let the words flow. Journal writing not only clarifies thinking and fosters creativity but also helps you feel more comfortable in the physical act of writing.

Keep your journal on loose-leaf notebook paper in your three-ring binder or on a computer, and write in it at least three times a week. You may want to set aside a special place and time, but planning is not necessary. By the end of the semester, your journals will contain at least thirty-six entries. Each should be at least a paragraph in length, clearly numbered, and dated. You may either write by hand or use a computer; if you write, please write legibly. Journals will be collected at announced due dates (see class plan), approximately every three to four weeks. Staple your entries together before turning them in.

An additional handout offers some suggestions for journal entries, but I would like for one journal entry a week to be a summary of and reaction to a magazine or newspaper article you have read or a book you have read. You may also react to situations or discussions that have occurred in this class or in any of your other classes.

In order to have the required number of entries, you will need to write in your journal only three times each week.

Suggested Journal Topics

1. React to a movie or TV show that you have seen recently. Give a summary, and then tell what you did or did not enjoy. Reflect on ideas the movie or show made you think about.

2. Name a city or town that you have been to and tell in detail what it is like. Use the senses (sight, hearing, smell, touch, taste) to create an image in the reader's mind.

3. Write a description of one of your favorite leisure-time activities.

4. Write a narrative by completing this statement: *I was never more scared than . . .*

5. Describe what you would like to be doing five years from now.

6. Complete the statement: *My most unusual teacher was . . .* (Explain why.)

7. Go for a walk, find some object, and describe it in detail.

8. Tell a friend or someone in your family about how to do a chore that you do.

9. Describe a person you have met. What qualities or characteristics impressed you?

10. Write a paragraph that describes your ideal job.

11. How are you different from your friends or family members? How are you similar?

12. Focusing on a current issue that interests you or that is important to you, write a letter to the editor of your campus or local newspaper.

13. Invent a product, and then write four or five complete sentences that highlight its strengths and that convince magazine or newspaper readers to buy the product.

14. Describe your feelings about a class that you dislike. How could it be improved?

15. Describe a class that you like. Why do you like it? How is it different from the others?

16. Find an online collection of quotations, choose one, and explain what it means to you.

17. Write down something funny, interesting, or thought provoking that you overheard. After you write down what you overheard, relate it to your own life and thoughts.

18. Write a poem.

19. Complete the statement: *I was doing well until . . .* or *I was not doing well until . . .*

20. Explain how you would teach this class if you were the professor.

21. Describe what you like most about yourself.

22. If you could change history or the recent past, explain what changes you would make.

23. Tell how one person has had an impact on your life.

24. Invent a holiday. Describe when it would appear on the calendar, how it would be celebrated, and why it should be a holiday.

25. Describe a goal you have set for yourself.

- Check your prediction after the prereading. Were you on target about what the full reading would say? If not, explain why in a few sentences.

- Summarize the reading in a short paragraph or a longer one if the reading is lengthy.

- What is the author's main point, and how does the author support it?

- Can you relate anything in the reading to your own life or to the lives of those around you? Connecting the reading to your own life may make a good topic.

Sample Reading Journal Entry for Langston Hughes's "Salvation"

(p. 691 of *Real Essays*)

Prediction: The author will talk about being saved in church.

Summary: The author describes going to a revival meeting as a kid and sitting on a bench with other children, waiting to be saved. The preacher asks, "Won't you come to Jesus?" but the author can't bring himself to do it. He has been told that he will see Jesus and feel different when he is saved, but because he doesn't, he doesn't leave the bench, even when adults gather around him and the other children and pray. Finally, the other children go to be saved, and the author is the only one left on the bench. In the end, he feels so ashamed that he goes to the preacher. Although the congregation is very happy about this, the author feels sad and guilty for lying about seeing Jesus. And he no longer believes in Jesus because Jesus didn't help him.

I couldn't find one sentence with the main point, but the author seems to be talking about how doing something we don't believe in can make us feel bad, even if we're doing it for what seem like good reasons. The author supports this point by including a lot of the boy's thoughts.

Relate to my life: Something kind of like this happened to me when I was a kid. I went to church with a friend several times, and every time the minister said, "If you haven't been saved, come up front and stand with me." Every time, I'd go up. My friend started to laugh at me, but I kept going up because I never felt saved. I'd like to write about how people's expectations for us can make us question ourselves or feel isolated.

Use the Writing Center

Sometimes the most useful instructional approach sends students out of the classroom—and to the writing center. Writing centers come in all sizes and philosophies. Some centers fall under the auspices of the English department, a developmental studies area, continuing education, or student services; others are part of a larger learning center or a separate entity. Some centers were established as labs for classes, some serve multiple disciplines, and some are learning centers that offer various review classes in grammar and writing.

Staffing is as varied as support and purpose. Many centers are staffed by a combination of paid and volunteer tutors. Some hire trained professional tutors with at least a bachelor's degree whereas others rely on faculty who volunteer or who are assigned as part of a teaching or lab load. Many hire peer tutors.

Hours and modes of operation also vary. Some centers operate on a set schedule; their tutors, who are assigned to different areas or teachers, meet regularly with students on an appointment basis. Others, perhaps more commonly, operate on a drop-in basis. Generally, the drop-in arrangement works well because of the unpredictability of the schedules of students who also work and have family responsibilities. In centers where students can drop in, there is a casual, comfortable atmosphere that can help reduce the tension of a tutoring session. Also, a drop-in arrangement may serve more students because they can visit the center on the spur of the moment. However, be aware that the limited number of hours such centers are open is often a problem. Students have such varied work schedules and obligations that writing centers that are not open at night and on weekends may not fit their needs.

No matter what their organization, most writing centers operate under the same general theory: Writing tutors can help students discover their abilities and thus become better writers, not just producers of better writing. For the most part, writing center staff will not give answers; they will only ask questions to help students focus, think, organize, take risks, and demonstrate their critical thinking skills.

If your college has a writing center or tutoring center, make sure your students are aware of it. If possible, take class time to walk your students to the center for a brief orientation. That way, they not only find out where the center is located but have the opportunity to meet the staff. Then they won't feel too uncomfortable when they go for help the first time. Encourage your students to use the support services. Their visits will save you time, and your students also will benefit from hearing directions from another point of view.

Meet with your writing center staff to determine what services are available. Some facilities offer guidance in audience and approach; and generally they will help the student edit, but they will not edit for the student. Some writing centers provide excellent handouts and writing aids that your students can apply to your class and other courses. Other facilities offer tutoring for students who have problems in grammar and writing. Some centers have computers that offer grammar exercises, writing assistance programs, and Internet access.

To ensure a successful experience for your students, you need to work with the staff. Don't send your students to the writing center "for help" without clear guidance. See if your center has a form that you can send with the student indicating what you want the student to work on. You can also create your own referral form, or write specific instructions on the student's paper. Ask if the staff would like you to send copies of your assignments (and samples of completed assignments) so that they know what to expect when your students come in.

Also, be sure the center's staff members know what you expect of them, and let your students know as well. Do you want the staff to question the student to help him or her find more supporting points? Do you want the staff to merely help with proofreading? Then, follow up on the students you have sent to the center (some centers send monthly reports to faculty regarding which students have visited the center, why, and for how long). By working closely with the staff, you will probably discover that the writing center will welcome you and your students with open arms, and you will all enjoy the relationship.

If your college does not have such a center, you may want to investigate some online writing centers. (See Resources for Developmental Professionals in Chapter 13 of this manual.)

10

Teaching ESL Students and Speakers of Nonstandard English

Revised by James May, *Valencia Community College*

A Word or Two about Language

Before beginning our discussion of ESL students, it may be a good idea to discuss the general concept of linguistic diversity. As a developmental writing teacher, you are likely to encounter three broad groups in your classes: students who speak standard American English, speakers of English as a second language, and native speakers who speak nonstandard dialects. The majority of this chapter is devoted to the linguistic and cultural needs of your second-language students; however, this beginning section will focus on the needs of students who do not speak standard American English as a native language.

As you read this chapter, you may notice that students who speak nonstandard dialects of English have much in common with second-language learners. Dialects are varieties of language that contrast in pronunciation, grammar, and vocabulary; they are also often associated with geographic areas and social class. Some examples of dialect differences in English include Indian English, Caribbean English, Midwestern English, Bostonian English, Southern English, Appalachian English, and Black English. Like learning a new language, learning a new dialect is a long, slow process.

Dialects are one of the most interesting features of language, but they are also one of the most controversial, particularly in schools. Speakers of standard English who hear a nonstandard dialect often make erroneous assumptions about the speaker's intelligence and motivation. Teachers of nonstandard-English-speaking students need to recognize that their students' linguistic differences rarely indicate true linguistic incompetence, and that speaking a nonstandard dialect does not impede cognitive development. In fact, years of sociolinguistic research have shown that dialects are not incorrect, but that they are merely different versions of the standard language. Correctness in language is a matter of social acceptability, and claims that some varieties are "proper" and others are "sloppy" reflect biased attitudes rather than true linguistic facts.

Keep in mind that such attitudes can negatively affect your students. Research has shown that a teacher's beliefs about students' abilities can act as a self-fulfilling prophecy. When educators underestimate students' abilities because of the dialect they speak, those students will do less well in school, perhaps as a direct result of the negative expectations. Cultural conflicts can also result from erroneous beliefs about dialect. A teacher who demonstrates a distaste for nonstandard dialects of English runs the risk of alienating students, who may see that teacher as elitist. And if this barrier forms between the teacher and the student, the student may lose interest in conforming to the patterns of standard English and may even become defensive of his or her dialect. Remember, research has shown that students have turned their backs on schools because what they learn there has conflicted with what they learn from their home cultures.

In addition, the high value that many teachers place on objectivity and explicitness, especially in writing, may conflict directly with the verbal styles of many nonstandard-English-speaking communities.

The following suggestions will help you enhance the learning opportunities for all your students: standard English speakers, speakers of nonstandard English dialects, and speakers of other languages.

- Model a positive attitude toward all varieties of language and culture. By creating a safe environment that respects all languages and cultures, you will prevent students from feeling a need to defend their linguistic and cultural identities.

- Develop a purpose for learning standard English. Many nonstandard-English-speaking students come from environments where standard English is not used; they may not understand why standard English is important.

- Allow for one-on-one conferences. Students may not know what to do with written feedback. One-on-one conferences allow you to clarify the meaning behind the feedback.

- Provide ample opportunities for students to gain reading experience, which plays an important role in developing writing abilities.

- Minimize formal instruction in grammar and mechanics. Instead, provide the most feedback about the aspects of students' writing that differ significantly from standard English.

- Provide regular, substantial practice designed to develop meaning and fluency in writing. Good writing takes practice, so spend less time on grammatical form and more time on actual writing.

- Make writing assignments realistic. If your students can develop real goals for writing, they may begin to see the benefits. You may also want to provide an opportunity to write for multiple audiences.

- Provide explicit instruction not only of the writing process but also of learning strategies.

- Use collaborative writing activities that allow students to benefit from seeing other writers at work. Pairing high- and low-level workers can create benefits for both.

- Allow for flexible grading that empowers students to take control of their own fate. Extra-credit assignments that allow students to better their grades through increased effort are effective motivators.

Teaching the ESL Student

ESL students are like native speakers: amazingly diverse. Some are truly interested in learning, and some don't want to put forth any effort. Some will have completed an ESL program, whereas others will have left a program too soon or will have never even been exposed to ESL courses. Even those students who have been exposed to such courses will vary considerably due to differences among ESL programs across the country.

Theories differ on how ESL students should be taught, and a discussion of the various theories of second-language acquisition is beyond the scope of this chapter. However, it may be a good idea to discuss how ESL students should be treated with respect to grading. One theory holds that ESL students working toward a degree in an American college or university should be assessed by the same criteria that apply to native speakers. Proponents of this theory argue that English-speaking students attending a foreign college would not receive special consideration for their lack of language skills and therefore the same should hold true for foreigners studying here. The truth of this contention remains to be seen. Clearly, however, this theory fails to make mention of the fact that many ESL students in the United States are actually U.S. citizens. Another theory holds that ESL students deserve special treatment and specialized criteria that overlook some of their language problems (idiom, pronoun, and article usage, for example). This approach may sound reasonable, but whether or not it prepares students to function in the real world also remains to be seen.

As a teacher of ESL students, you may want to put yourself in your students' position. What do you feel would be the best approach to learning a new language? What type of instruction would you find most beneficial? How would you like to be graded? Most of us would agree there should be some middle ground. ESL students may require extra help and assistance, but their writing must be acceptable in the real world if they are to succeed in their chosen careers.

Assessment and Placement

Proper placement of students helps both instructors and students, and including an ESL student in a developmental writing class designed for native speakers can create complications for all members of the class. Many of us are not trained to teach ESL students, and many of their writing problems are distinct from those of native speakers. Also, students who are not ready for regular English classes can become discouraged when faced with failure after failure, especially if the class moves too rapidly or doesn't cover in detail their types of problems. Proper placement is therefore something you will need to consider. If your college has an ESL program, work closely with the director of that program. Find out what ESL classes are available to students, how placement is determined, and how students advance out of ESL courses into mainstream English classes. If policies and processes are not in effect, offer to work with the ESL faculty to establish guidelines. Also, find out if your college will allow you to transfer a student from your developmental writing class into an ESL class within the first week or two of a semester.

Do not, however, attempt to automatically send a student out of your classroom. Determining who should be in an ESL class and who might succeed in a regular English class is not easy, but if you look for certain clues, you can make logical and objective decisions. Ask the student whether he or she has already completed some ESL classes. If so, the student may speak English somewhat fluently. However, be advised that there is a distinct difference between speaking and writing proficiency in English. Like other developmental writing students, ESL students may speak English quite proficiently while lacking literacy skills. The best way to assess your students is to ask for a writing sample and examine it carefully. If the ESL student's writing is filled with organizational errors, grammatical errors, vocabulary problems, and awkward or confusing syntactic structures—that is, if almost every sentence has some type of meaning or syntax problem—then the student probably would benefit from an ESL program instead of developmental writing. The following examples illustrate passages written by students who need to master more skills before they can successfully complete a developmental writing course. All three are filled with errors, and the students' ideas are hard to understand.

> No permitted with citizens who living in Texas carry weapon. After all amount accidents, we can realized almost that situation occur are by criminal they usually carrying a weapon with them whenever they go out, an make it happen wherever with anytime they don't scare who they are. The Texas Police department they really having that problem but they haven't been found the best way to solution yet, after each ocurred to make person who is a victim of the guns. For instant, if the legal of the Taxas absolutely

unallowable to selling guns also somehow they get all guns form any stores and controll on they hand. That would help people more safty.

> In the United States people legally carry weapon so you can safe by yourself but behind this reason, it makes you feel worry and also have more accident shoot each other. For example, last six months ago in the Plaza area on the Haltom road Da Lat was a place had happened an accident shooting a girl about 17 years old because this girl went with her new boyfriend and she did not break up her old boyfriend yet at that time, two these guys meet each other at that place driving an accident has happened the old her boyfriend had to shooted an minor person.

> The social will become unsafely if everybody can legally carry a weapon. It is easy to see on this point. Teenagers can also legally carry a guns, and they can active in anytime on their ages. The ages that make them feeling victory and ready to fighting with everybody; the ages that make them can not control by themselves. Among of them, we have not listed the groups of gangster that is one of the social's worry, and the police on the street.

One of the most obvious problems exhibited by these three samples is a complete lack of organization. Good paragraph construction in English typically follows a specific pattern of organization. As you know, paragraphs typically begin with a topic sentence, which in some way previews a pattern of support. The support points then follow this previewed pattern and relate back to the topic sentence. In the examples above, you may have had a difficult time identifying the topic sentences. Therefore, you had no way of guessing the possible pattern of organization and may simply have moved from word to word, attempting to make meaning out of the whole thing. It is more likely, however, that you got frustrated and stopped reading each paragraph after the first few sentences.

The point here is that these students not only have grammar, vocabulary, and syntax problems but also fail to recognize the organizational pattern of paragraphs in English. When assessing ESL students, keep in mind that different cultures often prefer different organizational patterns. Some cultures allow for more digression in their writing. Others allow for parallel structures—what we would consider redundancies. Still others follow circular patterns that may never mention the topic explicitly.

Not all ESL students write like those who produced the previous three samples. Other nonnative speakers have been in the United States longer, have studied English in their countries, or have immersed themselves in learning English. Their writing will be clearer and will have fewer errors. In fact, you may discover that most of the errors are merely a result of poor proofreading skills. The following examples illustrate passages written by two students who probably can succeed in a regular class. Both examples have errors, but their main ideas are readily understandable. Notice that the topic sentences in these passages are clearer, allowing readers to follow the writer's pattern of logic more easily.

> American citizens should have a right to carry concealed weapons. You never know whats going to happen, when you walk out of your house. The legislature of Texas made a great dession about this National Rifle Association. For an example when you walk out of your house front door, when someone try to mug you would you rather have a concealed weapon to protect yourself or not I would rather to have one and protect myself.

> Many people considered weapon carrying is a good way to protect themselves in any situation. But I oppose that view. I think that people should not legally carry a weapon because it is cause many accidental shootings. First of all, people's lives was threaten by legally carry a weapon. As we know that in society, such as in school, work place, hospital, we always have disagreement while we are argueing. Shooting is a good method to solve this problem. Perhaps, many people who misused gun will take this advantage to show of their power over the crowd that caused killed innocent citizen.

Obviously, the first paragraph is more polished than the second, but both of these students fall within the realm of acceptable writing for a nonnative speaker in a class of native speakers.

Instructional Strategies

Once you have determined which students belong in your class, what do you do with them? Whether you are working with a standard American English speaker, a speaker of a nonstandard English dialect, or an ESL student, your task as a teacher is to help all your students arrive at the same point: the acquisition of standard American English. A mixture of cultures can be a rewarding experience for you and for your entire class. However, you should not automatically assume that an ESL student knows what you expect of college students in the United

States. (Nor should you assume that ESL students know everything about their own culture, since many are American citizens.) Therefore, after you express your expectations orally, you need to provide a written explanation for future reference. This is a safe practice that can be employed with all your students.

Another way to help ESL students understand American academic culture is to have a class discussion in which students describe their conceptions of the academic expectations of college students. If students have experience studying in colleges abroad, you may want to ask about their academic experiences in those countries. Consider listing the findings on the board and then using that list to compile a written set of expectations for students in your class. This activity may help you understand your students' mind-sets and determine what assistance you may need to provide to make the transition into your class an easy one. Whether you have an entire ESL class or only one or two ESL students in your class, most students seem to enjoy learning about educational programs in other countries. This discussion also helps the students build a sense of community. By allowing all students to share aspects of their home culture, you can create a culturally inclusive environment in which your ESL students will feel safe to stray from their dependency on their native language.

Encourage students to write about their own experiences and to share their writing with their classmates. However, for students to feel comfortable enough to do so, you will need to model respect toward linguistic differences. Without considering them wrong or deficient, discuss how your ESL students are different so that they can scaffold their learning around those differences. Be careful not to overcorrect your nonnative speakers. Excessive overt correction may lead to a decrease in motivation and a lack of willingness to participate.

Once your ESL students have begun to share their work, watch whom they share with. Often, native speakers will pair off with other native speakers and nonnative speakers will pair off with other nonnative speakers. Assigning an ESL student a native-speaking partner can help both students learn and grow. Recall from Chapter 9 of this manual that active learning is the best form of learning. For a native speaker, teaching a nonnative-speaking partner represents a prime opportunity for active learning. And in some situations, you may find that an ESL student has more background knowledge than the native speaker. For example, if you teach in a computer classroom or lab, you may discover that the nonnative speakers take to the computers beautifully whereas some of your older native speakers approach the computer with much trepidation. Therefore, although the native speaker may be in a better position to offer guidance on language problems, the nonnative speaker may be in a better position to offer guidance on computer problems.

One area you may choose to be strict about is spoken language. Encourage all your students to speak in standard English while in the classroom. Remind your students that, although you respect their dialect or native language, they must practice standard English in order to learn the language. However, be careful about completely banning their native language from the classroom. If you hear two students conversing in their own language during work time, ask if they are having a problem with the assignment. If they are, then your question gives them the opportunity to ask you in English. If you are trying to explain something to a student and the student doesn't seem to understand, feel free to ask another student to help you out. Even native speakers won't always understand what you mean, and we sometimes have to ask someone else for another way of explaining the idea. Be prepared to employ multiple approaches for teaching the same concept. If you are not prepared to explain things in more than one way, tell students that you will get back to them when you come up with a more effective way of teaching it.

The classroom should be psychologically comfortable for all students to learn optimally; this is especially true for second-language learners. Because of language ego, many ESL students will feel uncomfortable producing in English unless they feel it is safe for them to do so. One theory even suggests that there is an affective filter that can block language learning unless students are made to feel comfortable and safe. To create a positive learning atmosphere for your ESL students (as well as for your other students), begin by modeling respect of language and culture. Allow students to see that you value their opinions and explanations, especially those that link learning to their own languages and experiences. For more specific suggestions on making your classroom comfortable for all students, see Chapter 3 of this manual.

Remember that in some cultures students must pass only a proficiency test to pass the class. Your students may not be accustomed to daily assignments and homework. Often a short study-skills lecture on the need for continuous repetition and reinforcement can help nonnative speakers understand the value of and the demand for this type of work. ESL students may benefit from explicit instruction of the cultural expectations of American schools. If you present this information at the beginning of the course, most students start out on the right foot. Unfortunately, you still may have a few bright students who resist the idea. However, if you sit down with them and explain that they can complete the course successfully only by following the requirements, most will settle down into the routine. Setting this priority early helps them not only in your class but in other classes as well.

To help ESL students with their writing, emphasize organization and encourage student–teacher conferences. Have students begin any writing assignment with some form of prewriting (freewriting, clustering, brainstorming); then show them how to turn the resulting information into an informal outline. Stress that the outline will help them stay focused on their topic and will relieve some of the pressure of deciding what to say as they are drafting. Provide samples from former students, newspapers, or the text for your students to examine and then follow. When students are ready to move from the drafting to the editing stage, help them with paragraph flow by explaining different techniques that provide transition. (See Chapters 4–9 of *Real Essays*.)

If your school requires students to perform timed writings, you may want to discuss how the timed writing process differs from the standard writing process. Your ESL students may show a lack of editing skills on timed tests. Remember these students are not writing in their native language and therefore require more time than native speakers do to monitor their output. In addition, your students may benefit from explicit instruction on how to turn prompts into thesis statements.

Many ESL students are extremely bright and know the grammar rules; often, the errors they make are a result of rushing their writing and not taking the time to edit carefully. When you have ESL students who consistently make the same type of error, sit down with them individually and ask them to explain the rule to you. Or have the students read their papers aloud. If they can correct the errors orally, then they understand the rule. In either case, you will know if the problem is due to lack of knowledge about editing or a lack of time. If the problem is due to lack of editing skills, stress the importance of this stage of the writing process. You may also want to encourage your students to take advantage of the writing centers and tutoring centers on campus. Tutors can give students interactive explanations of their errors, something you may not have the time to provide. However, you may need to explain what kind of help is acceptable and what kind becomes plagiarism. Plagiarism is not an internationally accepted concept. Some cultures even believe that copying someone else's work is a form of respect or flattery.

If you discover that your students do not know the grammar rules, explain the rules in a variety of ways and have students develop several original sentences applying them. Modeling is an excellent way to teach rules to both native and nonnative speakers. For instance, you can give students sample sentences and ask them to follow the same form to write their own sentences. You can go over the sentences with the students to determine if they now understand and can apply the rules to their own paragraphs and essays.

Instead of focusing on everything ESL students are doing wrong, look for aspects of language (plurals, gerund use, etc.) that they are sometimes using correctly. Have them focus on why they have used something correctly under one circumstance and incorrectly under another. Consider marking only one kind of problem in one of their drafts (verb problems, for example). The benefits of this approach are threefold. First, there will be less negative, and potentially discouraging, feedback on students' papers. Second, it will relieve the burden of your having to correct everything, which can be a daunting task. Third, if your ESL students are sometimes applying specific rules correctly and sometimes not, they may be stuck in one stage of development. Therefore, focusing on that stage of development may help them transition through it with greater ease.

How should you help ESL students overcome grammar problems while maintaining the focus of the course? Some ESL errors are common to both native and nonnative speakers and can easily be worked on in class: pronoun reference, subject-verb agreement, and *-s* endings on verbs, for example. Another major problem that both ESL and many native-speaking students face is spelling. If you assign weekly (or daily) spelling words from a list of one hundred commonly misspelled words (available online), you can incorporate both spelling and vocabulary into your students' weekly or daily routine. If you use computers, introduce ESL students to the spell checker. However, warn them about overuse of the thesaurus option. ESL students often fail to recognize the different connotations of English words.

Other problems are more specific to ESL students and require a variety of approaches. Incorrect usage of idioms should be dealt with as the situations arise, by pointing out the problem and explaining the proper use to the student. Some errors may be too complex and time-consuming to tackle in a developmental writing class: verb tenses, definite articles, and prepositions, for example. You should identify the problems and then offer outside assistance, send the student to the tutoring center, or assign individual work outside of class. Some of these typical ESL problems are addressed in Chapter 33 of *Real Essays* and in "ESL notes" that appear throughout the grammar chapters.

Most developmental students are nonreaders, and many ESL students are likely to fit into that category as well. Make up a list of books or bring old magazines from home. Encourage your ESL students to read the books or magazines and to write in their journals about what they've read. Explain that by reading in English they will learn vocabulary, sentence structure, and idioms.

Another problem that many nonnative speakers face is a lack of cultural background knowledge. Therefore, you may want to send ESL students to museums, parks, zoos, plays, community centers, hospitals, and the like to complete specific assignments and to report back to the class. In other words, they need 200 percent more exposure to the language and culture than other developmental students do. This is something that native speakers already have, and we as teachers often take for granted.

As you work with your ESL students, remember that just like all the special needs students in your class, they require a multisensory approach to learning. They also need an abundance of modeling to help them understand your expectations and to build their confidence and skills. You must be patient yet demanding, and you must be available to offer individual help if necessary. Although it may sometimes take many attempts before an ESL student understands a concept, if you are nurturing, your students will be motivated. As one instructor pointed out, this may be your student's first class, and his or her experience in the classroom with you and the other class members may determine whether this is his or her last class. Although working with ESL students (or any developmental students) can be trying at times, the rewards are limitless.

11

Assessing Student Writing and Progress

Revised by Karen Eisenhauer, *Brevard Community College*

Thoughtful evaluation is one of the most important services you offer as a teacher. Your evaluation begins the process of guiding your students, individually, to becoming better thinkers, more discerning judges, and better writers. This is where, as the saying goes, the rubber meets the road. But the task does not have to be painful for you or your students.

When we assess our students' writing, we meet them as individuals. Their writing difficulties may be commonplace or peculiar, but remedying those problems will usually require that we communicate to them as the unique individuals they are. We can recognize and comment on their particular strengths, and we can direct them to the most productive and important areas for improvement. This opportunity to have an individualized impact on each student in the class is an opportunity not offered in many other courses.

However, this "opportunity" can be a great deal of work. For your students, it is a risky undertaking, full of confidence-crushing danger. Fortunately, with some careful consideration of your objectives and thoughtful planning, you can avoid the pitfalls and make your course something that both you and your students look forward to.

Purpose and Philosophy of Assessment

There are two quick stories I would like to relate to you as we begin, incidents that helped me form my basic philosophy regarding the purpose and goal of assessing *any* work done by students. Both incidents occurred when I was a student teacher working

with Mrs. Dewey, a woman for whom I have vast respect: She is the teacher we all aspire to be.

Scene one: A student has not finished her exam during the allotted class period. She is concerned about not having finished and speaks to Mrs. Dewey as she is leaving class. Mrs. Dewey asks the student if she would like to come back during her lunch break to finish the exam. With profound gratitude, the student says that she will return. As she leaves the classroom, the rather naive intern (me) asks Mrs. Dewey if she is not concerned that the student will look up some of the answers to questions between now and lunchtime. Looking down her nose through her bifocals at the intern, Mrs. Dewey replies pithily, "Well, I should hope she would." Silence and chagrin are the response of the intern who suddenly realizes that learning, by whatever method, is the highest priority in this classroom.

Scene two: The intern is sitting in the large, open teachers' workroom when another English teacher comes in carrying an armload of cardboard posters, and plops them on her desk, complaining loudly, "Just look at these. I told the students to make a poster for their book report, and this is what I got." She holds up a plain white poster with three stick figures drawn on it in pencil, an effort that looks as if it were completed on the school bus this very morning. She demands to know, "How am I supposed to grade something like this?" The intern is again silent. She is embarrassed for the teacher standing in front of such disrespectful work. When the intern mentions the incident to Mrs. Dewey, she receives an acerbic response: "You get what you ask for. If you don't ask for much, you won't get much."

These incidents have become vital lessons for me:

- **THE BEST ASSESSMENTS EVALUATE *AND* TEACH.** Assessment, including exams, should not be only for the purpose of awarding grades. Evaluating student progress is useful, but the best assessments should be, primarily, another teaching tool, focusing on learning and improving. Students who care enough to ask for additional time to complete an exam, even though they may look up answers, can usually have a little extra time in my class. They learn more this way.

- **FOR QUALITY RESULTS, MAKE QUALITY ASSIGNMENTS.** Quality assignments are usually not made spontaneously. When students receive an assignment, they need to know what constitutes success. Therefore, you as the instructor must have defined beforehand, in concrete terms, the components of success. And you must share this information with your students.

Making the Assignment

If students are to be successful, they will need a road map, provided by you, on which the destination is clearly marked. This means that you must have a destination chosen ahead of time and be prepared to point out at least one potential route for reaching it. In practical terms, this means that you should plan your assessment strategy as you plan the assignment. And, when you give the assignment to your students, give them the basics of the assessment strategy at the same time.

Providing a road map for assignments does not mean you have to stifle creativity. There are usually many different routes to a single destination, and people will have different preferences for their journey. But regardless of the route, it is critical that everyone understand the destination.

Building assignments and assessments simultaneously requires that you determine which assessment method will work best with the assignment you have in mind. Some of the following considerations should help with these decisions:

- **KNOW WHAT YOU WILL BE LOOKING FOR AS YOU EVALUATE.** Establish the criteria for success and have these clear in your own mind as you build an assignment. It is also useful to have an idea of the relative importance of each criterion. Determine the basic components of a successful essay and make a list, ranking the list in order of importance.

- **ENSURE THAT STUDENTS CLEARLY UNDERSTAND YOUR RESPONSE TO THEIR WRITING.** If they do not understand, they will not be able to learn or improve and your efforts will be wasted. (Some strategies to help in this area are described later in this chapter.)

- **AVOID EXCESSIVE EVALUATION.** Providing too much feedback at once may cause students to become confused or to lose hope. Focus on the most important items first. If a paragraph contains a weak or inadequate topic sentence, what is the use of marking spelling errors?

- **STRESS THAT REVISION IS CRUCIAL TO IMPROVEMENT.** Make revision a normal and expected part of the routine. This will free you from having to mark everything on your first evaluation. For their first few assignments, I tell students that all papers will be revised until they are worthy of an A. (Portfolios are another strategy for dealing with the problems of too much evaluation and revision. Portfolio grading is discussed on p. 147.)

- **REMEMBER TO COMPLIMENT.** Students will work for compliments, and they will remember them longer than criticisms. They are likely to repeat behavior you praise, so make it a point to include a compliment or two.

- **MANAGE YOUR TIME.** Time management is crucial to *your* sanity. Determine what you will grade intensively, what you will check for completion, and what you will let students evaluate in class or on their own. It isn't necessary that every piece of work receive a score. Too many grades can also become overwhelming for students as well as for you.

- **PUT SUCCESS WITHIN STUDENTS' REACH.** If papers will be revised until they are worthy of an A, students will feel that success is possible and will have less incentive to cheat.

Communication Strategies

Helping Students Understand Your Evaluation

Have you ever watched a group of students, regardless of the course, as they receive newly graded papers? Even if the grade is on the front, they will immediately scan the rest of the paper for any written comments. Until they have read all comments, it is useless to try to get their attention. Comments are what students truly value in evaluation. Comments, both positive and negative, are what they will remember, and comments are your most powerful tool for guiding improvements. The following strategies may help:

- **BE CONSISTENT IN YOUR USE OF TERMS.** Will you be looking for a main point or a topic sentence? Do you talk about "run-ons" or "fused sentences"? It is usually best to use the same terminology as the text. If you vary from the text, provide students with a means to compare your terminology to that in their books.

- **DISTRIBUTE A CHART OF CORRECTION SYMBOLS.** Students need to know what the editor's marks on their papers mean. Include a sample of your handwriting on the chart so that they can see what your particular marks look like. *Real Essays* includes a chart of correction symbols in its back pages; you can photocopy it with your handwritten marks in the column titled "Your Instructor's Symbol."

- **READ A PAPER THROUGH BRIEFLY BEFORE MARKING IT.** This practice allows you to determine where you will focus your effort. You should not spend more time evaluating a paper than the student spent in writing it. If the paper lacks unity and coherence or has no main point, note these deficiencies and ignore the other problems until the next revision.

- **USE COLOR TO COMMUNICATE.** I use purple ink for content comments, green ink for grammar errors, red ink for grammar errors they really ought not to be making at this point, and a variety of highlighters for other necessary notes. Disorganized papers, for instance, may end up looking like a rainbow as I highlight each different idea and its companion sentences in different colors. Students soon get the idea that all the orange sentences should be grouped and not sprinkled throughout the paper. A colleague uses pink highlighter for "perfect"—a quick way to provide a compliment. While this may seem time consuming, if you can communicate effectively the first time, you will not have to repeat yourself on every subsequent paper.

- **CONFERENCE WITH STUDENTS BRIEFLY WHEN YOU HAND BACK THEIR PAPERS.** They will not understand everything you have marked, and will probably not ask what you mean, but if they have some individual time with you, they will ask questions. Organize classroom activity to allow for these miniconferences.

- **CONSIDER MAKING YOUR OWN RUBRIC FOR MARKING PAPERS.** Steps for building rubrics are discussed in detail later in this chapter.

- **PROVIDE PLANNING SHEETS TO BE FILLED IN AS A PREWRITING STRATEGY.** Collect these planning sheets and look them over. These are frequently helpful in spotting where a student is misunderstanding the writing process. You may also want your students to submit all stages of their writing: brainstorming, freewriting, initial drafts, peer-editing responses, and any additional drafts. This way, you can see where the student began and what thought processes he or she followed. In addition, when you are looking for positive comments, you can refer to the amount of work, the quality of revisions, or the evidence of development. (Note that forms for planning paragraphs are included in *Additional Resources to Accompany Real Essays*.)

- **DO NOT GRADE EVERYTHING.** You can require multiple drafts and only grade the final product. Initial drafts can be read for content only. Secondary drafts can be skimmed for content and organization. Mark grammatical, punctuation, and spelling errors in later drafts. This approach will emphasize writing as a process and will also avoid giving students too much to consider at once.

- **CONSIDER USING A COMPUTER.** For example, Microsoft Word has a comment feature, and *Comment*, a Web-based tool available with this book, makes commenting on papers quick and easy.

- **AND REMEMBER THAT SOME ASSIGNMENTS DO NOT REQUIRE GRADES.** Journals, drafts, and workshop materials may simply be checked.

Encouraging Revision

Because learning to write means learning to revise, consider allowing students who score below 70 to revise their assignments. It is also a good idea to put "Rewrite" or "Revise" on the paper rather than a grade. Some teachers promise students that they will grade only from the top, meaning they will score only the final version. A student who takes the time to revise an assignment using the instructor's comments will learn and improve his or her grade.

Other teachers believe that once they have read and marked an assignment, they have contributed too much to the assignment for the student to receive full credit. If you want to encourage students to revise on their own, without excessive editorial assistance from you, you could use a scale such as the one on page 141 to determine grades.

My policy has been to require developmental students to revise their first few papers until those papers are worthy of an A. I want them to know just how much work it will take to achieve that goal, and I also want them to know that they are capable of achieving it. With nondevelopmental students, I usually require rewrites for low-scoring papers on the first assignment. In this case, I want students to understand that I am willing and able to help them improve, and to also understand that I do not accept poorly written work.

Criteria for Evaluating Student Writing

As noted previously, you must establish the criteria for success and communicate these to your students. At a minimum, every successful paragraph or essay must have a main-point statement; support for the main point; unity; coherence; and standard forms of spelling, grammar, and punctuation. However, this is not a list students will initially understand. Instead, break this list down into concrete terms you can share with them. *Topic sentence,* for instance, may become *topic and main point about that topic.*

In many states, criteria have already been established for you by means of some standardized examination the students will take. If this is the case, obtain a copy of the criteria and base your own criteria on it. Another source to consider for criteria is your text.

Once you have your criteria listed, you will need to decide how you will determine whether the paper meets them. Two common methods of assessment are holistic scoring and analytic grading. In holistic scoring the grader bases the score on his or her impression of the overall quality of the paper. Numerical scores typically range from 1 to 4, or possibly from 1 to 6, but letter grades may also be used. In analytic scoring the grader analyzes and scores the components of the writing. Here the scores can be any sort of point value.

You may use any combination of scoring methods, depending on the assignment you have chosen and your purpose for assessing that assignment. Whichever method you choose, however, remember that it must successfully communicate to students the strengths and weaknesses of each particular work.

Whether you use holistic scoring, analytic scoring, or some other method, a checksheet or rubric of some sort is required in order to maintain consistency and objectivity in the grading process. In each of the sections that follow, a sample rubric is provided. However, the best rubric for you and your students will be one that you build yourself. Such a rubric will be the one you most thoroughly understand and will therefore use most effectively. It will also be far easier for you to explain the scoring process to your students when you are using your own instrument. The following sections present some common methods of holistic and analytic grading; after these, the chapter gives steps for building your own rubric.

Holistic Scoring

With holistic scoring, the grader reads through the student's work and appraises it as a whole according to a set of general criteria. The criteria address the quality of the essential elements of a paper: topic sentence or thesis, development, organization, logic, mechanics, and usage. A basic method of holistic scoring merely assigns an overall score of 1, 2, 3, or 4 according to the quality of these elements. There is a set of criteria for each possible score, and the grader matches the overall quality of the paper to one set of criteria to determine the score.

While holistic scoring is a tremendous time-saver for the teacher, to students it appears almost completely subjective unless they fully understand the criteria. Even if they do understand, the numerical score alone will not help them improve their writing. A further drawback is that it is difficult for one person to maintain consistency throughout a set of papers.

Holistic scoring is most often used by groups of teachers who get together to grade preliminary or end-of-semester placement paragraphs or essays from a whole set of classes. The teachers begin the scoring session by discussing the criteria and grading a set of control paragraphs or essays that represent the range of point values. The purpose is to have everyone apply the criteria in the same manner. Next, each paper to be scored is read by two graders, who must score them within a point of each other. If an essay receives more than a one-point separation, the paper is read by a third "master" grader. Many colleges report that this method of holistic scoring does provide a clear indication of students' abilities and that, amazingly, the scorers are seldom off by more than a point even when each grader cannot put aside his or her own writing priorities or prejudices.

If your school scores final paragraphs or essays holistically, it will be helpful to your students if you score some of their papers in this manner so that they will develop and understand what constitutes a passing paper. An easy way to manage this effort is to attach a copy of the criteria sheet to the paper and highlight each statement you feel applies to the paper. Some students may have one statement highlighted in each area.

The sample scoring guides on pages 137 and 139 illustrate two approaches to holistic scoring.

Sample Evaluation Guide—Holistic Scoring (Option 1)

A good paragraph or essay has an overall unity: a clear statement of purpose, and a continued focus on that purpose; a clear and semilogical progression of points and/or ideas with clear, semilogical, and specific development; and a sense of closure.

+ means excellent; *3* means adequate; – indicates weakness; *x* means not evident

_____ **Appropriateness:** Does the paragraph or essay adequately address the topic? Are the language and style appropriate to the audience stated in the prompt?

_____ **Unity/Focus:** Is a main idea or statement of purpose clear? Is a focus on that idea maintained throughout the sample?

_____ **Development:** Is the development appropriate to the topic and purpose? Is it adequately applied to a given point or idea? Is there enough of it?

_____ **Organization:** Is organization announced and adhered to, OR is it implied and then logically "unfolded" in some sort of order in the sample?

_____ **Sentence Structure:** *Overall:* Do the sentences effectively communicate an idea, or does grammar hold them back? *Specifically:* Do fragments, comma splices and run-ons, faulty parallelism, subject-verb agreement, pronoun reference (not number agreement), or dangling/misplaced modifiers seriously detract from the paper's quality?

_____ **Usage:** Are there errors in word choice, including homonym transposition (to/too/two, etc.), pronoun number agreement, errors in the use of negatives, ineffective repetition, or tense shifts?

_____ **Mechanical Conventions:** Are there problems with spelling, punctuation, or capitalization?

A graded paragraph or essay receives a score of 1 to 4; paragraphs or essays that score 3 or 4 pass; those that score 1 or 2 do not. Occasionally, a paragraph or essay will receive a 0.

0   The paper is not written in English, does not mention anything remotely close to the topic at least once, or is totally illegible.

1   The paper makes some reference to the topic but is weak in all areas.

2   The paper has weak organization (no logical flow) AND lacks adequate development. Grammar errors occur in almost every sentence, or there are two or more types of major errors that distract the reader.

3   The paper makes sense. It may start off weak but ends on a strong note (or vice versa). There may be some grammatical errors but no distracting ones.

4   The paper is well formed, has a clear focus, and has few errors.

Sample Evaluation Guide—Holistic Scoring (Option 2)

4 — Good to Excellent Paragraph or Essay
Organization and Development
- clearly established main idea
- good development with specific examples
- logical organization
- clear understanding of assignment

Sentence Structure
- sentence variety
- few major sentence errors

3 — Passing Paragraph or Essay
Organization and Development
- established central point (but weaker than a 4)
- attempt at organization and development
- adequate supporting details
- possible lapses in logic
- clear understanding of assignment

Sentence Structure
- attempts sentence variety
- weaker control over sentences than a 4

2 — Needs Remediation
Organization and Development
- unclear or misdirected central point
- some development but some irrelevant points
- few organizational skills
- assignment not fully addressed

Sentence Structure
- little or no sentence variety
- some problems with major sentence errors (fragments, run-ons, comma splices)

1 — Needs Remediation (perhaps ESL)
Organization and Development
- no discernible central point
- lack of development
- little if any connection to assignment

Sentence Structure
- seriously flawed
- numerous major sentence errors (fragments, run-ons, comma splices)

Analytic Grading

In analytic scoring, each criterion you have defined—for example, the presence of a topic sentence or thesis statement—is evaluated separately and converted to points. Totaling the points results in a percentage grade. Some instructors find comfort in the precision of numerical grades, while others shy away from such specificity.

When points are used, it is also necessary to determine how many points you wish to award for each item. Will an excellent topic sentence or thesis statement be worth 5 points and a poor one 2 points? Is an excellent topic sentence or thesis worth more points than the effective use of transitions? Taking the time to make these judgments may seem tedious, but it is a valuable exercise that will help you understand what you are actually doing as you evaluate.

Some teachers may be tempted to take off a certain number of points for each fragment or other serious errors, but unless you allow rewrites, you may want to avoid such an approach; think how demoralized a student would feel to receive a –50.

Marking points without explanations is also not an effective means of communicating with students. They will not understand, for instance, why their topic sentence or thesis statement is worth only 2 points while their neighbor's is worth 5. Comments should be included to help students understand the reasons for the score.

The following sections discuss percentage scoring and grid scoring, two common types of analytic grading.

PERCENTAGE SCORING. One popular analytic format is to divide the assignment into five elements and assign a percentage of the total points to each.

- Focus, with a clearly defined topic and relevant details (20%)

- Content that is well developed, with details and original ideas (25%)

- Organization that moves logically and smoothly from beginning to end (25%)

- Style that is appropriate for audience and topic (15%)

- Mechanics demonstrating an understanding of grammar, punctuation, and spelling rules (15%)

A second method looks like holistic grading but uses the criteria set to award percentages rather than whole numbers. The sample percentage scoring guide on page 143 illustrates this method of evaluation.

If you use percentage scoring and allow rewrites, you may wish to adopt a scale such as the following to encourage the best effort right from the start.

Grades on first effort:
90 – 100 = A
80 – 89 = B
70 – 79 = C
0 – 69 = R

(Rewrite)

Grades on second effort:
85 – 100 = B
70 – 84 = C
0 – 69 = R

(Rewrite)

Grades on third effort:
70 – 100 = C
0 – 69 = R

(Rewrite)

Although this scale assumes that students will be allowed to rewrite until they have produced at least a C paper, you may want to give a final grade below 70 if the student's work has not adequately improved by the third effort.

GRID SCORING. Some instructors avoid the problems of assigning grades by using a grid to analyze a piece of writing. Grids are simple checklists that divide the assignment into criteria and distinguish among "Strong," "OK," or "Weak." Grids have the advantage of being quick and nonpunitive. However, if you need to assign grades at the end of the semester rather than give a pass/fail indication, then you can convert the adjective to numbers. Grids may also not work for all assignments. Successful use of grids must also include comments explaining how or why the writing is strong or weak.

Although grids can be redesigned with each assignment, the sample on page 145 is a useful example.

Sample Evaluation Standard—Percentage Scoring

Grades on written work range from A to F and are based on content and form.

90–100   The **A** paper engages the reader's interest and shows strength in all areas of composition: clear, logical ideas; original thought; careful word choice and effective phrasing; no serious errors; and concentration on a main purpose, with strong development and support.

80–89   The **B** paper shows strength in most areas of composition: a clearly stated central purpose; logical and adequate development; and few serious or careless errors. Although showing competence, the B paper lacks the original thought and style that characterizes the A paper.

70–79   The **C** paper is a satisfactory composition with a worthwhile central idea. Although it may be organized clearly and logically, its paragraphs may not be as fully developed as those in the B paper. It avoids serious or careless errors in the use of English and may, in fact, have few correction marks on it, but it lacks the vigor and clarity of thought and expression to be considered above average.

60–69   The **D** paper indicates below-average achievement in expressing ideas correctly, sensibly, and effectively. Most D papers contain serious errors and fail to present a central idea or to develop it adequately. With more careful proofreading as well as fuller and more logical development, many D papers could receive a C.

Below 60   The **F** paper may have one or more of the following problems: serious errors in grammar, spelling, punctuation, and sentence structure; a missing or vague main idea; incomplete development or lack of specific support; failure to follow directions; or plagiarism.

SERIOUS ERRORS:

(1)   Inadequate statement of main idea
(2)   Inadequate or illogical paragraph development
(3)   Awkward sentence structure
(4)   Sentence fragments
(5)   Run-ons or comma splices
(6)   Lack of subject-verb or pronoun agreement
(7)   Problems with verb form or verb tense
(8)   Severe punctuation problems

Errors in any one of these categories can drop your paper one letter grade.
Errors in any two of these categories can drop your paper two letter grades.
Errors in any three of these categories can drop your paper three letter grades.

Sample Evaluation Standards—Grid Scoring

Example 1

	Strong	OK	Weak
Content, insights, thinking	———	———	———
Genuine revision: substantive changes—not just editing	———	———	———
Organization, structure, guiding the reader	———	———	———
Language: sentences, wording, voice	———	———	———
Mechanics: spelling, grammar, punctuation; proofreading	———	———	———
Overall impression	———	———	———

Example 2

	Outstanding	Satisfactory	Weak
Cover letter			
Thesis statements			
Topic sentences			
Supporting material			
Integration of reading and writing tasks			
Explanation and development			
Sentence style/complexity			
Grammar and mechanics			

Portfolios

A portfolio is a selective collection of a writer's work that is assembled for the purpose of assessment. One big advantage of using portfolios, according to Jack O'Keefe of Richard J. Daley College in Chicago, is that instructors can defer grading. Rather than grade each new paper with a number or letter grade, teachers can make comments on the papers and ask for revisions; students do not have to be afraid of a bad grade and negative input. Deferring grades may well encourage students to take more chances with their writing. After all, growth in writing fluency—perhaps the most important goal of the teacher—presumes an early abundance of errors. If the student is encouraged to be fluent, writing errors are simply part of the process—and, perhaps of even greater importance, are not held against the student.

Developmental writers are often afraid to write, afraid to make mistakes. If writing errors are not judged in a punitive way but are seen as a necessary part of becoming more fluent, students may improve their attitude toward writing and learn that communicating meaning, not avoiding error, is the goal of writing.

At some point in the semester, such as at midterm, the teacher can confer with each student and assign a grade to the portfolio for all papers written to that point. It is important to include in the portfolio the prewriting and earlier drafts, all showing evidence of the student's hard work and reminding him or her that writing is a process, not a one-time event. An individual teacher can use portfolios even if his or her department does not.

If you plan to incorporate portfolios into your curriculum, you should evaluate carefully the different forms this approach can take. Consider the following, keeping in mind the experiences of colleagues in your department who have used portfolios before and any requirements your department may have.

CONTENT. Identify the purpose of the portfolio. Do you want it to foster development, to demonstrate achievement, to show various ways of thinking/knowing/learning (quantitative or qualitative), or to encourage students to make connections among disciplines? Content varies, depending on the purpose of the portfolio. Often, it includes examples of various strategies and can include writings based on personal experiences, social issues, or readings. Students need to be aware of the content requirements from the beginning of the semester. Also, decide how much to include. For instance, you may not want to include any drafts, or you may ask for one assignment with all drafts, with complete annotations.

SELECTION. Decide who will determine the portfolio's contents: student, instructor, college. Will the selection be based on personal likes and dislikes, on established criteria, or on representative samples for certain categories?

REFLECTION. Reflection, a self-analysis of what the student has accomplished, can take various forms. You can require a table of contents, a letter of introduction, a reflective paragraph or essay on the entire semester, an annotation for each item, or a reflection on a single piece of work. Research shows that weak writers do better with a structured experience.

COMMUNICATION. Identify the criteria for success. Are you seeking evidence of connections made among disciplines, of the student's becoming more responsible for his or her own learning, or of the student's readiness for the next course? Clearly communicate the criteria to your students.

EVALUATION. Identify the means of assessment (letter of response, scoring guide, or dichotomous scale) as well as the approach (holistic or analytic). Although many colleges/instructors champion holistic grading, Peter Elbow recognizes a built-in problem with the approach. Because each student's portfolio is unique, the holistic grade may not work well. The grader is asked to compare all writers and their diverse selections on a single quantitative scale. For instance, how does one compare a strong narrative and a weak illustration paragraph with a strong illustration paragraph and a weak narrative? Granted, if all selections are strong or all are weak, graders can easily agree on "Excellent" or "Poor/Unsatisfactory" ratings, but the middle-range portfolios with the inconsistent paragraphs or essays prove the most challenging. However, if your only purpose is to determine which students can progress to the next level, which need to remain in remediation or enter remediation, or which will receive scholarships or awards, then holistic grading is efficient and fast.

For more information about teaching with portfolios, see Chapter 12, Using Writing Portfolios.

Self-Assessment

Find ways for students to participate in their own assessment. Not only does this foster active learning and a sense of responsibility, but it allows you to negotiate criteria for assessment that seem fair and relevant to everyone. Midway through the semester, and then again at the end, you may want to have students write a paragraph about what they have gained from the course so far and what they still want to master.

Consider letting students help establish the criteria by which they will be evaluated. At some point in the first week, have students form small groups and ask each group to brainstorm a list of course requirements, letting them know that whatever criteria the class as a whole comes up with will be used to evaluate them at the end of the semester. You may need to provide a few examples of what you mean (e.g., arrive on time, help others in the class, be creative), but let the lists be their own. Combine the lists and distribute the combined list to the entire class at the next class meeting, encouraging discussion of any criteria that seem unclear. Remind students that this list will be part of their final evaluation and that they will have to give themselves a grade. Throughout the semester, check in with individuals and the class to see how aware they are of the list and to ask whether anything should be changed. At the end of the semester, have students assign themselves a grade or a score based on how well they did; they can also write a one-paragraph description of how well they fulfilled the requirements.

You can also have students write self-evaluation paragraphs or essays at the end of the semester; this assignment often works well in combination with portfolios. Students should review any goals they set for themselves at the beginning of the course and look over their work for the entire semester. They can then comment on their worst piece of writing (why they think it's the worst, what about the process or the assignment made it turn out so poorly), their best piece of writing, their strengths and weaknesses as a writer, and what areas of their writing they intend to improve.

Building Your Own Rubric

A rubric that you design yourself can combine features from all the assessment methods listed above and become a valuable, personalized teaching tool. Essentially, it is a checklist for which you have determined which items will be evaluated, and how. A standard rubric allows students, through repeated exposure, to become thoroughly familiar with the qualities you expect to find in their papers, and to chart their progress over time. Students also tend to view this method as more objective than grading done without a rubric.

Building a rubric can be a valuable exercise for you because it forces you to list, in black and white, the exact criteria for success, and to then adhere to those criteria when grading. Having such a checklist is also helpful for maintaining focus on the selected criteria, thus keeping grading more consistent.

Sample rubrics have been included throughout this chapter, but building your own is a much better idea than copying one. It will be custom-made to suit your teaching style, it will contain your language and your values, and it should therefore be the best means you have for communicating your assessment methods to your students.

To build your own rubric, complete the following steps:

1. **LIST ALL ITEMS YOU WILL LOOK FOR WHEN GRADING.** This list should include all the basic parts of papers, such as a main-point statement, supporting points, development through details, and so on. It may also include other ideas you are emphasizing in class, such as use of transitions.

2. **PLACE CRITERIA IN THEIR ORDER OF IMPORTANCE.** My favorite rubric begins with the items "focused topic" and "main point."

3. **COMPARE YOUR LIST WITH ANY MANDATED RUBRICS.** If your state or school has mandated rubrics, make sure your students will be prepared for any required evaluations at this level.

4. **REVIEW THE SAMPLE RUBRIC IN THIS CHAPTER.** If there are any additional ideas you like in the sample, add them to your rubric.

5. **DETERMINE AN EVALUATION SCALE.** Decide how you will evaluate each item on your list. Is a simple "yes—it is present" or "no—it is not present" sufficient? Or do you want to indicate some sort of quality ranking?

6. **FORMAT YOUR LIST.** Put your criteria in a user-friendly format, maintaining the order of importance you determine in step 2. Include space for compliments and for specific suggestions for revision.

The sample rubric on page 149 is designed primarily for yes/no evaluation, with space to explain weak areas, if necessary. This rubric assumes that revision will occur several times. Points can be attached to each item, or the comments can stand alone with a grade of R being the grade of record until the paper is satisfactory.

Sample Custom Rubric

Grade for *first writing:* _____

Grade for *first revision:* _____

Grade for *second revision:* _____

Is the topic narrow or focused enough?

Is there a main point that can be *shown, explained, or proven?*

Are there supporting statements that *show, explain, or prove* the main point?

Are the connections between the supporting statements and the main point clear?

Do the supporting statements have enough details to make them convincing?

Is the information in the paper presented in a logical order?

Are there any detours in the paper?

Are there any sentence fragments?

Are there any run-ons or comma splices?

Are there any spelling errors or other word errors?

Congratulations for:

Suggestions for improving your paper:

Considerations for Statewide Standardized Tests

THEA

If you live in Texas, then you will need to consider the Texas Higher Education Assessment (THEA), formerly the Texas Academic Skills Program (TASP). It is offered as THEA Internet-Based Testing (IBT) or THEA Quick Test, which is taken on paper at designated sites. Students who are not eligible for an exemption or waiver may need to take the THEA before enrolling in Texas public colleges and universities.

The test has three sections: math, reading, and writing. The writing section has a multiple-choice portion and an essay portion. The former measures the student's ability to recognize purpose and audience; unity, focus, and development in writing; effective organization in writing; effective sentences; and edited American English usage. Students are asked to read several short essays and answer forty or so multiple-choice questions about word choice, organization, support, development, grammar, and sentence structure. The essay portion requires students to write an essay of three hundred to six hundred words on an assigned topic. The essay is graded holistically on its effectiveness in communicating a whole message to a specific audience for a specific purpose.

THEA essays are scored on a scale of 1 to 4 according to the following criteria: appropriateness, unity and focus, development, organization, sentence structure, usage, and mechanical conventions. Essays are scored by two readers who are trained and whose scoring is continually calibrated during the grading sessions. If readers are more than one point apart, then the essay is read a third time and the readers are evaluated to see if one is scoring too high or too low. Scores from both readers are added to give a final score of 2 to 8. If a student scores 4 or lower, the student does not pass the THEA and is often required to take developmental courses in order to remain in college. A student who scores 6 or better automatically passes the THEA and continues in regular college courses. If a student scores a 5, the objective test score is considered: Students who score at least 70 percent on the objective test pass the THEA, and those who score lower than 70 percent will need to take developmental courses. The essays of all students who do not pass the THEA are then analytically scored so that students know what areas they need to improve.

Some schools allow students who pass the THEA during a semester to receive automatic credit for the remedial course in which they are enrolled. Then, the students have the option of continuing to attend class or not returning for the remainder of the semester. A surprising number of students continue with the class to better prepare themselves for their credit courses.

Because the essay generally determines whether the student passes the THEA, your best approach to preparing students for the test is to emphasize the planning and organization of their essays. You might direct students to Chapter 9 of *Real Essays*. Of the seven criteria, four center on the organizational/content areas of the essay. Only three deal with grammar, usage, spelling, and punctuation. Therefore, even if students are weak spellers or don't know a comma from a semicolon, they still have an opportunity to pass the THEA if they can demonstrate an understanding of how to construct a persuasive essay.

To prepare students for the essay portion of the THEA, I would suggest that you begin the course with paragraph writing. A student who doesn't understand the concepts of topic sentence, specific and relevant support, and summary statement will not be able to write a passing essay. Because the basic structure of an essay is an exploded paragraph, students learn the basics (and teachers evaluate the writing) without the frustrations of hundreds of words and a multitude of sentences that don't blend smoothly. In fact, some instructors spend most of the semester on the paragraph and introduce the essay only during the final three weeks, yet the students have the concepts down so well that essays come more easily. I personally spend half the semester with grammar and paragraphs and don't begin the essay until midterm.

Give students plenty of practice writing THEA-style essays. Official THEA prompts briefly present two sides of an issue and then instruct the student to support one of the two sides in three hundred to six hundred words. Topics are such that students could use common knowledge and common sense to support their views. Any current event that has received media attention or any traditional controversy makes an excellent prompt for THEA practice. Sample topics might include uniforms for public school students, no pass/no play law for extracurricular activites, payment of student athletes, state-required placement tests, tax increases, or assisted suicide. Here are two sample prompts:

- When patients are in life-or-death situations, should they (or their family members) retain the right to make decisions about whether special measures should be taken to sustain life, or should doctors retain this right? Patients' rights advocates claim that an individual's right to choice does not cease when that person enters a hospital or becomes seriously ill. They believe that doctors and hospitals sometimes want to play God and don't necessarily understand a patient's will to live or wish for no extraordinary treatment measures. Those who believe that doctors should retain the right to decide a patient's treatment say that doctors—with their medical experience and knowledge of a patient's history—are in the best position to make this decision. They say that some families of seriously ill or injured patients give up too soon, while others hold on with false hopes. What is your opinion? Write a letter to the editorial editor of your local newspaper stating and defending your position with logical reasons and evidence.

• You are part of an advisory committee for your state board of education, which has been informed that the state is considering funding fully online schools. In these schools, instruction would take place entirely through the Internet, e-mail, and other online means. Proponents of the schools argue that they would allow better access to education to people living in rural areas, to those with extended or unusual work hours, and to working parents, among others. Opponents say that face-to-face interaction between students and teachers, and among students, is essential to socialization and learning; therefore, online schools would never offer a complete educational experience. In an essay to be read by your fellow committee members, discuss the advantages and/or disadvantages of the proposed online schools. Be sure to provide evidence for your choices.

For more information and a practice test, visit the THEA Web site at www.thea.ne5inc.com/.

PERT

BACKGROUND. From October 1982 to June 2009, students who were pursuing an A.A., B.A., or B.S. degree at a public college or university in Florida took the College-Level Academic Skills Test (CLAST), with sections in reading, math, and writing. CLAST was given to all college sophomores but is now no longer used. College Placement Test (CPT), an Accuplacer test, was also widely used as a placement tool and is still used at some schools in Florida. Most schools now use the new Postsecondary Education Readiness Test (PERT).

PERT'S USES, GOALS, AND PURPOSES. PERT comes in two forms. First is a placement test. Students will take this test if they do not have other tests scores, such as SAT or ACT scores, to show college readiness. One goal in developing the new test was to have a common definition of college readiness, so students and instructors (at both the high school and college levels) can be clear on what students are expected to know and be able to do upon reaching college. PERT, that is, has been carefully aligned to Florida's Postsecondary Readiness Competencies (PRCs).

Second, PERT is a diagnostic test. If students are placed into a college prep class, they will likely take the PERT diagnostic test, which is a fifty-question test designed to show which competencies they may have already mastered. Thus, the goal of many in Florida is to provide targeted remediation so that students can move through their prep courses more rapidly. Initially rolled out on a trial basis on October 25, 2010, tested throughout the spring and summer of 2011, and officially launched on August 10, 2011, PERT is a key part of the state's "redesign" initiative for higher education. In the new plan, underprepared students become college ready in a faster, more efficient manner so they can start taking their college-level courses as soon as possible. The hope is that accelerating the pace of students through developmental studies will decrease the number of students who become discouraged and drop out. PERT's diagnostics are thus calibrated to an important curriculum change: Two levels of developmental courses are now generally offered in reading, math, and writing, instead of the former three levels. A press release from Florida's Department of Education sums up the hopes for PERT: "New Placement Test Designed to Help Florida Increase College Graduation Rates."

The PERT placement tests will eventually be "computer-adaptive," meaning that the questions given to a test-taker depend on how he or she has done on prior questions.

To learn more (and for a study guide provided by McCann Associates, the developers of PERT), go to the Florida Department of Education's site at www.fldoe.org and type PERT in the site search box.

FLORIDA COLLEGE BASIC SKILLS EXIT TEST. At present, Florida no longer has a common required Basic Skills Exit Exam. Each college system—Miami Dade College, Broward, and so on—will choose its own exit exam. For exit exams, many college systems are having students take a multiple-choice objective test and write an essay, to be scored according to a holistic rubric.

Conclusion

As the previous sections indicate, multiple-choice writing and grammar questions are a standard feature of many standardized tests. To help students prepare for such tests, consider creating tests and quizzes from *Testing Tool Kit: A Writing and Grammar Test Bank* CD-ROM, available with *Real Essays*. A guide that correlates chapters in *Real Essays* with items in this test bank appears on the inside front cover of this book. No method of evaluation is perfect, primarily because no one method communicates to all students. Accept that regardless of the method you choose, personal communication, although time-consuming and labor-intensive, will always be best. Design evaluation to include a manageable mix of personal communication and standardized responses. Try to incorporate time for individual conferences—even two-minute ones—into your class schedule. Plan a group activity and pull students aside one at a time. Invite the writing tutor or perhaps a colleague to come to your class for half an hour to supervise the group work if possible. A calm and relatively stress-free instructor is a better instructor, always.

And regardless of your best-laid plans, inevitably a student, class, or situation will come along that just refuses to mold itself to your design. In that case, be flexible and be creative. One semester, for example, I had a class that would not function cohesively. There were too many distractors and too much bad chemistry. In order to salvage the situation, I put the entire class on individual study for the rest of the semester, providing packets of handouts and assignments to be completed. I didn't like it, but it was the best I could manage under the circumstances.

Assessing student writing is challenging. It is part skill, part art, but always a labor of love.

12

Using Writing Portfolios

Craig Kleinman, *City College of San Francisco*

What Is a Student Portfolio?

Portfolio keeping can greatly enhance learning and teaching as well as program assessment provided it is structured in a way that allows for reflection and communication. This is especially true in a developmental writing course, in which students with little or no experience writing academic essays need to embrace writing as a process and reading as an interactive event, and teachers need to see as much evidence of learning as possible. End-of-course process or learning portfolios enable teachers to help students recognize how much they have learned and grown as writers. Portfolio assessment offers teachers the opportunity to analyze the logic of course sequence and their understanding of students' course entry and exit skills, as well as the efficacy of writing and reading assignments designed for those courses.

But what exactly is a portfolio? A portfolio is a representative collection of a student's writing that "engage[s] students in a process of inquiry into what they have learned" while also "demonstrating the outcomes of learning" (Zubizaretta 28). Portfolios, provided they promote communication, process, and reflection, allow students to transcend the nuts and bolts of specific tasks and mechanical submission. When students develop an awareness and then a critical understanding of why they have been assigned specific tasks and why they are making specific choices during revision, what they learn will likely resonate with long-term meaning, especially when they can clearly convey the significance of what they have done. More and more colleges now use portfolios to determine upper division writing competency instead of an exam, and it is not unusual to find portfolios where a master's thesis may have been in the past.

Portfolios are also, of course, very much a part of the world outside the classroom. Photographers, contractors, musicians, dancers, architects, investors, designers, chefs, and a wide range of artists, administrators, and business professionals rely heavily upon portfolios to document and attract work. Teachers, as you may know all too well, are often required to maintain a teaching portfolio as part of tenure review, and many teachers may also create portfolios to (1) store successful or promising assignments, handouts, lesson plans, syllabi, and student work, (2) prepare for future job searches, and (3) share material with colleagues during curriculum development and assessment meetings. You might want to point out the "real-world" uses of the portfolio when you introduce the idea to your students at the beginning of the course.

Creating a Student Portfolio

Introducing Students to the Portfolio

When introducing the idea of a portfolio, ask if anybody in the class has put one together in the past. Some students will likely raise their hands, mentioning portfolios they've created in high school or other college courses. It's not unusual for students to say that they kept a poetry and prose portfolio or maybe a portfolio of designs or ads created in a graphics class. Ask them why their teachers required them to keep a portfolio. Likely they'll say, "To show what we could do." Not a bad answer, but ask them to go further.

- **Ask them how they decided which pieces to add.** Do not be surprised if many of the students say that they made no choices, that they just put everything from that semester or year into a folder. That, arguably, is not a portfolio; it is a sack, maybe even a dumpster. **Point out that selection process can make a crucial difference in the quality of the final portfolio.**

- **Ask them whether their view of the course, and what they accomplished in it, changed as they reviewed and evaluated their collection of work.** Discuss the benefits of selective revision and metacognition. A college composition course using a text such as *Real Writing* or *Real Essays* may be the first venue in which a student will be pushed into reflecting critically and examining *why*. Too often students do not have to think critically, and too often this is because they are so disconnected from the academic work required of them. So why not push them to examine the why's of their own rhetorical choices and discursive strategies?

- **Ask them what, in their opinion, are the advantages and disadvantages of a course that requires a portfolio, as opposed to a final exam.** It's likely that few students will actually prefer a final exam. Be sure to stress, however, that creating a portfolio is not less work than a final—it's a different (and for some of us, a more meaningful) way of measuring what was achieved over the course of a semester.

First Steps

REQUIRE STUDENTS FROM THE START OF THE SEMESTER TO MAINTAIN A WORKING FOLDER OF POTENTIAL PIECES FOR INCLUSION. Emphasize the fact that these pieces should show an evolution in the student's use of strategies, approach to a topic, or something similar—they should not simply be a collection of pieces that received the student's highest grades. Ideally, this will motivate students to think more about the revision process and what they should value in teacher feedback.

ESTABLISH A SCHEDULE OF STUDENT-TEACHER CONFERENCES. In working with students to create portfolios, periodic 20-minute conferences, or perhaps a longer conference with a small group of students, can be more productive than hours of written comments generated in isolation. Conferences can reinforce students' awareness of audience, not to mention showing students that teachers care about their portfolios and are invested in the process.

In their extremely helpful, practical, and thorough guide *Portfolio Teaching: A Guide for Instructors* (available free to users of any Bedford/St. Martin's text), Nedra Reynolds and Rich Rice suggest a series of conference questions that will push students to understand their choices and articulate how to show progress, independence, and creativity, for example:

- Which piece in the working folder deserves the most revision?

- Which piece did classmates enjoy the most?

- Which was the hardest task?

- Which piece makes the research process exciting?

- Which piece causes the most excitement over writing and revising?

- Are there still any unclear assignment requirements?

- How might the portfolio be organized?

- What do you hope will happen?

- Where are the opportunities in the portfolio to make those hopes a reality? (29).

What Should Go into a Portfolio?

As the teacher, you should direct what goes into your students' portfolios, according to the goals of your course. What are your priorities: development of strong paragraphs? Argumentation based on a consistent issue or theme? Mastery of rhetorical modes? Be sure to make students aware of what it is you want them to achieve in the course, and let them know that you will be measuring the portfolio by those standards.

Reynolds and Rice encourage teachers to allow variety in a portfolio's contents, since students have different strengths, are just beginning to explore those differences, and need practice making and presenting informed choices. If the primary text for a course is organized rhetorically, like *Real Essays,* then variety might come through in the different methods of development emphasized in the portfolio essays. However, variety can apply to such things as length, genre, and stages in the writing process. Evaluating such portfolios may be more challenging than if all students' contents were to match tightly drawn archetypes, but this variety can offer "a more complete picture of the student's writing competence" (8).

In a writing course in which five or six pieces of writing are graded, perhaps only two or three of those pieces would typically be included in the portfolio. Teachers who place a strong emphasis on active reading and the integration of reading and writing might also ask students to include one or two annotated assigned readings. Some teachers may want to see some grammar exercises, especially if the student can point out a connection between the work done in grammar and the work done in the essays. Other teachers may encourage students to include writing and images not created for the class but that nevertheless connect in significant ways to the work done in the writing class. What is important is that students learn how to evaluate and select pieces of their work that represent *a meaningful, representative collection.*

Unless a teacher wants only to see "best" work or most recent revisions, then drafts should be represented in the portfolio to validate and document the learning process: for example, marked or graded versions of the essays, plus outlines, drafts, brainstorms, freewrites, reading response sheets, and peer review sheets. If a teacher relies heavily on, say, weekly vignettes or brief write-to-learn pieces to sustain student engagement, then students should have the option to include some of these pieces in their portfolios. Teachers who have pushed students to write in a wide range of styles and situations would likely encourage variety in the portfolio.

Students should also compose a cover letter that discusses the evolution of their writing process across the semester. (See p. 157 for more on the cover letter, its importance, and possibilities.)

Types of Portfolios

Portfolios can take various forms, again depending on what you, the teacher, want to see. Two common forms are the process, or *learning portfolio,* which emphasizes process and a wide variety of evidence of learning, and a *best-works portfolio,* which emphasizes polished revision. And, of course, there are paper, electronic, and Web-based portfolios.

The presentation of the content will depend on the medium. *Paper portfolios* can take a variety of forms. The portfolio might be organized by assignment, with each assignment presented in a cluster together with its drafts and feedback, or as a "narrative," with a cover letter introducing the semester's work from the earliest to the latest days. Some teachers and students prefer a paper presentation for its "archival" qualities—for many, handwriting in particular adds to the personality of the portfolio and provides a clearer sense of its creator.

Electronic portfolios (or e-portfolios) that rely on programs such as Word or PowerPoint offer a practicality and efficiency that may be more appealing to some. Scans of marked work could be introduced or even hot-linked to specific passages for quick reference. If technological literacy has been stressed throughout the course, then an electronic portfolio may be the way to go. An idea-mapping program such as Inspiration can offer creative ways to plan and visualize the presentation.

Web-based (or online) portfolios can offer everything that the aforementioned electronic portfolio can provide, but even more possibilities exist for hyperlinks and wider-world context. Helping students acquire the skills to produce a strong online presence—while becoming better writers, readers, and critical thinkers—could have incredible long-term effects, especially in our media-driven culture. An online course management program such as *WritingClass* (Bedford/St. Martin's), which includes blogs and peer review tools, lends itself quite nicely to a course integrating online portfolios. Keep in mind, though, that necessary Web-tech skills might prove a barrier for some students, server space needs to be secured, and students, if they are not intimidated by Web creation, can sometimes be tempted to spend more time playing with, say, background colors, images, and hyperlinks, than actually revising their essays.

Guiding Student Reflection

Reflecting on Individual Pieces

It is essential that teachers promote critical reflection, for this enables students to articulate what, how, when, and why they are learning. Accordingly, as Reynolds and Rice point out, a portfolio is most effective when students "are invited to collect, select, and reflect on artifacts . . . that best represent their experience and engagement with the learning process" (2). Without reflection, the acts of collection and selection lose meaning, and the portfolio loses shape and rhythm, sagging, as Langston Hughes might say, "like a heavy load" back into undifferentiated storage status.

To help students reflect on individual pieces, you will need to provide guiding questions that correspond with the goals and outcomes listed in your syllabus. In my course, I gave students the following short list of questions to ask themselves after they revised a draft and as they reflected on pieces of writing for inclusion in their portfolios:

QUESTIONS FOR REFLECTING ON A PIECE OF WRITING

- How did my main point (or how I wrote my main point) change?

- What was changed in the introduction? Why was it changed?

- What additional support was needed, and where? Why?

- What additional research was required?

- What is my strongest point or example? How did that change from the draft? Why is it better?

- What was the weakest part of my draft?

- What corrections to grammar, punctuation, and mechanics were necessary? Are these errors I routinely make? How can I improve in these areas?

- Why is the revision better, and why do I care about that?

- What have I learned about writing and revision?

Questions you would use for the same purpose may be very different, depending on your own course goals and the goals of the particular assignment.

The Cover Letter: Reflective Introduction

The portfolio component that will most clearly synthesize reading, writing, and thinking is the cover letter, sometimes called a reflective introduction. Many teachers, in fact, consider the cover letter the most important document in the portfolio.

Cover letters give portfolio keepers a clear chance to appeal to readers (logos, pathos, ethos), to provide "insider" or "behind-the-scenes" details, and to promote the portfolio's strengths. Some portfolio writers use the cover letter to articulate areas of confusion and goals for future writing and reading. This informs readers that a writer who, for example, has struggled with fused sentences is aware of the struggle, making the error less of a distraction and more of a means of understanding that student's ongoing learning process.

Cover letters, like essays and portfolios, can vary in form, depending on a teacher's guidelines. Length can vary, but many instructors agree that the number of cover letter pages should roughly equal the number of essays or main pieces featured. That is, a three-page cover letter should provide enough room for students to comment on three main pieces or assignments and to demonstrate self-assessment.

The letter should contain focused, well-structured paragraphs and should point to specific examples from the essays, identified by title, that back the claims the writer makes about his or her progress over the course of the semester. Many cover letters are organized around the pieces of writing included or around course or personal goals. Many effective cover letters also include the following:

- Global and local, or higher-order and lower-order, changes that a student wants readers to notice

- What the portfolio illustrates about the student as writer, reader, and critical thinker

- The struggles the student encountered and what he or she did to overcome them

- Any patterns the student recognizes in his or her learning and writing processes

- Description of specific help given by a writing tutor, a classmate, or the teacher

- A revelatory moment during the course (an "aha!" moment)

- Future writing and reading goals

Note: Students may want to use the cover letter to praise the teacher and the class, and that is fine, if the claims are sincere and are supported with specific reasons and examples. You might want to advise students that overblown praise or claims will come off as insincere, holding back a careful reader or evaluator from embracing the remaining elements of the portfolio. Students may need to be told that the cover letter should not be used to "butter up" a teacher or, say, to appeal for an A.

Two sample portfolio assignments follow: the first used by me in one of my courses at the City College of San Francisco, and the second used by Jim Rice of Quinsigamond Community College. In the second assignment, note that, instead of a cover letter, students are required to write reflective essays on three topics:

1. How you write

2. How you use introductions and conclusions

3. How you would assess your best piece of writing

Sample Portfolio Assignment 1

Your final assignment of the semester is to create a portfolio. It is worth 40 percent of your grade. This is your opportunity to show how much you have learned during the semester. You will need to present your portfolio in a secure binder or folder that allows readers to fully appreciate your revision process.

Your Cover Letter

The cover letter, which should be 2–3 pages long (double-spaced), is your final self-assessment. It is your chance to show that you are fully aware of what you are capable of as a writer. Your cover letter should contain several well-focused and well-structured paragraphs, just like an essay. You might conclude your letter with remarks about your goals for continuing to develop your writing skills as you move through future college courses.

In your cover letter, you *must* do the following:

- Identify each of your portfolio's three essays by title.

- Demonstrate self-assessment; show that you are aware of yourself as a writer.

- Point to specific examples from the essays that prove your assertions about your writing.

You should also do *3 or 4* of the following things:

- Explain the revisions you made and the changes you want readers to notice.

- Demonstrate what this portfolio illustrates about you as a writer or critical thinker.

- Acknowledge your weaknesses while showing how you have worked to overcome them.

- Reflect on what you've learned about writing and reading.

- Discuss your strategies for writing and revising.

- Detail the process by which you solved a writing problem.

- Explain any patterns you see in your writing.

Your Essays

You must include three essays, one of which is an argument about [the last topic/issue of the term], and the other two of which are thoroughly revised essays written earlier in the semester. You may choose the order of the essays that you include, but you should explain the logic of that order in your cover letter.

One new essay:

Your final draft of the last essay of the semester will be included in the portfolio. You will not yet have received a grade on this paper. This is your chance to prove how well you can write without as much help from a teacher.

Two thoroughly revised essays written previously for this class:

Pick two of the essays you have done so far in the semester and revise them thoroughly. Part of the evaluation will be based on how thoroughly you have revised these essays, so don't just make a few little changes and call it done. Sincerely apply what you have learned about revision this semester.

After each essay, you must include the supplementary material that you produced to create that essay:

- Brainstorming sheets
- Outlines
- Ungraded drafts
- Graded versions

It is important for you to include this material since the process you went through to write these papers is extremely important.

Sample Portfolio Assignment 2

The Portfolio's Content

In keeping with the philosophy of portfolio writing, you will write three pieces dealing with three aspects of writing:

- How you write
- How you use introductions and conclusions
- How you would assess your best piece of writing

How You Write

Attach an example of your writing that demonstrates the entire process you use to write a paper.

The supporting materials should include all the work you have done to complete one essay. This may include brainstorming, prewriting, drafting, notes for each revision, peer review, conferences, and the final graded paper.

Your self-assessment should demonstrate your understanding that writing is a process which requires drafting, rewriting, editing, and revision. Write about each of the following categories:

- Clearly explain each step you take when writing an essay—from generating the idea and supporting details, through each stage of drafting, up to completion of the final paper.
- Which one part of this process did you find most valuable? Why?
- Quoting from any of your drafts and any notes you may have, show where you made significant changes as your essay developed. Explain why you made those changes and how they improved the essay. Be sure to point out the significant changes, not superficial changes in spelling and grammar.

Introductions and Conclusions

Take two essays you have written and compare and contrast the introductions and conclusions. Name the type of introduction and compare and/or contrast it with a second selection. Comment on the quality of the introduction, thesis, unity, and support of the introduction. Do the same with the conclusions. Use the attached list for the naming process.

Assess Your Best Piece of Writing

Attach the piece of writing you have done this semester which you consider to be your best work to date. Write persuasively to demonstrate why this sample is your best.

Write about both of the following categories:
- Identify three components of good writing. Explain why any piece of writing must have these components to ensure reader interest.
- Quoting examples from your work, demonstrate how your best work meets the criteria previously identified. Explain how your examples achieve what you say they do.

This brief essay should have the following:

- Accurate spelling

- Correct grammar

- Sentence variety

- Proper word usage

- An effective introduction and conclusion

- Thesis

- Paragraphs that have a clear topic sentence, keep to the topic, and progress in a logical order

Assessing the Portfolio

Putting together a successful portfolio takes time and effort: Students need to work hard both writing and critically reflecting on their writing, and you need to provide class time and careful, clear guidance on every step of the process. Assessment is the end game of the long, difficult, but hopefully rewarding process—an attempt to evaluate how successfully both you and your students have done your jobs. Portfolio teaching does not make assessment easier, but it doesn't make it harder either. Rather, portfolio assessment shifts some of the politics and responsibility of the process. Ultimately, a teacher's guidance is still at the core of the process, but the student has more control over the final product that's assessed. So what kind(s) of assessment work best with portfolios?

Holistic Evaluation

Provided that teachers have put the necessary amount of time throughout the semester into helping students become more critical writers and reflective learners, then they need not comment in detail when student work is presented in their final portfolios. This justifies a portfolio being evaluated *holistically*, despite its being composed of a number of pieces. While it's wonderful at the end of the semester to not annotate in detail or produce substantive comments, it's more wonderful to simply read the portfolios—to become a reader again—and absorb what students have (and have not) learned and what has happened in the class.

Make no mistake: Holistic evaluation is not simply grading from the gut. It requires consistency with the expectations established in the ongoing assessment of student work during the semester and a clear understanding of what was required in the portfolio. Have you clearly guided your students to build upon their reading assignments when composing their essays? Have you set up clear diction-, sentence- and paragraph-level expectations that enable students to put their exercises into practice in their essays? Then look for evidence of those things in their portfolios. Years of experience in evaluation certainly help, as do conversations with colleagues. (The latter will, of course, be much more formal if portfolio assessment is a departmental requirement or if colleagues assess one another's students' portfolios.)

But how much reflection is enough? Should more have been revised? How can improvement be accurately graded? Well, final evaluation is never simple, but Reynolds and Rice offer three helpful questions to consider when developing a grading guide:

- Do the reflective elements provide reasons for students' choices and identify the changes they have made to essays or projects in preparing the portfolio?

- Are the entries focused, developed, and organized, or do they reflect the qualities of good writing your course has emphasized?

- Is the arrangement and/or navigation scheme effective? (49)

Students should be aware of how important the cover letter will be in your assessment of the whole portfolio. A weak or strong cover letter can be a great illustration of what students have learned in the course. Letters that do not demonstrate metacognition and do not provide specific details, for example, can seriously detract from the strength of a portfolio, even if the essays themselves are quite strong. And letters that take a fresh approach, resisting formula by way of an intriguing metaphor or engaging anecdote, can strengthen the portfolio as a whole. For this reason, you should establish clear guidelines for what you expect in terms of the cover letter's content and style early in the semester.

Remember, though, the key is to look at the whole package. Overall, is the portfolio outstanding, satisfactory, or weak? Do not agonize over a single entry in the portfolio.

This basic rubric (opposite) could help with a holistic assessment of metacognition and writing.

The Question of Grades

For some students and teachers, grading works against learning. For them, grading is, as Erika Lindemann explains in *A Rhetoric for Writing Teachers,* a "destructive judgment valorizing product over process" (220). Many teachers who actually enjoy assessing and commenting on a student's paper resent evaluating it with a letter or number grade (even a high one).

Several legitimate questions arise in discussion of grading the work students do throughout the semester:

- Do grades distract learners from absorbing assessment or motivate them to absorb more?

- Will grades distort a student's selection process when picking pieces to revise for the portfolio (e.g., Why should I pick a paper that already received an A? Or, I'm not touching that D paper again.), or do grades provide a clearer understanding of what needs to be done?

If grades must be given to individual assignments, according to department requirements, or if a teacher simply wants to give grades, they can be useful—or at least used—when they do not undermine the benefits of process and reflection. In the context of the entire semester's work, most instructors make the finished portfolio count for the most significant percentage of the course grade. Writing submitted earlier in the semester typically carries a significantly lower percentage, because, in the view of most instructors who use portfolios, writers should be evaluated primarily on how their learning has added up during the course, not on their performance at the start of the course. In my opinion, some writing, for example write-to-learn pieces, should probably never be graded, only commented on. Grades or no grades during the semester, teachers must give students a chance to reflect and learn . . . and reflect again. Portfolios promote this practice.

In the end, whatever assessment methods you choose, you will most likely come to understand why so many of your colleagues are advocates of using portfolios in the writing classroom. After a semester of close work with your students, you will see their learning represented quite clearly in their portfolios. More important, so will they.

Works Cited

Lindemann, Erika. *A Rhetoric for Writing Teachers.* 3rd ed. New York: Oxford UP, 1995. Print.

Reynolds, Nedra, and Rich Rice. *Portfolio Teaching: A Guide for Instructors.* 2nd ed. Boston: Bedford/ St. Martin's, 2006. Print.

Zubizarreta, John. *The Learning Portfolio: Reflective Practice for Improving Student Learning.* Bolton: Anker, 2004. Print.

13

Surviving and Growing as a Professional

Developmental English has been a stepchild course in many institutions. However, with the advent of programs such as the THEA in Texas, the New Jersey College Basics Skills Placement Test (NJCB-SPT), and the PERT in Florida, more schools are having to put more effort into and focus more attention on their developmental courses. Unfortunately, many faculty members have neither the training nor the desire to teach students at this level, causing friction within departments. Furthermore, administrative concerns over performance-based funding and student retention can add to faculty frustrations. As teachers of developmental writers, however, we must stand up for their rights as learners. We must also work continually to establish ourselves as respected professionals. Following are (1) an overview of some of the sources of professional and institutional pressure you may encounter on your campus and (2) ideas for managing them. No matter what type of pressure you may feel from your institution, develop a cohesive group within your program and meet each issue with a united front. However, remember that change occurs slowly. Find a couple of colleagues who are committed to improving the developmental writing program, and work together to propose changes.

Admission and Credit Policies

If you are at a community college, your institution probably has an open-door policy. Even though such a policy should guarantee the survival of remediation, that remediation can take various forms. Some experts argue for separate courses that isolate those who need basic skills review or training; other experts push for mainstreaming, which either forces students to learn (or struggle or fail) on their own or requires attendance in a workshop or writing lab.

You can find research to back up either approach, so don't think that you must prefer one method or the other. The only true success is that which works at a particular time for a particular student. Those successes will vary from semester to semester, from student to student, and from teacher to teacher. (In fact, if your school requires a common syllabus, make sure that your administration realizes that no matter what the document, it will be interpreted differently by each and every teacher; therefore, even the best-planned ideas will not be carried out uniformly.) Regardless of the form, however, data support the positive effect of developmental programs on both retention and academic performance of entering college students who exhibit deficient skills.

Many experts believe that an ideal class size for developmental courses is around fifteen students. However, few of us are fortunate to teach in a school where this is possible. A more realistic class size to meet administrative approval will be probably around twenty-five. If you find yourself in a seemingly impossible situation, resolve to do the best you can. For instance, if you have, as one teacher did, a total of two hundred students with one section of fifty-four, your main priority will need to be personal survival. One solution is to mark the first couple of papers meticulously. For all other assignments, check only for surface errors and comment only on content and style. If you have access to a writing center, send students there for individual assistance and guidance. For error-filled papers, stop marking surface errors at a certain point. Indicate on the paper where you stopped marking and tell the student what to do next. (For other practical tips on grading papers, see Chapter 11 of this manual.)

A recent trend has relegated developmental courses to the noncredit realm. Therefore, many students do not feel a sense of obligation to a course that counts neither toward nor against their grade point average, nor toward their degree plans. If work in one class must suffer, it will probably be work for your developmental writing class. If students have a test in a credit class, they may decide to skip your class. When they can receive even "elective" credit, they take the course more seriously. Because that is not a possibility in many states, teachers must try to make students realize the personal benefits of remaining in and fully participating in developmental courses. You can offer success stories or testimonials from former students, mention colleagues who prefer students who have successfully completed developmental courses over those straight out of high school, or remind them that the skills they will learn in your course will help them make higher grades in their credit classes without as much effort on their part.

Teaching Assignments

One of the best-kept secrets in academia is the personal satisfaction instructors receive from teaching developmental writers. Because they don't recognize this benefit, many full-time English instructors try to avoid teaching developmental writing classes. Therefore, many departments rely heavily on adjunct instructors and instructors borrowed from other areas, assuming that anyone with a degree can teach a developmental writing class. (Too often, faculty from other disciplines are assigned these courses when enrollment is down in their areas.) In fact, developmental writing students deserve the best and most committed teachers. They need someone who is dedicated and willing to devote lots of energy to helping them learn. Seek out the best teachers and convince them that their skills are needed in the developmental writing classroom. But remember that even some of the best teachers will need training (forums, workshops) in teaching a second dialect or language.

A report about the former Texas Academic Skills Program (TASP)—now THEA—revealed that the quality of developmental education was below professional standards because the majority of teachers in developmental programs lack formal or even informal training in handling these classes effectively. Therefore, they could not implement the most current techniques for teaching underprepared students. (The report also found that faculty in two-year colleges were more likely than faculty in four-year colleges to consider developmental

instruction their profession, and that support staff in writing centers, whether in community colleges or universities, generally have a more professional attitude toward developmental education than do members of the faculty.) One solution to this lack of professionalism and training is to encourage attendance at conferences, workshops, and seminars. Perhaps you can even get your administration to fund a guest speaker who will offer advice on reaching the underprepared student. Numerous publications, books, journal articles, and conferences are available to help you become more familiar with developmental writing and thus a better teacher of it. See the bibliography at the end of this chapter for some suggestions.

A different problem can arise when developmental courses are grouped into a separate department away from the college's parallel courses. When placed in their own department, developmental instructors often feel marginalized or segregated from other colleagues because they aren't allowed to teach other levels of students. Although this type of arrangement helps the instructor concentrate his or her energies on the developmental writer, it may lead to discouragement. In addition, someone who teaches only developmental courses can lose sight of exceptional writing. We sometimes become excited if we get a paragraph without a major sentence error and forget that style and content are just as important. To maintain perspective, join in departmental and college activities—both professional development and social. Merely having lunch with other instructors can help you refocus on standard communication skills.

If your developmental courses are part of the English department, ask for class assignments that will balance your lower-level courses. For instance, although I did so for years, many of us prefer not to teach first-semester Freshman Composition while also teaching developmental English. By skipping to at least second-semester courses, you have gained a level of proficiency among the students and given yourself a break from the lower levels. In addition, such skipping can prevent developmental students from following you into their Freshman Composition classes just because they feel comfortable with you personally. You may discover that you need a break not only from the courses but also from the same students. You could ask for a rotating schedule in which you teach the developmental course every other semester.

If developmental courses are in a separate department, check with the administrators in charge to see if you can teach in both areas. Work closely with both departments; perhaps you could write a proposal suggesting that the two areas be combined or that instructors be allowed to teach in both areas. Point out that both programs will benefit from shared knowledge of students and that the developmental students will receive better preparation for Freshman Composition and upper-level courses when everyone is working together for the students' best interests.

New adjunct instructors often find themselves in the developmental classroom if full-time teachers don't want to teach the course. If this is your situation, seek out a full-time person to serve as your mentor or guide. Ask questions, and check on departmental guidelines, handouts, and requirements. Exchange information about your classes and your students. You will probably discover that teachers of developmental writing want to share their successes as well as their frustrations. Also, see Chapter 2, Tips for New Instructors, for specific suggestions.

Retention

All good instructors have one major characteristic in common: the desire for all students to succeed. They want students to want to come to class, to enjoy learning, and to leave their classes prepared for other college courses. However, you cannot assume total responsibility for your students' successes or failures. You can make your class as interesting and as relevant as possible; you can offer every student your concern and encouragement, but you cannot make your students attend class or do their homework, and you cannot solve all the personal problems that interfere with their attendance. With declining budgets, administrators often want larger class sizes and seek to hold teachers responsible for students who drop the course. Given the types of students who enroll in developmental courses, some instructors feel a tremendous amount of pressure and a great deal of frustration.

You must remember, and try to get your administration to realize, that open-door students often come to college with health problems, lack of adequate child care, unreliable or nonexistent transportation, inadequate educational backgrounds, and financial problems. And these situations don't disappear just because a student enrolls in college. He or she will continue to have economic, family, and social pressures. Students may enroll in a Monday, Wednesday, Friday class even when they know they don't have a ride to school on Wednesdays. Young students may be under pressure from parents to

hold down jobs and earn high grades in college although they never succeeded in high school. In addition, because of their youth, some students are easily swayed by peers to cut class or stay out late. Older students face other difficulties: They have to work overtime, their children's schools take a holiday, or their children get sick and no babysitter is available.

Retention is not just a classroom issue for the instructor. The entire college must become involved. One of the best retention strategies is an orientation. Students need an orientation to the institution, to classes, and to the idea of assessment and placement; they also need to develop a sense of community. Orientation sessions can provide all of that. If your college has an orientation session, find out what kinds of topics are included. If there is no orientation session, propose that the college start offering one. It's amazing that most universities, despite their high standards for admission, provide a week-long orientation for entering students (even longer for foreign students), yet many community colleges, with their open-door policies, don't even hold a single, two-hour session. Orientation should provide reality checks for students. They need information on how to study, read textbooks, take notes, find the support they need, talk with an instructor, and work in groups. Colleges could even use upper-level students to conduct the orientations, an excellent way of helping students meet one another and making the orientation even more meaningful.

Resources for Developmental Professionals

As I mentioned earlier in this chapter, the majority of developmental instructors are not trained to teach developmental courses. Even if you don't have formal training, you can teach yourself (become an active learner) by reading publications in the field and corresponding with others who teach developmental courses. Also, find the money and the time to attend conferences sponsored by professional organizations. Besides the obvious benefits of hearing speakers and obtaining handouts to take back to your own classroom, you can expand your circle of colleagues and learn even more outside the formal sessions. The personal and professional benefits are worth the money, even if you have to pay for the trip (in whole or in part) yourself. In fact, you may get more out of the conference if you are paying the bills.

Too often, developmental instructors fail to take advantage of the resources for professional growth that are available to them. This is hardly surprising, given the institutional pressures described in this chapter, but it creates a vicious circle: If our teaching situations make it impossible for us to connect with other members of our profession—whether by reading what they have said or by meeting up with them at conferences—we miss out on opportunities to improve those very situations.

The following is a brief list of resources you can use to maintain contact with current thinking by other writing instructors. In addition, please get yourself a copy of *Background Readings,* a thoroughly useful collection of professional articles on developmental education compiled by Susan Naomi Bernstein and offered free of charge to all users of *Real Essays.*

Professional Organizations

College Reading and Learning Association (CRLA)
The CRLA is a group of student-oriented professionals active in the fields of reading, learning assistance, developmental education, and tutorial services at the college/adult level. Membership information can be obtained at the Web site: **www .crla.net**. (See also Publications.)

Conference on Basic Writing (CBW)
With a mission to create a network of developmental writing professionals, CBW encourages conversations on pedagogy, curriculum, administration, and social issues affecting developmental writing. Contact the membership Web site at **orgs.tamu -commerce.edu/cbw/membership.html**. (See also Listserv.)

National Association for Developmental Education (NADE)
NADE seeks to improve the theory and practice of developmental education in postsecondary education, the professional capabilities of developmental educators, and the design of programs to prepare developmental educators. For more information, contact **www.nade.net**.

National Council of Teachers of English (NCTE)
This organization of sixty thousand members is devoted to the improvement of the teaching of English and the language arts at all levels of education. To learn more, check the NCTE Web site: **www .ncte.org/**.

Teachers of English to Speakers of Other Languages (TESOL)
With a membership of twelve thousand from more than one hundred countries, TESOL seeks to develop expertise and foster communication among teachers teaching English in diverse settings. Search the TESOL Web site: **www.tesol.org/**.

Books

Bates, Linda, Janet Lane, and Ellen Lange. *Writing Clearly: Responding to ESL Compositions.* Boston: Heinle & Heinle, 1993. Print.

Chaffee, John, and Roberta Wright. *Instructor's Resource Manual: Thinking Critically.* 3rd ed. Boston: Houghton, 1991. Print.

Enos, Theresa. *A Sourcebook for Basic Writing Teachers.* New York: McGraw-Hill, 1987. Print.

Gray-Rosendale, Laura. *Rethinking Basic Writing.* Mahwah: Erlbaum, 2000. Print.

Halasek, Kay, and Nels P. Highberg. *Landmark Essays on Basic Writing.* Mahwah: Erlbaum, 2001. Print.

Harklau, Linda, Kay M. Losey, and Meryl Siegal, eds. *Generation 1.5 Meets College Composition: Issues in the Teaching of Writing to U.S.-Educated Learners of ESL.* Mahwah: Erlbaum, 1999. Print.

Kells, Michelle Hall, and Valerie Balester. *Attending to the Margins: Writing, Researching, and Teaching on the Front Lines.* Portsmouth: Boynton/ Cook, 1999. Print.

McNenny, Gerri, and Sallyanne H. Fitzgerald, eds. *Mainstreaming Basic Writers: Politics and Pedagogies of Access.* Mahwah: Erlbaum, 2001. Print.

Rose, Mike. *Lives on the Boundary: A Moving Account of the Struggles and Achievements of America's Educationally Underprepared.* New York: Penguin, 1989. Print.

Shaughnessy, Mina P. *Errors and Expectations: A Guide for the Teaching of Basic Writing.* New York: Oxford UP, 1977. Print.

Publications

College Composition and Communication. 4 issues/ year; addresses the concerns of writing specialists, researchers, and teachers of college-level composition courses, through articles on theory, practice, and teaching of composition. NCTE, 1111 West Kenyon Road, Urbana, IL 61801-1096, or (877) 369-6283 or (213) 328-3870. To become a subscriber, contact the Web site: www.ncte.org/cccc/ccc-.

College English. 12 issues/year; articles about literature, critical theory, language and applied linguistics, literacy, rhetoric, composition, and professional issues related to the teaching of English. The major publication of the National Council for Teachers of English (NCTE), located at 1111 West Kenyon Road, Urbana, IL 61801–1096; (877) 369-6283 or (213) 328-3870. Contact the Web site to become a subscriber: www.ncte.org/journals/ce.

Journal of Basic Writing. 2 issues/year, published with support from the City University of New York. For a subscription, contact *Journal of Basic Writing,* P.O. Box 465, Hanover, PA 17331; (717) 632-3535. Or visit tamu-commerce .edu/cbw/cbw/JBW.html.

Journal of College Reading and Learning. 2 issues/year; contains theory, research, practice, and policy reflecting the voice of professionals dedicated to postsecondary reading and learning. Contact the Web site to become a subscriber: www .crla.net/journal.htm.

Journal of Developmental Education. 3 issues/year; published by the National Center of Developmental Education, Appalachian State University, Boone, NC 28608. Focuses on research, trends, and news related to postsecondary developmental education and encompasses writing, mathematics, reading, tutoring, and more. For subscription information, visit **www.ncde .appstate.edu/publications/jde/.**

Teaching English in the Two-Year College (TETYC). 4 issues/year; for the two-year college English teacher as well as for freshman and sophomore composition teachers in four-year schools; focuses on the teaching of composition: basic writing, grammar, business and technical writing. NCTE, 1111 West Kenyon Road, Urbana, IL 61801-1096, or (877) 369-6283 or (213) 328-3870. Contact the Web site to become a subscriber: www.ncte.org/journals/tetyc.

Teachers of English to Speakers of Other Languages (TESOL) Quarterly. 4 issues/year; bridges theory and practice for teachers, researchers, and scholars in linguistic disciplines. To subscribe, contact **www.tesol.org/.**

Web Sites

Conference on Basic Writing (CBW)
orgs.tamu-commerce.edu/cbw
This site contains professional and personal conversations on pedagogy, curriculum, administration, and social issues affecting basic writing, with links to basic writing e-journals and online resources.

National Association for Developmental Education (NADE)
www.nade.net/
This forum is intended to improve the theory and practice of developmental education. Links include collaborative learning and computer-based instruction.

National Council for Teachers of English (NCTE)
www.ncte.org
NCTE's mission is the advancement of the teaching of English and language arts at all levels of education. This Web site has links to journals and ideas.

Re: Writing
www.bedfordstmartins.com/rewriting
Developed by Bedford/St. Martin's, this site includes a wealth of professional resources, including online workshops, bibliographies, and journals for professional development. Re: Writing provides access to *The Bedford Bibliography for Teachers of Basic Writing,* an annotated list of books, articles, and periodicals selected specifically for their value to teachers of basic writing.

Teachers of English to Speakers of Other Languages (TESOL)
www.tesol.org/
TESOL's mission is to develop expertise in teaching English to speakers of other languages. This Web site offers links to education programs and publications.

Listservs

A listserv is an e-mail discussion group. Each listserv has two addresses, and it is important to distinguish between them: One is the administrative address, and the other is the discussion address. The administrative address provides access to information about the list whereas the other address is for the discussion itself; you will receive this address once you subscribe to the listserv, and any messages you send to that location will reach everyone on the list. Be sure to send all administrative queries to the correct address as it is a faux pas to send to the entire membership.

The addresses listed below are the administrative locations for each listserv. If you would like a fuller explanation of what subject matter a particular listserv covers, e-mail the administrator with the command "INFO [name of listserv]" in the body of the message. Another good command to know is HELP. The administrator will respond with a list of commands and functions relevant to his or her listserv. Should you choose to go ahead and subscribe to that list, you can e-mail the administrator with the command "SUBSCRIBE [name of listserv] [your first name, your last name]" in the body of the message. (Try this first, and if it fails to work, substitute your e-mail address for your name.) Finally, having subscribed to the list, you will first receive a Frequently Asked Questions (FAQ) file. It will have important information about how the listserv operates, including information on how to unsubscribe. We recommend printing the FAQ and filing it for future reference.

AEDNET: Adult Education Discussion
listserv@alpha.acast.nova.edu

BGEDU-L: Educator's Forum on Reform
listserv@ukcc.uky.edu

CBW-L: Conference on Basic Writing
listserv@tc.umn.edu

ECOMP-L: College English Composition
listserv@listserv.nodak.edu

LRNASST-L: Learning Assistance Listserv
listserv@lists.ufl.edu

MULTC-ED: Multicultural Education Discussion
listserve@umdd.umd.edu

NCTE listservs
To subscribe, visit www.ncte.org/listsubscribe, choose your desired listserv, and fill out the registration form.

TechRhet, sponsored by the Interversity Teaching and Learning Cooperative
To subscribe, fill out the registration form at www.interversity.org/lists/techrhet/subscribe.html.

Appendix: Readability Scores for Selections in Part 8: Readings for Writers

The following are grade-level scores of selections in *Real Essays,* Part 8, Readings for Writers. Two scores are shown for each selection, using two widely used methods for assessing readability: (1) Fry Readability Graph and (2) Flesch-Kincaid Grade Level.

Readability Scores			
Chapter	Essay Title	Fry	Flesch-Kincaid
41	Beth Trimmer, *Birdshot*	7	6.6
41	Langston Hughes, *Salvation*	5	3.9
41	M. Catherine Maternowska, *Truck-Stop Girls*	6	5.9
42	Tam Nguyen, *Reflection*	8	8.2
42	Kathleen Vail, *Words That Wound*	9	9
42	Deborah L. Rhode, *Why Looks Are the Last Bastion of Discrimination*	15	12.4
43	Heaven Morrison, *My Kingdom*	6	5.5
43	Alex Espinoza, *An American in Mexico*	8	7.8
43	Mary Brave Bird, *The Sweat Bath Ritual*	7	6
44	Katie Whitehead, *How to Avoid Carpal Tunnel Syndrome*	7	7.1
44	Farhad Manjoo, *Fix Your Terrible, Insecure Passwords in Five Minutes*	9	8.6
44	Malcolm X, *My First Conk*	6	5.6
45	Beth Trimmer, *Birth Order*	15	11.2
45	Amy Tan, *Mother Tongue*	9	9
45	Martin Luther King Jr., *The Ways of Meeting Oppression*	10	9.1
46	Kevin Willey, *The Optimistic Generation*	9	9.2
46	Nancy Mairs, *On Being a Cripple*	10	9
46	Juliet B. Schor, *Age Compression*	12	11.5
47	Rui Dai, *A Whiff of Memory*	12	10.3
47	Dave Barry, *The Ugly Truth about Beauty*	8	8.2
47	Nicholas Kristof, *Two Men and Two Paths*	12	10.6
48	Michael Jernigan, *Living the Dream*	7	5.9
48	Brent Staples, *Just Walk on By: Black Men and Public Space*	10	9.8
48	Amy L. Beck, *Struggling for Perfection*	13	12.9
49	Barbara Huttmann, *A Crime of Compassion*	8	7.7
49	Marc Siegel, *Treating the Pain by Ending a Life*	9	10.1
49	Jerry Fensterman, *I See Why Others Choose to Die*	13	8.1
49	Marilyn Golden, *Why Progressives Should Oppose the Legalization of Assisted Suicide*	13	13.8
49	Herbert Hendin, *The Case against Physician-Assisted Suicide: For the Right to End-of-Life Care*	13	13.4

Student Paper Submission Form

Instructors: Please use duplicates of this form for each piece of student writing that you submit for possible publication in future editions of *Real Essays, Real Writing,* or *Real Skills* by Susan Anker. In order to get permission from, and pay, students whose papers we decide to publish, it is very important that we know how to contact them. With that in mind, please make sure to include students' addresses and phone numbers.

Please submit the completed form(s) and paper(s) to:

Real Essays/Real Writing/Real Skills Paper Submissions
Bedford/St. Martin's
75 Arlington Street, 8th Floor
Boston, MA 02116

For each student paragraph or essay that we publish in future editions of *Real Essays, Real Writing,* or *Real Skills,* we will pay you and the student each $100.

Information about you:

Instructor's Name _____ Title _____

Department _____ Office phone _____
  (area code)

School_____

Mailing address _____
        (city)   (state)   (zip code)

E-mail address _____

Information about the paper you are submitting:

Student's name _____

Student's address _____
        (city)   (state)   (zip code)

Student's phone number _____
          (area code)

E-mail address _____

Title of the paper _____

Real Essays, Real Writing, or *Real Skills* assignment for which the paper was written: _____

_____

_____